SPORTS HAS BEEN a consuming interest for Jonathan Kolatch since childhood. At Queens College, where he received a B.A. in mathematics and was elected to Phi Beta Kappa, he was a catcher on the baseball team. After earning his B.A., he turned his attention to Oriental languages, and was awarded a Master's degree from Harvard University in Chinese Studies. While a student at Harvard, he served as a baseball coach at neighboring M.I.T. Dr. Kolatch received his Ph.D. in Chinese Studies from Columbia University in 1970. His research on Chinese sports is the first effort of this type to be undertaken by any scholar.

A native of Forest Hills, New York, Jonathan Kolatch has traveled extensively in Europe, Asia, and Africa. He recently returned from a year's stay in the Middle East where he perfected his skills in Hebrew and Arabic. He has just completed a translation, from the Hebrew, of David Ben-Gurion's *Ben-Gurion Looks at the Bible*. He is currently editing a football guide by a prominent sports personality.

SPORTS POLITICS AND IDEOLOGY IN CHINA

Jonathan Kolatch

JONATHAN DAVID PUBLISHERS • NEW YORK

SPORTS, POLITICS AND
IDEOLOGY IN CHINA
Copyright 1972
by
JONATHAN KOLATCH

No part of this book may be reproduced in any way without written permission from the publisher.

Address all inquiries to:
JONATHAN DAVID PUBLISHERS
Middle Village, N. Y. 11379

Library of Congress Catalogue Card No. 71-171702

ISBN 0-8246-0130-0

PRINTED IN THE UNITED STATES OF AMERICA

GV
651
K6

PTD

161187

SPORTS POLITICS AND IDEOLOGY IN CHINA

Contents

Preface xi
Sports in Traditional China—A Prologue xv

PART I—THE PRE-COMMUNIST PERIOD
1 THE PERIOD UNTIL 1928: THE YMCA ERA 3
    The First Programs of Physical Education 4
    Modern School Physical Education in the Military Tradition 5
    The YMCA's Physical Education Program 8
    The National Athletic Meet Series and the Establishment of Regional Athletic Associations 11
    The Formation of National Athletic Associations ... 17
    YMCA Involvement in Chinese Sports—1911-1927 . 19

CONTENTS (Cont'd)

2 THE PERIOD 1928-1949: THE ERA OF GOVERNMENT CONTROL 31
    The Beginning of Non-Military Modern School Physical Education 31
    Early Reforms Under the Nationalist Government... 33
    The First National Physical Education Conference and Its Aftermath 38
    The National Athletic Meets Under the Nationalist Government 42
    China and the Olympic Games 45
    Physical Education During the Sino-Japanese War.. 46
    The Financing of Physical Education 48

3 THE FAR EASTERN CHAMPIONSHIP GAMES: THE FIRST INTERNATIONAL ATHLETIC COMPETITION IN THE FAR EAST 51
    The Inception of the Far Eastern Championship Games 52
    Level of Athletic Performance at the FECG 66
    Indirect Influences of the FECG 66

PART II—THE COMMUNIST PERIOD

4 THE CHINESE COMMUNIST IDEOLOGICAL VIEW OF PHYSICAL CULTURE 75
    Mao Tse-tung's "A Study of Physical Culture" of 1917 77
    Chinese Communist Physical Culture in Pre-1949 China 82
    Sanction and Justification 85
    The Chinese Communist Policy of Physical Culture. 88

5 THE ORGANIZATION AND ADMINISTRATION OF PHYSICAL CULTURE IN MAINLAND CHINA 97

6 PHYSICAL EDUCATION IN CHINESE SCHOOLS 110
    The Primary and Middle School Program 110
    The General Education Physical Education Program in Schools of Higher Education 120

	Specialized Physical Education Schools	122
	University Level Training in Physical Culture	122
	Physical Culture in Middle School Level Normal Schools	126
	Spare-time Athletic Schools	127
	In-Service Training of Physical Education Teachers	130
7	MASS SPORTS AND THE CONCEPT OF NATIONAL DEFENSE PHYSICAL CULTURE	133
	The "Labor-Defense System"—1951-1958	135
	The Labor-Defense System in 1958	140
	Sports in Factories	144
	Sports in Communes	145
	Equipment	145
	Broadcast Exercises	145
	Sports for National Defense	146
	Military Camping	148
	Land Activities	149
	Aviation Activities	152
	Navigation Activities	154
	The Period After 1958	155
	Postscript	164
8	SPORTS AND INTERNATIONAL RELATIONS, A CASE STUDY: CHINA, THE OLYMPIC GAMES, AND THE GAMES OF THE NEW EMERGING FORCES	166
	Background	170
	The 1952 Olympic Games	171
	Developments Between the 1952 Games and the 1956 Games	174
	China's Preparation for the 1956 Games	178
	The Withdrawal	180
	The Events of 1958	184
	Aftermath to the Change of Status of Taiwan	187
	The 1960 Summer Games at Rome	189
	Events Preceding the Games of the New Emerging Forces	189

CONTENTS (Cont'd)

The Resignation and Expulsion of Indonesia from the IOC and the Beginning of the Games of the New Emerging Forces 190
The GANEFO Meeting (November 10-22, 1963) .. 193
A Different Perspective on GANEFO 195
Were the Indonesians the Real Force Behind the First GANEFO? 195
Events Since the First GANEFO 196

Summary 202

Notes 209

Bibliography 229

Index 241

Preface

IMPROVEMENTS in United States-Chinese relations continue at an ever-increasing pace. As these developments keep gathering momentum, we search for deeper understanding of the Chinese people and government with whom we have now made contact after a generation of isolation.

One of the most fruitful starting points in our search is the area of sports. There is little doubt, as the table tennis episodes of early 1971 have shown, that there is much understanding and trust that can develop through international sports activity and much to be gleaned about China from a study of the Chinese approach toward sports. These pages attempt to take a step in this direction.

As a pioneering study in a virgin field, *Sports, Politics and Ideology in China* presents the particular factors and forces which have been responsible for the development of modern sports in China, from a very modest beginning at the turn of the century, to a point where it has now become an integral part of the political, educational, military, and recreational life of contemporary China.

The phrase "modern sports" is used here so as to differentiate between the organized, competitive and non-competitive sports familiar to people in western countries, and traditional Chinese sports, such as the *wu shu* (a group of Chinese gymnastic exercises), which have existed in China for centuries. While these latter activities continue to exist today, they are now less popular then modern sports.

The study of athletics in China offers a unique opportunity for us to examine the impact of the West on traditional Chinese life. Although *wu shu* and various ancient forms of football, wrestling, and fencing existed in Chinese traditional society during the first millenium of this era, with the increasing importance of the civil service examination system during the Ming and Ch'ing dynasties (1368-1912), physical activity was frowned upon by the more sophisticated elements. The rapidity with which this attitude has taken an about-face within the last 70 years is one indication of the extent to which the patterns of traditional Chinese society have changed.

By far the greatest development in sports has taken place during the last 20 years. Sports such as track and field, swimming, soccer, table tennis, and basketball have become the preoccupation of large segments of the population under Communist encouragement. One strong indication of the importance that the Mainland Chinese now attach to athletics is evidenced by the effort that they have expended in setting up an organization outside of the jurisdiction of the International Olympic Committee—an effort made when they found themselves unable to compete in the Olympic Games. Another is the degree of importance which their political ideology attaches to sports.

This study covers a somewhat lengthy period. Accordingly, it is divided into two parts. Part I is a detailed survey tracing highlights in the development of modern physical culture in China from its inception, near the end of the nineteenth century, until the Communist takeover in 1949. Part II, comprising the bulk of the book, goes into much greater detail as it develops the major themes in physical culture for the first 20 years of Communist rule.

One thing which will become apparent in these pages is that there exists an institutional continuity in the area of sports between the Republican period (1912-1949), and the Communist period. Thus, the inclusion of physical education in the curriculum of the Communist education system can be seen as a legacy of similar attempts during the Republican period. The seeds for the establishment of international athletic relations by the Mainland Chinese, as exemplified by the large number of international dual meets in which they compete, as well as the Games of the New Emerging Forces, were planted when the Far Eastern Championship Games were first held in 1913. Similarly, the precedent for the National Athletic Meets now held every few years on the Mainland is as much traceable to a similar series held there between 1910 and 1948 as to the *spartakiady* periodically held in Russia. The emphasis on military sports, so visible on the Mainland, can be traced to the early years of the Sino-Japanese conflict in the 1930's. Many changes have taken place. Yet it seems safe to say that, at least in the realm of sports, the Communists have failed to break their ties with the Republican period.

The narrative here is carried to the beginning of the Cultural Revolution in 1966. The Cultural Revolution is a convenient breaking off point for us because sports passed through a period of what might be called suspended animation during the years 1966-1970. The study, therefore, is basically up-to-date, and present indications would lead us to the conclusion that in the 1970's sports on the Mainland will continue to follow the paths which it cut out for itself in the first two decades of Communist rule.

The phrase "physical culture" used widely here will probably confuse some readers. It is, in fact, a literal translation of the word *t'i yü*—the closest Chinese equivalent of our word "sports." It is used here because, as will be seen—especially in Part II—the Chinese interpretation of what is a sport and what should not be considered a sport sometimes differs radically from our own conception. The term "physical culture" then, should serve to remind us of this difference.

A word about the footnotes: The text is intended to stand by itself. For the most part, when clarification is required for an understanding of the text, it will be found at the bottom of the page. The casual reader need not feel that he is missing something by skipping the footnotes. Anyone who may care to delve into any particular topic more deeply, however, would profit from the notes and bibliography following the text.

I would like to say a special thank you here to Professor Bernard S. Solomon of the Department of Classical and Oriental Languages at Queens College under whom I first started to learn Chinese and who eased me over most of the rough spots during my academic career.

JONATHAN KOLATCH

Forest Hills, N. Y.
September, 1971

Sports in Traditional China

A PROLOGUE

PHYSICAL CULTURE in pre-modern China was frequently linked with military training and many of the activities which we today call "sports" assumed military significance at their earliest stages. The term *wu shu*—which has now become a synonym for traditional sports—can be rendered literally as "military skills." *Wu shu* originally included archery, fencing, wrestling, and a variety of activities revolving about the handling of clubs, spears, and swords. As Chinese boxing emerged during the T'ang dynasty (618-906), *ch'üan shu* (pugilistic skills) were added to the above activities under the heading, *wu shu*. Gradually, *ch'üan shu*, which includes such sub-categories as *t'ai chi ch'üan* and *shao lin ch'üan*, became the dominant aspect of *wu shu*.

Wrestling and archery are the two oldest *wu shu*. Archery dates back almost to the beginning of Chinese civilization, and during the Chou dynasty (1122-255 B.C.) became one of the "five arts" which consisted of music, archery, charioteering, writing, and mathematics. These were the essence of feudal education.[1] The *Book of Rites,* the *Spring and Autumn Annals,* as well as other writings of the Warring States period (403-221

B.C.) give accounts of the nobility participating in ceremonial tournaments which included archery. During the Chou dynasty, archery became a regular festival game for both the masses and the nobility. Contests were conducted on horseback and on foot to test proficiency in marksmanship and distance.[2]

Wrestling is mentioned in the literature of the Chou period, when it was allegedly popular among kings, princes, dukes, warriors, and even common people. Open competition is known to have been held in 113 B.C. during the Han dynasty (206 B.C.-220 A.D.).[3]

Before the sixth century A.D., boxing and wrestling were quite likely closely related. The *Shih Ching* (*Classic of Songs*) notes that

> If one has neither boxing ability nor courage,
> Such may usually be the cause of uprisings
>   and disturbances.

Prime Minister Kuan-tzu of the Chou state of Ch'i chose the best boxers in Ch'i to defend the state and felt that a state which is constantly engaged in defense training would remain free.[4]

Chinese boxing as it is known today is thought to have been brought to China from India with the first apostles of Buddhism during the first centuries of this era. The indigenous Chinese boxing and wrestling traditions, nevertheless, seem to have carried great influence into the future, for a set of exercises based on the movements of the tiger, deer, bear, monkey and bird, allegedly developed by the Han medical specialist Hua T'o, are still recognizable today in Chinese boxing.[5]

The present form of Chinese boxing (generally known as *ch'üan shu*) was originated during the Liang dynasty (502-557) by the monk Bodhidharma (Ta Mo) of the Shao Lin Temple in Honan. Bodhidharma noticed that those of his students who were frail used to fall asleep during his lectures, so he devised a system of 18 movements to be performed each morning in order to improve their health. These movements became the core of the Shao Lin style of boxing.[6]

In 722, according to legend, the boxing monks at Shao Lin received special acclaim when they performed admirably in response to an appeal by T'ang T'ai Tsung who was conducting a campaign to recruit soldiers. Thereafter, Shao Lin became known as the cradle of Chinese boxing.[7]

During the Yüan dynasty (1279-1368), Chüeh Yüan reworked Bodhidharma's 18 movements into 72, and later collaborated with Pai Yu-feng of Shansi, expanding the 72 into 170 movements, which form the present basis of Shao Lin boxing.[8]

Chinese boxing emerged into two basic schools. The "outer" school, of which Shao Lin is the most widely practiced style, stressed the development of strength, speed, and power. The word "outer" refers to the primacy of developing oneself physically—in contrast to "inner" spiritual cultivation. Thus, Shao Lin and its sister styles stress quick movement, leaps and kicks, and often imitate animals. Karate is a derivative of this school.

The "inner" school of which *t'ai chi ch'üan* is the best known form is characterized by slow movements which avoid jumping or running. It puts a great deal of stress on the coordination of breathing with movement. In modern day China, *t'ai chi ch'üan* is the most widely practiced of the traditional sports.[9]

Initially, Chinese boxing started out as a series of exercises geared toward the development of a healthy body. It then developed into a lethal martial art which caused alarm among foreign dynasties which ruled China (especially the Ch'ing—1644-1911) because of its potential use as an instrument to further revolt. They therefore attempted to suppress it periodically. These attempts and the increasing emphasis placed on literary achievement beginning with the Ming dynasty (1368-1644), seem to have contributed to a decline of boxing as a sport in China.[10] At present Chinese boxing exists in a form largely devoid of aggressiveness, which can be considered more a gymnastic exercise intended to promote good health.

Ball games, likewise, have a long history in China. According to legend, football was first used in the training of soldiers by the mythical Emperor Huang (1267 B.C.). Its aim was to infuse a feeling for team unity. The strategy and coordination leading to this unity and team strength would hopefully be transferred to military operations. The Han historian Ssu-ma Ch'ien notes of the Chou state of Ch'i: "There were not among its inhabitants those who did not perform on the pipes, or some stringed instrument, fight cocks, race dogs, dice, or play football." During the Han, a handbook on football in 25 chapters is said to have existed. The *Mirror of History* relates that the T'ang emperor, Hsi Tsung, devoted a substantial portion of his time to football, while the popular Yüan novel, *Shui Hu Chuan,* gives vivid testimony to the popularity of the game among the masses.

Not a great deal is known about the exact nature of ancient Chinese football, but it appears to have been comparable to our game of soccer, with use of the hands prohibited and the object being to kick the ball through a goal often demarcated by bamboo poles. The ball was originally made of leather stuffed with hair and feathers. During the T'ang this was replaced by a ball that could be inflated.[11]

Polo seems to have been known in China after 600 A.D. and was probably learned from the Tartars who were at home on horseback. A reference exists to an order given by the T'ang emperor in 710 that all higher ranking court officials participate in a polo match. On more than one occasion this emperor was memorialized for overexerting himself in polo. What might well have been the first artificial athletic field-covering was proposed by the reigning Sung emperor in 1163 who ordered that, in case of rain, the polo field be covered with an oiled cloth sprinkled with sand. As with other sports, polo decreased in popularity in Ming and Ch'ing times.[12]

References to the sport of "hawking" or falconry (taming hawks and using them in conjunction with dogs in hunting) are found as far back as the third century B.C. Despite these few references it was not until the second century of this era that falconry seems to have emerged as a sport. During the four centuries between the Han and the T'ang, falconry continued in popularity, and in the seventh and eighth centuries it reached its peak. In 608, over 10,000 people reportedly assembled in Loyang in response to a call for all professional falconers to appear before the emperor. Both emperors T'ai Tsung and Hsüan Tsung were enthusiastic falconers who distressed their advisors by this preoccupation. The lament that

> He took no pleasure in reading books
> His only joy was in hawks and horses

does not seem to have been atypical of T'ang royal advisors. Falcon hunts continued into the Yüan dynasty, but apparently waned thereafter.[13]

In addition to the above athletic activities, references to other sports are found in Chinese writings. Over 2,000 years ago, China was said to have had a water army which could dive, tread water and do the backstroke. The Sung (960-1279) poet Su Tung-po reported that many South China six and seven year-olds were adept at swimming and diving. In the frigid North, ice sports were already popular during the pre-modern period.[14] As early as the third century B.C. weightlifting in the form of lifting large bronze cauldrons was known.[15] Acrobatics are mentioned as early as the Han, and Sung books have pictures of tightrope walking and similar feats.[16]

This survey suggests that sports has had a long tradition in China. It is difficult to estimate the strength of this athletic tradition in the last few centuries preceding this one. The concentration of the available written record on the upper classes in China tends to ignore the life of the broad masses among whom athletics conceivably could have been more popular than among the literati. Nevertheless, the apparent decrease in recreational physical activity during the Ming and its even weaker position during the Ch'ing, coupled with the manner in which the modern movement in athletics emerged, leads us to conclude that any pre-modern athletic tradition that may have existed contributed little to modern day athletics in China.

Part I
THE PRE-COMMUNIST PERIOD

1

The Period Until 1928: The YMCA Era

THOUGH THE DEVELOPMENT of western sports in China was inspired by foreigners, one cannot ignore the climate prevalent in China in the late nineteenth century. The treaties resulting from the Opium War had provided more Westerners with freer access to China than had ever been the case before. The "self-strengthening" movement, led by such people as Tseng Kuo-fan, began to sanction the importation of western ideas and western inventions. The reforms of 1898 brought China still closer to westernization.

Few of the famous names associated with the intellectual ferment of the last half of that century had a deep interest in physical education *per se*. But, they were all vitally concerned with rejuvenating the Chinese fabric, and one would expect that they would have approved of any efforts encouraging physical cultivation for Chinese. Occasionally, specific support for physical education was given. The Thatched Hut Among Ten Thousand Trees School (*Wan Mu Ts'ao T'ang*), organized by K'ang Yu-wei in Canton before 1890, included calisthenics and military drill in its curriculum.[1] In the "Bushido of China" Liang Ch'i-ch'ao shows his appreciation for the necessity of bodily cultivation.[2] However, of all the giants of that era, it was probably Yen Fu—no doubt because he had been rejected by the traditional system, and had been exposed to the West more so than the others—who most clearly saw the need to inform the Chinese people of the value of physical fitness. Benjamin Schwartz writes that physical fitness ". . . is closely associated in his mind with the psychological values of physical courage and the power of physical endurance. In some ways, the affirmation of man's physical powers, and what might be called the physical virtues would provide for him the most dramatic manifestation of the new transformation of values." Yen Fu went so far as to espouse physical education for women on the grounds that healthier mothers would bear stronger children.[3]

What effect the support for physical education by people like Yen Fu had upon the development of modern athletics in China is, of course, quite difficult to assess. Yet, such advocacy should be noted as possibly having broadened the appeal of western physical culture in China.

THE FIRST PROGRAMS OF PHYSICAL EDUCATION

The first formal programs of physical education in the late nineteenth century followed two distinctly different trends with further diversity within each trend. At first, the concern was not really with sports, but with military exercise and a type of formal gymnastics. With the establishment of the Nanking Military Academy in 1875, the first course in physical training was introduced. The Tientsin Naval Academy, opened in 1881 under the patronage of Li Hung-chang, the military academy established by Li in Tientsin in 1885, and the academy set up in 1895 in Hupei by Chang Chih-tung also had exercise programs. These limited programs generally were directed by German or Japanese instructors of military training and did not include sports competition.[4] These early programs in physical exercise could not have had much influence, for enrollment in the military schools was small and the type of student studying there—having opted to pursue a career via a route other than the civil service system at a time when the system was still in full force—was far from an "average" Chinese.

MODERN SCHOOL PHYSICAL EDUCATION IN THE MILITARY TRADITION

In spite of its limited acceptance, it was the military-flavored physical exercise known as *t'i ts'ao* (as compared to the more sports oriented term *t'i yü*) which provided most of the physical training that was available in Chinese schools during the first 10 or 15 years of the twentieth century. And it was this type of exercise which was prescribed by the Board of Education (*Hsüeh Pu*) —the first organized government control over modern education—when it stipulated two to three hours per week of physical exercise for upper and lower elementary schools in 1905.[5] Subsequently, physical education was made a required course in middle schools, higher schools, lower normal schools, and lower agricultural schools. In 1907, a physical education curriculum was devised for women's normal schools. Periodic changes were made in these directives and in 1909 the time allotted for physical education in lower elementary schools was raised to four hours per week. At that time, urban schools were required to give physical training as a required course and rural schools, as an optional course.[6]

An evaluation of the extent to which school physical education reached Chinese children in the first 20 years of this century must take account of the low level of development of the Chinese educational system at the time. In 1905, only 102,767 Chinese children were in public schools out of a school-age population of approximately 33 million. In 1910, the figure reached 5% (1,625,534 children in school).[7] In 1915, 8.6%[8] and in 1925, 19%.[9]* Though the school system was certainly growing admirably, it still left the bulk of Chinese youth without education. Even if we credit half of the schools in existence with physical education programs (a figure which appears generous in view of the shortage of physical education personnel and general lack of interest in it), we see that physical education did not reach the preponderance of Chinese youth.

Those schools which did comply with the physical education directives of the Board of Education were staffed with German or Japanese instructors who advocated a spartan-like method

---

* Such figures are only estimates, for exact figures on China's population were not available and statistical reporting was in an early stage of development.

of training.¹⁰ Among the government schools of that era, only Nanyang (Shanghai), Peiyang (Tientsin), Haichün (Woosung), and several others had actual sports programs.¹¹ The average physical education programs in Chinese schools at that time probably were similar to the description provided by Martin Yang of physical education in the rural Shantung village of Taitou about 1915. The physical training provided there consisted mainly of military drill. Since the aim of the program was to make the boys good soldiers, marching, saluting, and military terminology were stressed so as to resemble a military camp. Teachers appealed to their students to train their bodies so that they would be able to defend their homes and their nation.¹²

This tradition of military drill maintained influence for the greater part of the first twenty years of this century. North China, having received a stronger German influence than the South, reflected more the German physical education tradition, while in South China, the Japanese influence was more in evidence. It was not until the 1920's that the Chinese term *t'i yü* (used today and having more of a sporting connotation) replaced the term *t'i ts'ao*.¹³

The need for physical education in Chinese schools in the first decade of this century stimulated the first Chinese schools and courses for physical education teachers. These schools were generally staffed by either Japanese, or by Chinese who had studied in Japan. The first such course was opened in 1903 at the Kiangsu Higher Normal School in Soochow. It was taught by a Japanese whose background was essentially in German and Swedish military gymnastics.¹⁴ A similar course was set up in Chekiang. The courses offered were limited in scope, generally lasting only one year, and included anatomy, physiology, exercise theory, and a few basic athletic skills.¹⁵

The first school dedicated solely to training physical educators was the Chinese Physical Training School (*Chung Kuo T'i Ts'ao Hsüeh Hsiao*). It was opened in 1904, in Shanghai, by Hsü Fu-lin. Hsü and his co-workers (Hsü Yi-ping and Liu Ch'eng-lieh) had been among those who had studied in Japan and brought back the Japanese exercise system. Outwardly, these people advocated a "national physical education" (*kuo min t'i yü*), while under cover they preached revolution and contributed to the downfall of the Ch'ing dynasty in 1911. Hsü himself translated a book from Japanese entitled *Swedish Curative Exercises.*

By the time the school was forced to close down in 1927, after having been ravaged during the Warlord conflicts, it had graduated 1,531 students from its two-year courses. The Chinese Physical Training School was extremely influential in its day and produced most of the heads of physical education departments until the government began opening physical education departments in its normal schools in 1915 and 1916.

The Hsüs were truly the first family of Chinese physical education. In 1905, Hsü Fu-lin's wife founded the Shanghai Chinese Girls' Physical Education School which continued in operation until the Japanese war.[16]

With the establishment of the Republic of China in 1911, the Board of Education gave way to the Ministry of Education (*Chiao Yü Pu*). The Ministry had little more machinery to implement its directives than had the Board. Nevertheless, it seemed to be more vigorous in its attitudes toward physical training. It reiterated earlier directives and called for three hours per week of physical education in elementary and middle schools. In December, 1912, it gave a bit more direction to future physical education programs by stating its aim: "The essentials of physical exercise are to cause all parts of the body to develop equally, to strengthen the body, to enliven the spirit, and to cultivate the habits of discipline and harmony." As to whether physical drill or military exercise was to receive more stress, the latter was to be given preference.[17]

Of greater significance from a historical point of view, as far as the development of western non-military physical education in China is concerned, are the sports activities which were first introduced in the Christian schools as early as 1888.[18] Here, for the first time, Chinese youngsters became acquainted with western sports. In 1890, at St. John's University in Shanghai, track and field was formally adopted as a sport and a Canadian who taught there organized a semi-annual sports meet. Sports activity spread to many of the church-affiliated schools while the government schools lagged behind in this respect. Development was so one-sided in favor of the church schools that at the first National Athletic Meet in 1910 most of the athletes were from missionary schools and almost none from government schools.[19] A gradual change occurred between 1910 and 1920 as the YMCA began to initiate sports programs in government schools.

The missionary schools initially conceived of sports as something divorced from education, intended merely for recreational purposes. The faculty members who took charge of the sports program were not specialists in physical education. Most frequently they had developed an interest in sports while attending school and served as volunteer supervisors at the missionary schools. It remained for the YMCA to take the first step (between 1895 and 1908) in turning a haphazard system of physical education into a more formalized one.[20]

THE YMCA'S PHYSICAL EDUCATION PROGRAM

The YMCA began its program in China when it sent a Secretary (i.e. a general administrator) to Tientsin in 1895 in the person of Dr. D. Willard Lyon. Lyon became responsible for initiating the YMCA's physical education program in addition to his other responsibilities. Although the YMCA had as its ideal the balanced development in young men of "mind, body, and spirit," the Y's athletic program in China proceeded slowly during its first years, largely because no formal provision had yet been made for a physical program (as they called their physical education work). At first, the nature of the program depended largely on the background of the Secretary at the particular YMCA branch in question. In 1898, three additional Foreign Secretaries—Robert R. Gailey, R. E. Lewis, and Fletcher S. Brockman—all of whom had some interest in sports, were sent to China to join Lyon. Gradually the sports program began to expand; especially in the Tientsin Association run by Gailey, a former football All-American at Princeton.[21]

Despite limited manpower, the Y was able to make definite, though slow, progress. Basketball was introduced at Tientsin in January, 1896, having been invented in Springfield, Massachusetts only several years prior. From the Tientsin Y it spread to the neighboring government middle school, the First Private Middle School, and the YMCA sponsored P'u T'ung (Common) School. In 1907, baseball was introduced in Peking.[22]

It was during this first period (1895-1908) that the YMCA

set the pattern for its most fruitful period of activity in physical education—1908-1928. Though they seemed to be everywhere, non-Chinese Y Physical Secretaries were limited in number, never numbering more than 18 to 20.[23] The Secretaries' greatest value to China was thus through activities in which they could reach a maximum number of people with a minimum staff: as coordinators of programs in Chinese and mission schools, as promoters of athletic meets, as trainers of native leadership personnel, and as propagandists for increased support for physical education programs among government officials and private citizens. As early as 1896, the Tientsin YMCA embarked on a program of promoting athletic competition in schools. C. H. Robertson, YMCA Secretary in Tientsin who arrived in China in 1902, spent part of his time teaching physical education in local Chinese schools, and an American teacher of physical education was placed by the Association on a full-time basis in the Tientsin school system. With both Gailey and Robertson taking an interest in physical education, in addition to their regular duties, Tientsin took the lead among YMCA chapters in the development of physical programs in the days before Shanghai became the center. In 1902, the first Annual Athletic Meet was held by the YMCA for Y members and students in Tientsin schools.[24] Interest was so high in these meets that by the time the sixth meet in this series was being held in 1908, the question was already being raised as to when China would be able to send a team to the Olympic Games.[25] By 1908, the YMCA had been instrumental in the promotion of track and field meets in Tientsin, Peking, Shanghai, Foochow, and at least 10 other cities. These early meets furnished the foundation for future interscholastic meets and the first athletic associations in China.[26]

Before 1908, the YMCA physical education program was not coordinated on a national level. Each local Association Secretary arranged his own program. In October, 1908, Dr. Max J. Exner arrived in Shanghai to serve as the first National Physical Director for China. What this did, in effect, was to create the first machinery for a national athletic program in China. Although the YMCA never served as an official national athletic body, the fact that it was the only organization seriously concerned with athletics, and had branches in various parts of China, made it uniquely fit to serve unofficially in this capacity.

Exner's stay in China was a short but fruitful one. He arrived in October, 1908, and by 1911 tuberculosis had forced him to relinquish his post. In the intervening years the YMCA was able to set up the apparatus for its physical education work for the next 20 years.

Exner arrived with definite goals in mind and plans with which to implement them. The aim of physical training for him was "to secure for the individual the physical basis for the largest and most efficient life for which it is possible for him to live; and to increase the capacity of the race."[27] He immediately announced the opening of a two year course to begin in October, 1909, for the training of Physical Directors, to include training in all branches of athletics in addition to textbook work and lectures in anatomy, physiology, hygiene, tests and measurements, the history of physical training, and Bible study. The trainees would receive pedagogical experience at the Shanghai YMCA. Exner's first class of trainees contained 14 students and by the spring of 1910, he was able to put on an athletic demonstration in the Shanghai gymnasium (which he had equipped) before 200 spectators.[28] Though only C. G. Hoh, from this original class, eventually became a YMCA Physical Secretary, the undertaking started the Y on a program which turned out some of China's first native experts in western physical education.

The years 1908-1911 were busy ones for Exner. In addition to directing the national physical education program, he was in charge of the local program at the Shanghai YMCA. The Shanghai Association, better equipped than most other YMCA branches, contained a quarter mile running track, a field for soccer and other games, four tennis courts, and locker facilities, in addition to the gymnasium. The most popular class was the evening men's gymnasium class generally consisting of about 25 men. Classes in physical education were also held for the 250 students at the Shanghai YMCA Day School, though many Chinese parents, true to the traditional bias against physical exertion, would not let their children participate. In addition to the class for Physical Directors, a special "Leader's Class" was organized whose members formed a trained group for exhibition purposes and at least once per week assisted Exner in the teaching. The organization of local meets was another time-consumer,[29] as were the hours spent in the preparation of instructional booklets suitable for translation into Chinese. (Exner himself was unable to write Chinese.)[30] Exner's most far reaching contribution was the initiation of the National Athletic Meet series which began in October, 1910.

THE NATIONAL ATHLETIC MEET SERIES AND THE ESTABLISHMENT OF REGIONAL ATHLETIC ASSOCIATIONS

With the initiation of the National Athletic Meet series in 1910, the YMCA turned the corner from being an active participant in Chinese physical education, to being its leader. What the YMCA, and especially Exner, who was its motivating force, hoped to gain from this effort is openly discussed by Exner himself. Despite a constant increase in the number of meets and the introduction of physical training courses in Chinese schools, physical education had merely scratched the surface in China by 1910. Exner and other YMCA leaders felt that by running a national athletic meet, nation-wide attention and interest in athletics would be aroused and at the same time standardization of athletic practices would be achieved. The YMCA was also concerned about its own image. It had found that its sports program gave it an inroad into government schools and groups which initially might be prejudiced against a Christian institution.[31] Once the foothold was gained through sports, the Y was then free to implement its many other programs. Among these was a program of religious indoctrination.

In the spring of 1910, Exner and other Y leaders approached the promoters of the National Industrial Exposition in Nanking about using the Exposition grounds for a national athletic meet. They were initially turned down, but subsequently reapproached by the Exposition directors who had concluded by the success of other meets held around that time, that a national athletic meet would be a likely money-maker. Under the arrangement worked out with the Exposition, the YMCA of China national office would bear the bulk of the financial burden ($2,500), and would provide the prizes. Teams would pay their own travel expenses, and the Exposition would provide for the entertainment of the athletes during their stay in Nanking.[32]

In order to facilitate the administration of the meet, Exner divided China into five sections originally designated Shanghai, Nanking-Soochow, North China, Wuhan, and South China. Later they were renamed North China, South China, East China, Central China, and West China.[33] Within each section a committee was appointed which was made up of both Chinese and foreigners and chaired by a YMCA Secretary. Each committee stimulated interest within its own section, held preliminary contests to chose the team which would represent the section, and raised the needed funds. The five committees together made up the National Committee, the Shanghai Committee served as the Executive Committee, and Exner as the National Committee chairman. The managers and referees of the meet itself were all foreigners.

No effort was spared in making the meet a success. In the case of the Nanking-Soochow section, which was athletically backward, YMCA physical men offered special assistance in training. Because their interest in sports lagged far behind that of the church schools, special efforts were made to secure the participation of government schools in the meet. The results here were slow in coming. They were better seen in subsequent national meets and in smaller meets following the national meet, where representatives from government schools participated in increasing numbers.

The first National Athletic Meet, held October 18-22, 1910, was actually six meets in one: 1) a national track and field meet for teams representing the five sections, 2) a middle school national track and field meet for the five sections, 3) an intercollegiate track and field meet, 4) a national tennis tournament, 5) a national soccer tournament, and 6) a national basketball tournament.[34] Attendance-wise the meet was considered a success with a daily average of 40,000.[35]

An amusing sidelight to this first national meet, which illustrates the conflict between modernization and tradition in China in those years, is given by the case of Sun Pao-hsin, a high jumper from Tientsin. Sun was eliminated from the competition because his queue constantly knocked the bar off of its standards. When he arrived home that evening, he promptly shaved off his queue and came back the next day to jump higher than anyone in China previously had.[36]

Although athletic standards at the first National Athletic Meet were of a high level for China at that time, they were far behind the world standards of that period. The following table briefly compares Chinese and American records in several events as of 1912.[37]

EVENT	CHINESE RECORD	AMERICAN AAU RECORD
100 yards	10.6 sec.	9.6 sec.
220 yards	24 sec.	21.2 sec.
440 yards	55 sec.	47 sec.
880 yards	2:13 min.	1:52.8 min.
high jump	5' 5½"	6' 5⅝"
broad jump	20' 3"	24' 7¼"
pole vault	10' 2"	12' 9½"
12 lb. shot put	38' 9¼"	57' 3"
12 lb. hammer throw	130'	207' 7¾"

On May 21-22, 1914, at the Temple of Heaven in Peking, the second meet in this series was held. It was of added significance because it also served as a tryout for the Chinese team to the second Far Eastern Championship Games to be held in 1915 in Shanghai (see chapter 3). This meet, like the first, was chiefly under YMCA supervision. A. N. Hoagland, Secretary of the Peking YMCA and General-Secretary of the North China Athletic Association, served as General Manager of the meet. Once again preliminary meets were held in each section to determine that section's representatives to the meet. However, each of the four sections (East, South, West, and North) entered only one team. Baseball and volleyball were added to the program for the first time.[38]

Reports from the period tell us that the National Games held in 1910 and 1914 (in addition to the Far Eastern Championship Games held in 1915 in Shanghai) contributed greatly to Chinese interest in sports. One of the tangible indicators of this is the formation of sectional and national athletic associations in China between 1910 and the third National Athletic Meet in 1924. The growth of these associations, together

THE NATIONAL ATHLETIC MEET SERIES[39]

MEET	DATE	PLACE	ORGANIZER	PARTICIPATING UNITS	EVENTS	NUMBER COMPETITORS	CHAMP.
1	Oct. 18-22, 1910	Nanking	YMCA	Sections: Wuhan, Soochow-Nanking, Shanghai, N. China, S. China	track and field, soccer, tennis, basketball	140 plus teams	None
2	May 21-22, 1914	Peking	YMCA and Peking Athletic Assoc.	E. China, S. China, W. China, N. China	Above plus volleyball and baseball	298	None
3	May 22-24, 1924	Wuchang	China Ama. Athletic Union	Same as above	Same as above plus swimming	520	North China
4	Apr. 1-10, 1930	Hangchow	China Nat. Ama. Ath. Fed.	22 teams from provinces, municipalities and overseas Chinese	Same as above plus women's track and field, tennis, basketball, volleyball	1631	Shanghai and Kwangtung
5	Oct. 10-20, 1933	Nanking	Nat. gov't.	33 teams as above	Above plus women's softball and national sports for men and women	2248	Shanghai
6	Oct. 10-20, 1935	Shanghai	Nat. gov't.	38 teams as above	As above	2700	Shanghai
7	May 5-15, 1948	Shanghai	Nat. gov't.	58 as above	As above plus men's weightlifting and boxing and men's and women's table tennis	2233	None

Note: For detailed scoring of the meets see Wu, *T'i Yü Shih*, pp. 407-428, and Hoh, *Physical Education in China*.

with other factors, ultimately contributed to a reduction of YMCA influence in Chinese athletics.

References exist to a South China Amateur Athletic Federation active in Kwangtung and Hong Kong as early as 1904.[40] However, it was in Peking that the first noteworthy athletic association got its start. In 1910, the Peking Athletic Association (*Pei Ching T'i Yü Ching Chin Hui*) was started, both as a response to the need for some formal sports organization to aid in the choosing of athletes for the first National Meet[41] and as the expression of a desire on the part of the American Indemnity College (later known as Tsinghua), North China Union College, and Peking University to bind together for contests in track and field, soccer, tennis, and baseball. With A. N. Hoagland as one of the General-Secretaries of this association, the YMCA had an interest in it.[42]

Preliminary discussions were held among top athletic officials in North China before the first North China Athletic Meet on May 24, 1913. At this time a committee chaired by Dr. Arthur Shoemaker, Athletic Director at Tsinghua and a YMCA man as well, was delegated to prepare a constitution for a North China Athletic Association. The constitution was adopted at a meeting of the representatives of all educational institutions represented at the first North China Athletic Meet. (Competition outside of the school framework was little known at that time.) Since the Peking Athletic Association was already an established body, for the first year it served as the executive committee of what was officially known as the North China Amateur Athletic Federation. At the time of the second North China Athletic Meet, May 18-19, 1914, the Peking A.A. was relieved of this responsibility.

The North China Amateur Athletic Federation—the most stable of all regional athletic associations in Republican China —held a total of 18 meets between 1913 and 1934. The first five meets were held in Peking and Tientsin, but thereafter they were rotated among the major cities in North China including Shenyang, Kaifeng, Taiyüan, Chinan, and Tsingtao. Up until 1923, foreigners took an active part in the management of the meets, but thereafter, they were entirely managed by Chinese.[43]

The next section to organize was East China, though with much less success than North China. On Jan. 2, 1914, representatives of various athletic interests in East China (i.e. Kiangsu and Chekiang) met to form the East China Athletic Federation. A. H. Swan (elected Chairman), J. H. Crocker (Secretary), T. B. Chang, and H. C. Chen all represented the Shanghai YMCA. Other groups represented included St. John's University, Nanyang University, the Chinese Public School, Soochow University and the Far Eastern Athletic Association. The Federation disbanded in 1915 because of internal friction. However, prior to the disbandment (May 15, 1914), the East China Intercollegiate Athletic Association was organized at the initiative of R. D. Smart, head of the Athletic Committee at Soochow University. This group was appreciably more successful than its predecessor and can be credited with the maintenance of athletic interest in the East China section during the following few years. The Association broadened its scope in 1921 to include non-collegiates and was able to hold six meets until it was forced to disband because of its association with missionaries in the wake of the May 30, 1925 incident, which saw British police shoot at Chinese. It was replaced by the Kiangnan Intercollegiate Athletic Federation[44] and intercollegiate athletic associations continued to exist in East China into the 1930's profiting from their proximity to the headquarters of the China National Amateur Athletic Federation which was based in Shanghai.[45]

Regional organization in Central China (the provinces of Anhwei, Kiangsi, Hunan, and Hupei) was very late in getting started. For one thing, it was reached by foreign physical educators at a later date than either East or North China. The YMCA did not begin to do extensive work in athletics in Wuchang (Hupei province) until 1916. In 1917, an athletic organization was provisionally formed among missionary and government schools in the areas of Wuchang and Hankow. This organization soon broke down leaving only the YMCA to maintain athletic interest in the area.

Sparked by the enthusiasm of Paul R. Sung, Executive Secretary of the Wuchang YMCA, the first Central China Athletic Meet (which included competition for women) was held at the Hupei Recreational Grounds in May, 1923.[46] Subsequent meets in this series were held in Nanchang in 1925, in Anking in 1930,[47] in Hankow in 1934, and in Changsha in 1936. Annual provincial meets were held in Hunan from 1917.

In 1924, following the second Central China Athletic Meet, the Central China Athletic Federation was formally established.[48]

Unlike the North, East, and Central China sections, South China (Kwangtung, Fukien, and later Kwangsi provinces and Hong Kong), although rich in athletic tradition, was never able to form an official sectional organization. Instead, many local athletic organizations were formed, generally involving the two chief athletic centers of the region, Canton and Hong Kong. Hong Kong, though a part of the British Empire, participated actively in Chinese sports and contributed athletes to teams which represented China overseas. The South China Athletic Association of Hong Kong, officially formed in 1908 but dating back to 1904, is the earliest athletic association known in China. The Kwangtung Athletic Federation, which held its first formal meet in 1909 in Canton, was another early pioneer in this area. After 1916, the Canton YMCA organized the Canton Athletic League—with competition on several age levels, as well as the Canton Tennis and Volleyball League for Girls.

Fukien's first such organization was the South Fukien Amateur Athletic Association formed at Kulangsoo in 1912. In its first years it held yearly local track and field meets, and in 1915, under the influence of T. M. Elliot of the Amoy YMCA, the first Southern Fukien Athletic Meet was held.[49]

THE FORMATION OF NATIONAL ATHLETIC ASSOCIATIONS

The formation of the regional and local sports associations described above contributed significantly to the general development of physical education by reducing the chaos on the sporting scene brought about by the lack of central control, and by encouraging competition on a local level. However, if China was to progress athletically as a nation and develop some degree of uniformity in her athletic standards, a national athletic federation was needed. Such an organization would be able to coordinate local programs into a national program, as well as supervise international competition.

Accordingly, in the spring of 1919, the representatives of North, South, and East China, who accompanied the Chinese

Far Eastern Games team to Manila, appointed a committee to draft a provisional constitution for a national athletic organization. The fruit of this was the formation of the China Amateur Athletic Union (*Chung Hua Yeh Yü Yün Tung Lien Ho Hui*) in November of that year. Some 19 Chinese cities were represented at the organizational meetings and three of the members of the Executive Committee were foreigners. The YMCA was represented on the committee by C. G. Hoh, who, by virtue of having studied in the United States, had a western outlook. Other Y personnel, such as J. H. Gray, were also deeply involved in the Union.

The Union's constitution provided for six geographic sections (North, East, South, West, and Central China, and Manchuria), each of which was to have a Secretary-at-Large. From the six sections were to emanate local branches. The Union was to generally oversee all athletic competition in China, to be the custodian of athletic records, and to encourage sports participation at all age levels and levels of competence. It also took upon itself the responsibility of organizing the Chinese Far Eastern Championship Games team. In 1924, the Union was replaced by the China National Amateur Athletic Federation.[50]

The biggest domestic achievement of the China Amateur Athletic Union was the part it played in conducting the third National Athletic Meet, May 22-24, 1924, in Wuchang, Hupei —a meet full of firsts for China. For one thing, Chinese took an increasing part in the administration of the meet. Hsü Ping-san was the chief official and Chang Po-ling, the referee-in-chief. Except for swimming and baseball, all referees were Chinese.[51] In an attempt to unify athletics in China, Far Eastern Athletic Association rules were employed for the first time. Thirteen provinces competed in the meet as well as a Chinese basketball team from Manila (the first overseas Chinese team to take part in the meet).

The meet was actually three competitions in one: an open championship for any individual or team in China; a provincial championship scored on a point basis; and a sectional championship, also scored on a point basis.[52] For the first time competition was provided for women, though the results did not contribute to the team standings. They competed in basketball, softball, volleyball, and group gymnastics.[53]

During the course of the meet initial steps were taken toward the formation of the China National Amateur Athletic Federation (*Chung Hua Ch'uan Kuo T'i Yü Hsieh Chin Hui*) which took over the functions of the China Amateur Athletic Union, and proved to be a more productive organization than the Union. C. T. Wang was its Honorary President, and Chang Po-ling was head of the Management Committee. The YMCA, in the person of J. H. Gray, National YMCA Physical Director, was influential in this body through 1927. In 1930, the Federation was granted official recognition by the Nationalist government, significantly increasing its powers. The Federation affiliated with various international athletic organizations including the International Olympic Committee, and the international associations for swimming, soccer, track and field, gymnastics, tennis, weightlifting, and basketball. In 1932, 1936, and 1948, the Federation sent Chinese teams to the Olympic Games.[54]

YMCA INVOLVEMENT IN CHINESE SPORTS— 1911-1927

After Exner's forced return to the United States in 1911, the YMCA physical program continued to grow. Exner was replaced by J. H. Crocker as National YMCA Physical Director. Between that time and the arrival of J. H. Gray in 1919 as the last National Physical Director, the YMCA reached its highpoint in physical education work.

The YMCA physical education effort in China took two broad paths. The first involved programs initiated and run by the Y using its own facilities. The second path was that of "service activities" (i.e. services rendered by the YMCA to outside organizations). In this latter category fall programs started by the Y Physical Department in Chinese government schools, speeches made on behalf of physical education throughout China, and the coordination of such meets as the National Athletic Meet series. It is difficult to attach greater importance to either of these aspects. The latter certainly had a more far-reaching effect in the long run. However, it was through the former that the YMCA first gained the confidence of others and thus made the Chinese receptive to its service programs.

The YMCA's own physical education programs were limited to those cities where there were Association chapters. It was thus able to reach rural areas only indirectly. The YMCA's first branch was set up in Tientsin, and from there it spread to Shanghai, Peking, Foochow, and Canton. Of the 22 YMCA's in 1920, 15 were coastal, five were located in Central China, and only two were in West and Southwest China.[55]

It is difficult to talk about the physical program in Y branches in a general way. Facilities differed greatly as did the number and quality of the trained staff. Originally, most of the Y physical work had to be done outdoors. Gradually, the number of indoor facilities increased so that by 1914 there were five gymnasiums; by 1918, eight;[56] and by 1923, twelve.[57] The first swimming pool was opened at the Shanghai Association in January, 1915.[58]

One can get a feel for the YMCA physical training operation by looking at the program in the Shanghai Association. With the arrival of Exner in 1908, the Shanghai YMCA became the center of Y physical work in China. The local program, which was developed there between 1912 and 1917 under Alfred H. Swan, became a model for physical work in other Y chapters.

The basic work of the Association's Physical Department was accomplished via the large gymnasium class, similar to that used by Y associations in the U.S. at that time. As late as 1912, due in no small part to the cultural bias against physical activity still evident in China, the Shanghai YMCA had difficulty attracting participants to its programs. To counter lagging attendance two steps were taken. To appeal to the traditional inclination of many Chinese, a course in Chinese boxing was opened. Men that were willing to come for Chinese boxing were found later to be more receptive to such western games as volleyball.[59] In addition, Y members not ordinarily entitled to physical education privileges were accommodated gratis. As attendance increased, a more stringent admissions policy was instituted.

As the YMCA physical education program gradually caught on, the sports area became a busy place, open some ten hours per day, six days per week. In 1915, this involved some 3,000 participants per week. The following "typical day" at the Shanghai YMCA shows the scope of the operation.

9:30 A.M.   Gym practice for physical director trainees
11:00 A.M. Gym class for students in YMCA day school
1:00 P.M.   Gym class for students in YMCA day school
3:00 P.M.   Gym class for students in YMCA day school
4:00 P.M.   Boy's full-member gym, bath, and swim
5:15 P.M.   Business men's class
5:30-7:00 P.M. Swimming pool open for men
8:00-9:00 P.M. Orphan boys' gym class
9:00-9:30 P.M. Evening school students' gym, bath, and swim

The physical program at the Shanghai YMCA was never a luxury operation. As the program expanded, the budget constantly grew (from $3,445 in 1910 to $13,921 in 1916).* However, the struggle for operating expenses was ever present, and somewhat of a fetish was made of the constant check on the cost of showers, towels, and soap. Despite the fact that they were a service organization, the YMCA did not cater to a lower class of Chinese. Use of facilities was strictly limited to members and this required spare money, something which most Chinese lacked.[60]

THE GROWTH OF THE PHYSICAL EDUCATION PROGRAM AT THE SHANGHAI YMCA[61]

	1912-13	1913-14	1914-15	1915-16	1916-17
Total use of gymnasium	3,786	5,223	8,686	28,511	30,269
Total use of recreation grounds	1,978	1,690	2,126	2,861	2,869
Total use of pool			1,374	26,862	31,257
Total number of baths	12,788	11,829	31,422	61,138	72,183
Number of senior members registered in phys. dept.	50	90	200	480	648
Number of jr. members registered in phys. dept.	60	100	350	600	700

* Although this was a great deal of money to the Chinese, it was barely sufficient for the YMCA's program.

Growth in other YMCA Physical Departments was as steady as it was in Shanghai. In 1917, in all YMCA chapters combined, 130,890 attended gymnasium classes. In 1918, this increased to 224,197, and in 1922 to 725,062.[62] In 1923, the approximate total membership in all Y Physical Departments combined was 20,000 men and 5,000 boys. They were instructed by 46 full-time directors (36 of them Chinese), most of whom had had a middle school course plus a technical course in physical education.[63]

In order to encourage the participation of boys and young men in its program, the National Office of the YMCA Physical Department devised several programs which were run on a national scale. One of the most successful was the "Hexathlon Championships" adapted from a Y program developed in the United States. It involved competition between Y city associations, with each association divided into junior and senior (18 and over) divisions. Six events made up the competition: 1) 60 yard potato race, 2) 160 yard potato race, 3) standing broad jump, 4) running high jump, 5) fence vault (target throw for younger boys, and 6) shot put.[64] Each city association entered as many competitors as it wished, but only recorded the six best scores in each event. Each team competed individually, and the results were then forwarded to the national YMCA office which announced the winners. The Hexathlon Championship began in China in 1915 and continued into the mid-1920's.[65]

In 1917, the National Committee of the YMCA of China published a "Standard Program for Boys" which provided for five rankings of the traits of boys ages 12-20 in each of four categories: mental, physical, religious, and social. The five physical standards were 1) health, 2) swimming or walking, 3) jumping, 4) running, and 5) games.[66] In 1918, a "Four-Fold Program" was established in which physical fitness and healthy living were included.[67] Both of these programs viewed physical training as having an integral part in the development of the complete Christian man.

Because the YMCA saw itself responsible for developing a program which would eventually be totally Chinese-directed, a great deal of its time was spent in the planning and carrying out of programs which would train the future leaders of YMCA Physical Departments.

Dr. Max J. Exner first established the pattern for the training of Physical Directors when he opened his course in Shanghai in 1909. Essentially this method involved the training of a small group of men by one Physical Director. A. H. Swan, who became the Physical Director at the Shanghai YMCA in 1912, used this same basic idea when he organized a similar course for directors in 1914. Five students were in this class the first year and seven the next.[68] In the fall of 1915, The Tientsin Association opened a similar training school for six students.[69]

The YMCA also attempted to alleviate the shortage of trained physical training personnel by running summer sessions. The first summer course was given in 1911 and was intended mainly as supplemental work for people already working as Y Secretaries and Physical Directors.[70] In 1914, the first such session for Chinese was run at Mokanshan with 29 in attendance. Lectures were given in Chinese by C. H. McCloy (the school's Director), C. A. Siler, and A. H. Swan.[71] The summer session program continued into the 1920's under the direction of J. H. Gray.[72]

The method of training Physical Directors initiated by Exner, and known as the "Training Center Method," proved to be generally ineffective. This was chiefly because it duplicated efforts in several Association chapters each of which was in itself ill-equipped to run such a training program. Nevertheless, during the Second Conference of Employed Officers of the YMCA in China held in Hangchow in November, 1915, it was decided to continue with the training center and summer school programs while the planning for a centrally operated YMCA physical training school continued.[73] In compliance with the decisions of this conference, the First Physical Directors' Conference (also held in Hangchow) decided in March, 1916, that the training center scheme would be continued in several of the larger Association chapters with no central training school of physical education to be established for at least three years.[74]

Soon after the Physical Directors had voted to comply with the decisions of the Employed Officers' Conference, they realized that they had made a mistake. The continuation of the training of Physical Directors at local associations would consume too much of the local Director's time and force him to assign tasks that he should be performing himself to an ill-trained assistant. J. H. Crocker, the National YMCA Physical Secretary, himself recommended that, in place of the system then in effect, a *regional* training center system be adopted with two Directors at each regional center.[75]

The Physical Directors then called a second conference in December, 1916, at which time they modified their previous endorsement of official YMCA policy. They recommended that physical work within the Association be given first priority, and that work outside of the Association (e.g. in government schools) be attempted only when adequate personnel was available. Further, they decided that local associations should divorce themselves from the future training of Physical Directors which hereafter would be confined to a central YMCA physical training school which would be established immediately under the supervision of C. A. Siler, C. H. McCloy, and A. H. Swan.[76]

The YMCA School of Physical Education of the Association College of China was officially opened in January, 1918, with twelve students, nine of whom had come from YMCA branches. The program offered was intended for college graduates, but also accepted middle school graduates. The course itself was comprehensive and included training in physical education, the biological sciences, English, and pedagogy, in addition to instruction in religion and Bible. After two years of formal study, the students were to engage in practical work. Those who elected to terminate their studies after two years would be awarded the title of "Instructor of Physical Training." Those who continued for two more years of formal study would be awarded diplomas as "Director of Physical Education."

Students sent to the school by YMCA branches had their entire tuition covered by the National YMCA Office. Local Association chapters and/or the students themselves had to meet all other expenses. Students not coming from a Y affiliate had to pay a yearly tuition of $100 if sent by a church affiliated organization; or $300 if not. Provision was made for remission of these fees for graduates later serving the YMCA for a specified period.[77]

Despite these elaborate plans, so long in the making, the school closed down in June, 1919, after a mere year and a half of existence. World War I had imposed financial hardships on the YMCA in China, but contributing even more to the closing of the school was the fact that Siler, McCloy, and Swan all went on furlough at the same time and could not be replaced. Swan never returned to China; Siler went into the missionary field; and McCloy later became Chairman of the Physical Education Department at the National Southeastern University in Nanking.[78]

The closing of this school was not linked in any way to the failure of its program. From an initial enrollment of twelve, in January, 1918, the school increased to twenty-six students at the time of its closing. By 1920, former students were serving in Associations in Peking, Tientsin, Tsinan, Shanghai, Nanchang, Changsha, Foochow, Amoy, Hong Kong, and Canton.[79] The undertaking of the above school was certainly one of the most ambitious programs attempted by the YMCA Physical Department in China. Had it been continued, it probably would have considerably altered the course of physical education in China for the remainder of the Nationalist period. Its closing was the first real setback in physical education of the YMCA in China.[80]

The failure of the YMCA plan to train Chinese Physical Directors in China necessitated a basic change in policy which commenced with the appointment of Dr. J. H. Gray as National Physical Director in 1919. Promising Chinese were now to be sent to Springfield College in Massachusetts, which was affiliated with the YMCA. It consisted of Tung Shou-yi, Gunsun Hoh, Hui Min-fei, and Liu Hsüeh-sung (known as Snowpine Liu in the U.S.). All of the above became leading physical educators in China upon their return, and served in the China National Amateur Athletic Federation. Tung became Professor of Physical Education at Peking Normal University, and after 1949, a top Communist sports official. Hoh taught in the Department of Physical Education at Nanking Normal University and is now a top Formosan sports official. Hui served as President of the Kwangtung Physical Education College.[81]

As already pointed out, the YMCA, as a Christian organization, was very interested in the expansion of its various programs as a means of gaining a foothold in areas and among groups which would ordinarily be closed to more openly missionary groups. This, in turn would facilitate their propagation of Christianity. Had the Y limited itself to programs in its own limited number of centers throughout China, its influence would not have been what it was. A definite positive factor in the Y's development was the freedom which its Secretaries enjoyed to travel free of the suspicion which often greeted locally-based organizations in an area.[82] In the area of physical education, these service activities were especially significant.

The YMCA first became known in this connection as a coordinator and sponsor of athletic meets. The Y is best known for having initiated the two important series of meets during the Nationalist period: the National Athletic Meets, and the Far Eastern Championship Games (see chapter 3). However, the YMCA spent a much greater proportion of its time in the organization of many smaller, less-prestigious meets. The first YMCA sponsorship of an athletic meet took place in 1902 in Tientsin.[83] At the outset, the Y usually fielded a team in the competitions which it arranged with local schools. In subsequent years, however, the Y devoted itself increasingly to the management of meets.

In the same vein, the YMCA hosted "athletic days" whereby people interested in a particular sport, on an informal level of competition, would report to the YMCA athletic field for several hours of recreation.[84] The continuous sponsorship of small scale athletic meets and informal recreation through sports, during the first quarter of this century, carried on by no other group than the YMCA, was the chief reason why more formal athletics on a large scale were able to develop in Republican China. Without these opportunities, the skills necessary for national and international competition could never have been developed.

As mentioned above, the top YMCA Physical Directors (Crocker, McCloy, Swan, and Siler) spent a great deal of their time traveling and promoting the idea of physical education. They gave many lectures throughout China, both urban and rural. Consequently, the YMCA became synonymous with physical education in China, and when a government school or a municipal government began to think of initiating a physical education program, it was natural for them to turn to the Y for advice.

The YMCA was able to help them in several ways. If it was

a school seeking advice and it was located in the geographic area of a YMCA branch, the Physical Secretary of the branch sometimes taught a course there. At other times, the YMCA supplied government schools with teachers of regular subjects from the West, who by virtue of an athletic background were able to organize an active sports program there.[85] The Y was also able to supply in-service training for physical education teachers in government schools and during the 1913-14 school year, 11 schools in Shanghai sent staff members to the Shanghai YMCA once weekly for physical education training.[86]

From 1914 to 1916 YMCA Secretaries were constantly approached to organize physical education programs in various schools, especially in Peking and Shanghai. In 1914, the Peking YMCA directed physical education programs in the Peking Union Medical College and other local schools.[87] In 1915, the Chinese government, in conjunction with the YMCA, decided to organize departments of physical education in five normal universities. The first was founded in 1915 in Nanking, with the YMCA's Charles H. McCloy heading the department. In 1916, similar departments were founded in Peking, Szechwan, Wuchang, and Kwangtung. In each case, the YMCA was behind the organization of the department, and, in each case, the fact that the YMCA could only initiate the program, and did not have sufficient manpower to continue to direct it, resulted in the deterioration of the program. Only in the latter 1920's, when qualified Chinese physical education instructors trained abroad began to return, did these schools begin to fulfil their expectations.[88]

Although most of the programs which the YMCA set up for others involved educational institutions, this was not always the case. In November, 1915, John H. Crocker, accepted an invitation from the Kiangsu Educational Association and delivered a series of talks entitled "Why China Needs Physical Education." The lectures had a stirring effect on those assembled. This fact added to the favorable impressions which American playgrounds had made upon Huang Yen-pei (Secretary of the Kiangsu Educational Association) on a visit to the United States, caused him to petition the Provincial Governor of Kiangsu to establish a playground in every county in the province. The Governor agreed and ordered that some 60 playgrounds be built and that two men from each county be sent to a central location for three or four months of special training.⁸⁹ The YMCA was asked to run this special course. It opened in Shanghai, on November 26, 1915, with 145 students, all of whom had been graduates of Chinese or Japanese schools of physical education. The teachers were chosen from the YMCA's top physical men (Swan, Crocker, McCloy, and C. G. Hoh).⁹⁰

The YMCA physical education program between 1920 and 1927 continued along the lines which had been developed between 1908 and 1920. As was shown above, participation in the physical education program mushroomed during the 1920-1927 period under the leadership of J. H. Gray. The hexathlon competition continued and a boy's club pentathlon was introduced. Summer seminars were also continued.⁹¹ The YMCA continued to be involved in the administration of the National Athletic Meets and the Far Eastern Championship Games. It was also under YMCA auspices that Chinese soccer teams visited Australia in 1923 and New Zealand in 1924.⁹²

And yet, as the Physical Department continued to thrive statistically, it began to stagnate. The outstanding cause for this seems to have been the manpower shortage which plagued the program from its inception. By the 1920's, Chinese leadership at most YMCA branches had been sufficiently trained so that it could efficiently run the gymnasium classes and playground programs started years before. Athletic meets initiated by the Y were also, in the main, efficiently conducted by native Chinese. What was lacking, however, was the top leadership, the personnel which could produce creative new programs without which any organization, however successful, eventually begins to deteriorate. It was for this reason that the failure of the YMCA College of Physical Education in June, 1919, was so significant. The YMCA, despite all of its programs, was never able to develop the creative native physical education leadership which it craved. Most of the top American physical education leaders left China or turned to other pursuits around 1920. When, on top of this, many of the most promising Chinese went to the United States to study, the weight of maintaining the entire operation fell on Gray. Though he was a capable man, his primary energies had to be directed toward the continuation of what already existed. He never really had the freedom to breathe fresh air into the program.

The success of the YMCA effort in passing over the leadership of Chinese athletics to the Chinese gradually contributed to a reduction in its own influence. It was largely, if not completely, through the flow of events started by the YMCA, that the China Amateur Athletic Union and the China National Amateur Athletic Federation were started. As these organizations gained in strength, they gradually took over the control of domestic physical education which heretofore had been the province of the YMCA. Thus, the YMCA, which had gained so much of its status as an organizer of athletic meets, lost a primary source of influence. In time its overall status on the Chinese scene declined.

In the final analysis, it was the times themselves which drew the curtain on YMCA influence in China. Anti-foreign feeling began to grow in the mid-1920's. The May 30, 1925 incident in Shanghai in which 12 Chinese were killed at the command of a British police officer heightened these tensions. The YMCA, with its national offices in Shanghai, probably suffered accordingly. In addition, with the establishment of the Nationalist government in 1927-28, provincial and national physical education institutes began to be established in large numbers, and private control of physical education by groups such as the YMCA was discouraged.[93] With the return of J. H. Gray to the U.S. in 1927, the YMCA ceased its active role in Chinese physical education, and an era was brought to an end.

One cannot really summarize the success or failure of the YMCA physical education program. When the YMCA started this program, little organized physical education existed in China; when Chinese began to assume full responsibility over it in 1927, there existed a program organized on a national basis. Between 1900 and 1927 the YMCA was the dominant factor in physical education in China. What we have thus tried to do in this chapter is to point up the obstacles which the YMCA faced in building up this program, and show how they handled their difficulties, where they placed their emphasis, and where and why they were unsuccessful.

To appreciate their success, we must recall their difficulties. Foremost was the problem of language. National YMCA Physical Secretaries differed in their language competence (as did local Secretaries). Exner was able to develop a successful program without any knowledge of Chinese. McCloy and Siler were the most proficient in Chinese. Crocker was somewhere in between. Despite the fact that much success was often achieved without a knowledge of Chinese, there is little doubt that such a shortcoming carried with it a heavy burden. J. H. Crocker, who was the National Physical Secretary during the physical program's most successful years, made this clear in his correspondence, just before he left China.[94] Limitations in language frequently made the use of translators (in short supply themselves) necessary. A translator, however, interfered with the growth of a personal relationship between teacher and student. Yet, without one, comprehension often became difficult if not impossible.

To try to bridge the language gap, YMCA physical men were constantly preparing written material. If they were able, they prepared them in Chinese. Otherwise, they were prepared in English and later translated into Chinese. The YMCA publication department prepared rule books in Chinese and in English for various sports. Special pamphlets and texts were designed with titles such as "Physical Department Handbook," "Nomenclature," "Apparatus Work," "Track and Field Technique," and "Construction of By-laws of Athletic Governing Bodies."[95] Before 1915, the rules of the various sports had been transmitted orally.[96] Thus, the YMCA's translation and publication service was a definite step forward. Unfortunately, in preparing written material, the few YMCA men trained in physical education were robbed of time which ideally should have been spent in the field.

It was a severe shortage of manpower that prevented the YMCA physical program from developing further. As the program became more successful, the pressure of time on the top Physical Directors increased. Each new program that was developed brought with it new requests for lectures and new requests for advice. The YMCA was not geared to meet this demand.

It can be said that the YMCA had an orientational effect on Chinese physical education. When the YMCA started their work in China, physical education was little known and little understood as a modern phenomenon. Through their work in this area, China was put on the road toward breaking a traditional bias. This not only had a long range effect on the Chinese attitude towards play, but also contributed to a more positive attitude towards physical labor. That the Y did not completely succeed in rebuilding this attitude is not to its discredit; such a goal would have been visionary.

2

The Period 1928-1949: The Era of Government Control

WITH THE FORMATION of the Nanking government in October, 1928, an entirely new era in physical education was inaugurated. Physical training now became a concern of government and emphasis shifted to legislation and provision for physical education within the government bureaucratic structure. The practical consideration shifted to the physical education program in the school curriculum.

Conditions were so varied in different parts of China during the Republican period that accurate statements can only be made for the situation in limited geographic areas. Our emphasis here, therefore, will be on the formal aspects: government directives, legislation, and conferences.

THE BEGINNING OF NON-MILITARY MODERN SCHOOL PHYSICAL EDUCATION

The German-Japanese military tradition which was dominant in physical education at the beginning of the century did not go unopposed. The National Athletic Meets of 1910 and 1914, and the Far Eastern Championships, held in Shanghai in 1915, introduced western sports to many Chinese youths for the first time. Little by little, sports was incorporated into the curriculum of Chinese government schools. Eventually, the "dual track school physical education system" (*shuang kuei chih hsüeh hsiao t'i yü*) was developed in which military physical exercises were stressed in class and western sports given time after school.[1]

Between 1910 and 1920 there was a spurt in the growth of physical education teacher training schools. Other private physical training schools in Hangchow and Nanking joined the Chinese Physical Training School.[2] And, as previously mentioned, in 1915-16 the Chinese government and the YMCA jointly started physical education departments in five higher normal schools. The YMCA increased its own training program during this period. In 1915, the YWCA established a two-year physical training course for women which in 1925 became part of Ginling College in Nanking.[3]

As the 1920's approached, Japanese influence in education started to wane as American influence increased and progressive Chinese educators began to pay more attention to physical education. At the Fourth Annual Conference of the National Federation of Educational Associations in 1918, it was suggested that men be sent abroad to study physical education and that courses in it be required in normal schools. The conference also recommended the establishment of physical education associations in all provinces and municipalities. In order to extend military training, it called for boxing, fencing, and physical drill. The Ministry of Education endorsed these recommendations.[4]

At the first Conference of the Chinese Progressive Education Association in July, 1922, a subcommittee was appointed to debate the topic "Physical Education and National Games." In its four sessions, the subcommittee debated the entire range of topics under the general heading "Physical Education." It came out with recommendations to establish additional physical education specialists' training schools, both on a provincial and a national level; to establish full physical education curriculums in higher middle schools and normal schools so as to facilitate the training of elementary and other sundry physical education personnel; to work for more recreation grounds and programs for the masses; to establish a Chinese National Physical Education Research Association (*Chung Hua Ch'uan Kuo T'i Yü*

Yen Chiu Hui) which would be part of the Chinese Progressive Education Association; to offer military training as an elective in post-secondary schools and universities, but *not* as a replacement for physical education.[5]

The most significant outgrowth of the conference's discussion of physical education was the formation of the Physical Education Research Association, headed by C. H. McCloy. McCloy had left the YMCA in 1919 and returned to the United States for two years of research. He returned in 1921 to form the Physical Education Department of Southeastern University in Nanking. McCloy was especially interested in the development of modern teaching methods and materials. During his stay in the U.S., he had developed his own theories based on psychology and biology which he incorporated into the program at Southeastern. He emerged as the leader of progressive physical education in China between 1921 and his departure from China in 1926. Programs that he worked out during the 1920's for the training of physical education teachers were used by the Chinese government in the 1930's.[6]

One of McCloy's pet projects was the *Physical Education Quarterly* (*T'i Yü Chi K'an*) which he published almost single-handedly between 1922 and 1925. The journal was supposed to be an organ of the Physical Education Research Association, but he received little help with it and was compelled to fill most of its pages with his own findings and those of his colleagues at Southeastern University. Its articles usually dealt with teaching standards, health, teaching programs, and bodily development. Before McCloy left China, the journal had already ceased publication.[7] McCloy, working by himself, could not have the influence on Chinese physical education that he would have had, had there been a strong supporting cast behind him.

EARLY REFORMS UNDER THE NATIONALIST GOVERNMENT

As Chiang Kai-shek pressed on toward the unification of China in 1927-28, physical education, for the first time, began to receive real government attention. The changes effected eventually established the first total official government control over physical education.

The first step in this process took place in December, 1927, when the University Council (*Ta Hsüeh Yüan*)—which had been created in 1927 at the urging of Ts'ai Yüan-p'ei, to take the place of the Ministry of Education—established a National Committee for Physical Education under its auspices, headed by Liu Chia-hsiu. It was composed of well known athletes and specialists in physical education whose collective aim was to promote physical culture on a large scale. The Committee was largely ineffectual; partly because its members were scattered throughout China and could not be easily convened. The Committee was abandoned in 1928.[8]

In May, 1928, the University Council convened the First National Educational Conference. The outstanding resolution of this conference was that henceforth education would conform to the Three People's Principles of Sun Yat-sen. The two-week conference resolved, among other things, that "to promote nationalism, education should seek . . . to raise the general level of moral integrity and physical vigor of the people. . . ."[9] Specifically, the third point of the conference's 15 point resolution noted the importance of "stressing the training of national physical strength."[10]

The Three People's Principles were concerned in part with stimulating a national spirit, a spirit of sacrifice, and a sense of discipline. The Kuomintang wanted to do away with individualism and help forge group consciousness. They apparently were impressed by the notion that Britain's political leaders were developed "on the playing fields of Eton" and felt that by encouraging the people to work together and to learn to endure physical hardship through physical training and athletics, they would contribute toward a national sense of unity. It was further hoped that strengthening the body would increase the intellectual capacity of the nation.

The Three People's Principles Physical Education Program later spelled out the goals of physical education:

1) to emphasize training of character and disposition
2) to advocate military physical education
3) to expand mass physical education
4) to advocate physical education for women
5) to stress development for physical toil and intellectual thought

6) to contribute to family life, education and art education[11]

This new thrust in physical education in the late 1920's brought with it a readoption of the spartan military spirit that was a part of Chinese physical education in the first years of this century. American physical educators, with their emphasis on games and sports, who just ten years prior were invited to teach in Chinese schools, now began to be replaced by German methods, materials, and manpower. Colleges with professional physical education departments now began to invite German directors to head them. Chinese physical education students now began to be sent to Germany instead of the United States. This increasingly militaristic physical education, based on the German model, was predominant until 1948. It joined with, however, rather than replaced, the interest in sports which the Americans had helped create.[12]

The National Physical Education Law of April, 1929, stands out as the highlight of the first years of Nationalist government rule in the area of physical education. The law was amended in September, 1941, but its main provisions as ratified by the Legislative Yüan, and presented in their entirety below, remained in effect until 1949.

THE 1929 NATIONAL PHYSICAL EDUCATION LAW[13]

1) The young men and women of the Chinese Republic have a responsibility to be the recipients of physical education and parents or guardians have the responsibility of enforcing it.

2) The aims of physical education are to bring about orderly development, suitable health, as well as physical power and the power to resist, together with the growth of all faculties of the body so as to enable [each Chinese] to be able to endure every type of labor and exceptionally telling tasks.

3) In planning physical education programs, whether for boys or for girls, age and individual bodily strengths and weaknesses must be paid attention to; and its management

and methods should follow the declarations of the Training Commissioner's Department and the Ministry of Education.

4) All customs and habits which hinder the regular growth of the bodies of young men and young women should be strictly prohibited by the administrative organs of counties, municipalities, towns, villages and hamlets; and its program should be fixed by the Ministry of Education Committee and the Training Commissioner's Department.

5) Each self-governing hamlet, village, town and municipality must erect public sports grounds.

6) Schools at the upper middle school level and above must all establish physical education as a required subject and must, at the same time, comply with the previously announced military physical education program.

7) All physical education committees established among the people must be registered under the supervision of the local government, and make application to the Ministry of the Interior, and consult with the Training Commissioner's Department. However, those people who are serving the people's physical education in scientific research and in investigation of teaching materials are not bound by this limitation.
In matters of budget, all physical education authorities should be closely controlled by the local government which must watch its financial situation and call in higher government control bodies to help it in making decisions.

8) The physical education organized in each county, municipality, village, town, and hamlet must accept the control of the local government and be under that organization which controls education.

9) All physical education personnel responsible for school or people's physical education committees must have proper credentials. The regulations regarding the nature of the credentials are to be fixed by the Training Commissioner's Office.

10) All physical education personnel who have served for three years or more in good standing should be given

The Period 1928-1949: The Era of Government Control 37

suitable rewards by the Training Commissioner's Department, with the Department to work out details.

11) The Training Commissioner's Department should set up a special high level physical education committee to deal with the research findings of special organizations and to examine foreign situations so as to serve the objective of the people's physical education.

12) All physical education groups must inject group traits into the government program.

13) This law takes effect from the day on which it is issued.

The Kuomintang saw physical education as one means of developing a national spirit of unity which would enable China to emerge as a modern state capable of defending herself. For this reason, the 1929 law stresses national control of physical education. The phrase "group traits" mentioned in article 12 refers to the national feeling of oneness which the Kuomintang hoped to foster. National administration of physical education would also permit more efficient use of the limited top-level physical education personnel that was available. The Training Commissioner's Department* would be the organ of government responsible for overseeing the national program.

Article 4 addresses itself to the need to work against traditional attitudes which would undermine attempts at a successful physical education program. As late as 1929, there were still many parents opposed to their children's participation in physical education—a remnant of the Ch'ing view of what education should be. To them, shedding the traditional gown to participate in athletics was still an unthinkable step.

In compliance with the 1929 Law, many provincial and municipal educational administrative bodies (e.g. Kansu, Chekiang, Anhwei, Hupei, Shantung, Shanghai, and Peking) began to establish physical education committees staffed by physical education specialists.[14]

---

* No national physical education authority existed in 1929 since the National Committee for Physical Education was abolished in 1928. Reviving such a body was apparently contemplated at the time that the 1929 law was written.

In the same month that the National Physical Education Law was ratified, the government published a specific set of guidelines on education. The seventh article of this document stated that "each school grade and social group should uniformly stress the people's physical education. Middle school and university [physical education] specialists must receive military training, develop the aims of physical education, and make it their responsibility to increase the people's physical strength, train a stronger and healthier spirit, and cultivate disciplined habits." About this time, the Ministry of Education announced two and one-half to three hours per week of compulsory physical education for elementary school students, with from two to three hours per week required for other levels of education. The programs were to include marching, exercise, rhythm activities, sports skills and games, and traditional Chinese sports.[15] As tensions increased after the Mukden Incident in Manchuria in September, 1931, military training received more and more stress in school physical education programs.

THE FIRST NATIONAL PHYSICAL EDUCATION CONFERENCE AND ITS AFTERMATH

The 1929 National Physical Education Law had established the basis for a physical education program on a nationwide scale. However, it had provided no specific plan to be carried out, nor any administrative machinery. These were provided as a result of the First National Physical Education Conference called by the Ministry of Education, and held in Nanking, August 16-21, 1932.[16]

At the Conference's six sessions, the 400 delegates debated the full scope of physical education: school physical education, military training, administration, physical training for children, physical training for women, sports for the masses, traditional Chinese sports. What emerged from the over 280 resolutions put forward was a statement of the broad aims of physical education, together with recommendations for specific actions which should be taken to achieve these broad goals.

In the former vein, it was decided: 1) that the people must receive sufficient opportunity to develop their bodies, 2) that they be trained to exercise in order to adapt to external conditions, 3) that the spirit of cooperation and unity be cultivated together with courage, endurance, and nationalism, and 4) that the habit of participating in sports as recreation be developed among the people.

Most of the progressive steps taken in the area of physical education during the next few years stem from the resolutions of this conference: the appointment of a National Director of Physical Education and an advisory committee; the organization of physical education committees within provincial bureaus of education and municipal boards of education; the sponsorship of in-service summer school sessions by the Ministry of Education; the planning of physical education curricula for primary and middle schools; government takeover of the National Athletic Meet (to be held at two year intervals); support for annual meets in provinces, counties, and municipalities.[17]

In October, 1932, the first official Nationalist government administrative body for physical education was formed as the Physical Education Committee (*T'i Yü Wei Yüan Hui*) of the Ministry of Education. The Committee, staffed by such notables as C. T. Wang and Chang Po-ling, had broad responsibilities. The scope of their activity included the creation of plans for the national development of physical education, inspection to see that government directives in physical education were carried out, the formation of a strong academic physical education program, and the creation of a national physical education bureaucracy and budgetary apparatus.

The Committee was able to make moderate progress in most of these areas, though it suffered from limited manpower and power of enforcement. Its "National Physical Education Plan" (*Kuo Min T'i Yü Shih Shih Fang An*), which was issued in 1933 and which reflected the decisions made at the 1932 National Physical Education Conference, was largely sound and comprehensive. By 1935, the Committee was able to oversee the formation of 23 physical education committees in provinces, municipalities, and special districts.[18]

The Committee's greatest achievements were in the planning of national curricula. Its first action in this realm came in 1932-33 when the physical education directive of 1929 was revised. For the first four primary school grades, 150 minutes per week of physical education were required. Suggested activities included games, outings, traditional sports, hill climbing, calisthenics, and ball games. The requirement was lengthened to 180 minutes per week for fifth and sixth graders. At this level boys and girls were separated and more strenuous activities were introduced. All students were required to participate in after-school sports and exercise programs.

For lower middle school students, three hours per week plus ten minutes daily of morning exercise and 30 minutes daily of after-school exercise or recreation were required. The program stipulated was to include gymnastic exercises, corrective exercises, ball games, and track and field. The program for upper middle school students was the same except that it required two hours per week instead of three, and 50 minutes daily after school.[19] In 1936, the Ministry of Education began to publish outlines for university physical education requiring two hours per week. Military training was an integral part of the course.[20]

The pattern established by the Physical Education Committee (with minor revisions in 1942) remained the program in effect up until the end of Nationalist rule of the Mainland in 1949. In 1934, a formal national physical education curriculum was established which echoed the above program and reflected the "four-fold" program developed earlier by the YMCA.[21] With the official publication of the formal curricula, the Ministry of Education now deemed it improper for teachers to plan their own courses.[22]

What is so striking to us today about these curricula is the similarity between the school physical education pattern developed during the Republican period and that adopted by the Communists after their takeover (see chapter 6). The school physical education program has been viewed in both cases as a three-pronged entity. At the heart of the program is the regular physical education class *(cheng k'e)* during which time the basic work is done. The early morning exercise *(tsao ts'ao)* period, in both cases, has been regarded as a warm-up. In the colder winter months it has often been held in-between classes. Similarly, both the Nationalists and the Communists have used the extra-curricular *(k'e wai)* sessions to reinforce that which was learned in class and to foster sports competition.

The Period 1928-1949: The Era of Government Control

Physical education during the Republican period, however, did not enjoy the government support or the relative peacetime conditions which existed after 1949. Very often lack of staff and shortages of equipment caused the elimination of the regular class-time period. The early morning period seems to have only been successful in those instances where students lived on or near the campus and could arrive sufficiently early. It often resulted that the extra-curricular sports program, manned voluntarily for interested students by a faculty member who saw the need for such a program, was the only physical education available to a student.[23]

The Physical Education Committee also succeeded in setting up broad requirements for teacher training courses. This

REQUIRED EDUCATION FOR PHYSICAL EDUCATION PERSONNEL

NATURE OF EMPLOYMENT	REQUIRED EDUCATION
Elementary school teachers and junior staff members involved in public playgrounds and in administration work.	Four years of normal school training after elementary school or Three years of normal school training after junior high school.
High school physical education.	Five-year physical education.
Teachers and senior staff members in public playgrounds and involved in administration work.	Course after junior high school or Two-year physical education course after high school.
Top level administrators; physical education teachers in colleges, and leadership training institutions; directors at public playgrounds.	Five years of training in a department of physical education of a teacher training college after high school.

became an increased necessity in the 1930's. For, all told, between 1927 and 1949, 22 physical education training institutions were founded. In the main, the courses of study in these institutions (outlined below) were formulated by the Ministry of Education based on a program worked out by Charles H. McCloy at the National Southeastern University between 1921 and 1926.[24]

With the formal inclusion of physical education in the school curriculum, the need for printed material in Chinese became more acute. In 1933, a committee made up of primary and secondary physical education teachers was appointed to compile textbooks and other printed material. By the end of 1934, the committee had produced three volumes on physical education for the primary school level and six for the middle school level.[25] In 1935, the Ministry of Education entered into an agreement with the Commercial Press and the Ch'in Fen Book Company to print various athletic rules manuals.[26]

THE NATIONAL ATHLETIC MEETS UNDER THE NATIONALIST GOVERNMENT

After the completion of the third National Athletic Meet in 1924, plans had been worked out to hold the next meet in 1926 in Canton. The civil war, going on in China at the time, however, played havoc with these plans and it was not until 1930 that the fourth meet in this series was held in Hangchow, Chekiang. China took a step forward athletically with this meet due to the fact that the China National Amateur Athletic Federation took complete charge. The Chekiang provincial government also took an active role and bore $100,000 of the $260,000 budget. For the first time Chinese took complete charge of directing and refereeing the meet.[27] Chinese schools also took an increasing part in the meet as the majority of athletes now came from Chinese government schools.[28]

An innovation at the meet was the cessation of competition on the basis of geographic section (each consisting of several provinces) as had been the case previously. Instead, the unit of competition became the province and the municipality, of which 22 entered the 1930 competition.

Chinese government leaders were impressed with the potential which the meet held for national unity and, at its conclusion, took steps to put its control under the Ministry of Education. The Ministry set up an organizing committee and voted to hold the fifth meet in Nanking, in 1931. The Mukden Incident, in which the Japanese invaded Manchuria, forced its postponement until 1933.

Both the fifth and the sixth National Athletic Meets were run by the Chinese government. The previously unmatched scope of the meets, and the money spent on making them a success in times of increasing national tension, seem to indicate an effort on the part of the government to uplift morale and convey a feeling of normalcy. To this end, both meets were held on October 10th—the national holiday of independence.

President Wang Ching-wei expressed the government's feelings about the national meets in formal terms at the open ceremonies of the 1933 meet:[29]

> In the present-day world the struggle for survival depends not only on human energy but also on the utilization of material forces. That China at the present moment needs more adequate material resources there can be no doubt whatsoever, but this utilization of material forces depends essentially on the vigor of the human spirit. We can utilize these forces only when we are in healthful spirits, otherwise we shall be simply utilized by them instead. A healthy mind always dwells in a healthy body. With a sound body, one can carry on any struggle to the finish, and not give up midway, but an unswerving spirit in an unhealthy body cannot lead us to ultimate victory. In this lies the significance of athletics.

> Though in past athletic meets the training and health as well as the skill of our students have been amply demonstrated, yet, according to the reports of the Ministry of Education, the number of Senior Middle School graduates who are able to fulfill the requirements of the military physical examination is still not very large. The reasons for this state of affairs are manifold, but neglect of sports is one of the chief causes. My hope for the present National Athletic Meet is that the occasion may reveal both our strong and weak points in the matter of physical health, in order that we may promote the former and

rectify the latter. The aim of the athletes present today should be not merely to win personal honours, but more especially to contribute towards the strengthening of the country and the race. To impart this new spirit, this desire to fortify the country and the race, to the masses of the people, is therefore the primary aim of the National Athletic Meet. Over 100,000 people are present at this Meet today, and I hope that every one of them will become strong and healthy, so that they may with greater advantage share the responsibility of overcoming the national crisis.

The 1933 meet attracted 2,248 athletes (including 706 women) from 33 provinces and municipalities including athletes from the provinces of beleaguered Manchuria. For the occasion, the country's largest steel and concrete sports arena was constructed, near the Ming Tombs, at a cost of from one to one and a half million dollars. Some 300,000 spectators filled the grounds during the 10 days of competition. They were joined by over 300 newspaper correspondents and 100 photographers from 134 newspapers and news agencies, as well as several film companies. Management of the meet by China's top sports administrators—Chang Po-ling, C. T. Wang, Gunsun Hoh, and Tung Shou-yi—ensured its smooth completion.[30]

The Shanghai Meet of 1935 had a similar story behind it. The Shanghai municipal government received permission from the national government to float a public bond of 3,500,000 *yüan* to finance the meet. A new 70,000 seat stadium was built at the Kiangwan Civic Center[31] adjoined by a swimming pool, a gymnasium, and numerous sports fields.[32] The more than one million spectators present made the meet a financial success as well.[33]

A seventh meet had been planned for 1937 in Nanking, but the Marco Polo Bridge Incident, and subsequent Japanese occupation, postponed this meet until May, 1948, when it was held in Shanghai.[34] Chiang Kai-shek apparently used this meet as a show of the strength of his government. Although he was able to secure 58 teams (over 2,000 athletes) from provinces, municipalities, overseas Chinese and the military, attendance was only 10% of the 1935 meet.[35] Soon after, the Nationalist government collapsed and the National Athletic Meet series came to an end.

CHINA AND THE OLYMPIC GAMES

China's first contact with the Olympic movement came in 1922 when she became a member of the International Olympic Committee. This membership was initially inactive, and it wasn't until 1928, at the Ninth Olympiad in Amsterdam, that China participated in an IOC meeting. When China's representative at Amsterdam, Paul Sung (who was also a YMCA man) returned, his impressions were published by the Commercial Press under the title *Olympia (Wo-neng-pi-ya)*.

In spite of this visit, China did not consider herself ready to send athletes to compete in the Games on a regular basis, and probably would have waited many years before doing so had it not been for the conflict with Japan. Several months before the 1932 Games were scheduled to open in Los Angeles, it came to the attention of the China National Amateur Athletic Federation that Japan was intending to send Chinese athletes to Los Angeles in the name of the Manchukuo (the puppet government of the Japanese in Manchuria). To counter this, the CNAAF hastily decided to send two Chinese athletes to these Games. They finally succeeded in sending one athlete —sprinter Liu Ch'ang-ch'un—who competed without distinction, accompanied by an official of the CNAAF.

Preparations for participation in the Tenth Olympiad in Berlin in 1936 were made in a more orderly fashion. They began with the setting up of a training camp by the CNAAF in the summer of 1935 at Tsingtao. All track and field winners at the 1935 National Athletic Meet were invited to the camp and a German coach was brought in to train the group. In the early part of 1936, a more advanced eight-week camp was set up at Tsinghua University, with the final tryout held in June, 1936. The final team consisted of 107 male and female athletes and officials in basketball, track and field, soccer, swimming, cycling, weightlifting, boxing, and Chinese boxing. In preparation for the Games, the soccer and basketball teams made an extended tour of Southeast Asia including Manila, Indochina, Burma, India, Java, Thailand, and Malaya. Chinese athletes met with little success at the Games in Berlin.

In addition to the official delegation to Berlin, a group of 34 physical educators, under the leadership of Dr. T. L. Yuan of the Peking National Normal University made the trip to

Germany in order to study physical education in Europe. Several of the group remained in Germany until September of that year.

The final Chinese delegation sent to the Olympics under the Nationalist flag represented China at the 1948 Games in London. A team of 37 participated in track and field, swimming, soccer, basketball, and cycling, again without distinction.[36]

PHYSICAL EDUCATION DURING THE SINO-JAPANESE WAR

All contemporary observers seem to agree that Chinese physical education suffered severe setbacks during the period of confrontation with Japan (1931-45). Nevertheless, the Nationalist government, because it saw physical education as a means of strengthening the people, continued to give it support throughout this period.

In 1936, the Physical Education Committee, which enjoyed a somewhat low status in the Ministry of Education, was elevated to the Department of Physical Education (*T'i Yü Tsu*). As such, it became responsible for the coordination of all matters having to deal with physical education, boy scouts (*t'ung tzu chün*), hygiene education, and student military training. Concurrently, physical education departments were established in increasing numbers at the provincial and municipal level.

After the government was forced to move from Nanking to Chungking, Szechwan, in 1937, the Ministry of Education of necessity underwent a streamlining. In September, 1939, the Department of Physical Education was abolished, and replaced by an enlarged form of the Physical Education Committee which had existed prior to 1936. The Committee consisted of one standing member and departments of planning and publication. In 1940, the names of these departments were changed to School Physical Education and Social Physical Education. Gradually, the Physical Education Committee began to increase its staff size and regained some of the functions of the 1936 Department of Physical Education. In September, 1941, a department in charge of research and publication was added to the two already existing. At this time, boy scout work, hygiene education, and school military training were transferred to other departments and committees of the ministry. The Committee—which in the interim changed its name to the National Physical Education Committee *(Kuo Min T'i Yü Wei Yüan Hui)*—continued to be enlarged and undergo minor structural changes through 1945.[37]

The early 1940's were years in which the Physical Education Committee was actively trying to plan for the future. At the same time, it had to take into account the limitations imposed upon it by the war in progress. In October, 1940, the Second National Physical Education Conference was held in Chungking with the emphasis on deciding upon a national physical education program which stressed China's war needs. The outgrowth of this conference was a reissuance of directives for all grade levels and the establishment of a four-month course to train high level municipal and provincial physical education administrators. On September 9, 1941, the 1929 National Physical Education Law was reissued in revised form and that day declared an annual physical education holiday. Except to reflect the new government machinery created to administer physical education since 1929, and to decree that all national, provincial and municipal budgets must list allotments for physical education, both the 1929 and the 1941 forms of the law were equivalent. In the same year the "National Physical Education Plan" (now called *Kuo Min T'i Yü Shih Shih Fang Chen*) was also reissued.

It was not until the 1940's that the Nationalist government took its first effective step toward enforcing its physical education directives. In 1940, the Ministry of Education published methods of instruction and criteria for evaluation of athletic skills and bodily growth. Testing groups were organized to visit the schools and examine weight, height, bodily development, and athletic skills. Boys were examined in 35 phases of track and field, ball games, and apparatus, while girls were tested in 24 areas of track and field and ball games. Such testing teams were able to visit every county and municipality in Szechwan in 1940, testing 18,000 middle school students. Similar testing efforts were continued through 1944. In the period 1945-47, when the convening of physical education committees became impossible, physical education personnel were dispatched on a tour of accessible areas (chiefly limited to Szechwan) to promote physical education.[38] Thus, although the level of accomplishment was low, the government effort in physical education continued virtually until the Communists took control.

The China National Amateur Athletic Federation also made an effort to continue with its efforts during the war years. Beginning in 1941, it banded together with referee associations, and formed branches in the rear areas. In 1943, there were 12 branches of the Federation in provinces, counties, and municipalities, and nine referee associations.[39] The China National Amateur Athletic Federation remained active until 1949 and thereafter continued its work on Taiwan.

THE FINANCING OF PHYSICAL EDUCATION

Before the Sino-Japanese War, little provision was made for specific financing of physical education programs on the local level. Funds for physical education had to come from the school's general budget. Unless the particular school in question had extensive resources or the school principal looked at physical education in a particularly favorable light, the chances were that little from the school budget would be appropriated for physical education. The program generally depended on student contributions to maintain itself, resulting in a great variation of quality from school to school. Only in

CENTRAL GOVERNMENT PHYSICAL EDUCATION APPROPRIATIONS (1939-1947) [41]*

YEAR	APPROPRIATION (YÜAN)	AUGMENTATION	SUM
1939	88,000	——	88,000
1940	88,000	——	88,000
1941	88,000	——	88,000
1942	800,000	——	800,000
1943	1,318,000	692,000	2,010,000
1944	2,405,000	697,280	3,102,680
1945	3,303,900	——	3,303,900
1946	10,000,000	3,000,000	13,000,000
1947	50,000,000	——	50,000,000

* Any consideration of the above figures must take into account the runaway inflation plaguing China at the time. This inflation can be summarized as follows using July 1937 as the base year (1.0): June 1938 (1.4), June 1939 (2.3), June 1940 (4.9), June 1941 (11), June 1942 (36), June 1943 (132), June 1944 (466), June 1945 (2,167), August 1946 (5,485), June 1947 (36,872).[42]
From this it can be computed that central government appropriations for physical education generally *declined* during this period. In terms of 1937 currency, the appropriations for physical education from 1939-1947 were approximately: 38,300; 18,000; 8,000; 22,200; 15,200; 6,660; 1,525; 2,370; and 1,360 *yüan.*

PROVINCIAL GOVERNMENT PHYSICAL EDUCATION APPROPRIATIONS (1939-1946) [43]

YEAR	ANHWEI	KIANGSI	SHANTUNG	HUNAN	SHENSI	KIRIN
1939	—	—	—	—	—	—
1940	—	—	—	—	—	—
1941	5,000	—	—	83,078	—	—
1942	25,000	—	—	2,078,509	7,000	—
1943	27,000	unknown	—	unknown	17,160	—
1944	50,000	100,000	—	unknown	10,000	—
1945	68,720	200,000	102,000	unknown	unknown	—
1946	50,000	500,000	8,847,200	117,000	unknown	427,407

YEAR	LIAONING	SUIYÜAN	KWANGTUNG	KWANGSI	KWEICHOW	CHEKIANG
1939	—	—	—	—	19,870	1,800
1940	—	—	—	—	25,435	7,000
1941	—	4,585	1,200	—	56,790	13,000
1942	—	15,000	15,187	—	98,000	12,000
1943	—	119,927	286,000	—	253,000	67,000
1944	—	296,800	unknown	unknown	500,000	80,000
1945	—	212,112	1,553,000	6,197,500	1,300,000	150,000
1946	5.325 (million)	12.317 (million)	18.058[a] (million)	62.808[b] (million)	200,000	831,000[a]

YEAR	YÜNNAN	FUKIEN	SHANGHAI	TIENTSIN	PEKING	NANKING
1939	—	4,000	—	—	—	—
1940	—	5,400	—	—	—	—
1941	—	8,064	—	—	—	—
1942	—	14,000	—	—	—	—
1943	—	172,000	—	—	—	—
1944	200,000	210,600	—	—	—	—
1945	300,000	436,192	—	—	—	—
1946	900,000	910,000	120,000,000	2,676,240[c]	22,000,000	753,400

Appropriations given in *yüan*
a Includes playgrounds and sports committee budget
b Includes other items
c Includes sports committee budget

church schools or progressive schools (e.g. the Nankai Middle School) was physical education properly budgeted.[40]

Beginning in the mid-1930's, government appropriations to physical education programs were made on a more regular basis, though there was still no official line in the budget for them. In 1939, the central government began to make specific allocations in its budget for physical education. Article VIII of the 1941 Physical Education Law took the final step by requiring separate budgeting for physical education by central, provincial, and municipal governments.

We have attempted here to portray the development of physical education in China during the 1928-1949 period. Our presentation undoubtedly has been uneven. In certain areas, abundant information is available, while in others, only the barest outline is to be found. In a sense, this lack of uniformity portrays better than words, the true situation in Chinese athletics at that time. Sports and physical culture never managed to emerge from the developmental stages during the Republican period.

Practically speaking, sports development in these years was foredoomed. The Kuomintang government ruled over China in name, but in fact, China, with the Japanese controlling some areas, Nationalists others, and Communists still others, was as divided politically as she had ever been. What this element of disunity did was to drain an already weak potential for physical education development. Instead of developing a unified administrative command which could tap China's meager reservoir of manpower and establish a central physical education institute to train the badly needed leadership, each faction was left to fend for itself. Teachers reflected Japanese, German, or American influence. But no influence was sufficiently evident to establish the basis of a lasting tradition.

It is difficult to pass judgment on the achievements of the Nationalist government in physical education. For one thing, written records which are passed down to us tend, in all their maze of detail, to cover up the fact that by 1949 the vast majority of Chinese had not only never participated in sports, but had never even been to school. We have no standards against which to judge Kuomintang physical education achievements, because the Nationalists inherited a system which was in its infancy. For it to have flourished, ideal conditions would have had to prevail. There was nothing ideal about the conditions in China from 1928 to 1949.

It is thus, on the efforts of the Chinese, rather than on their achievements, that we have concentrated. We have seen that despite continuous war pressures, despite a lack of funds, despite insufficient leadership, despite improper equipment, the Chinese government saw enough significance in physical education to give it support as best it could. All this leads us to believe that under more normal conditions, physical education—which suffered stunted growth during the last 20 years of the Republican period—would have seen a much happier fate.

3

The Far Eastern Championship Games: The First International Athletic Competition in the Far East

IN THE TWO PRECEDING chapters, we have highlighted the development of western sports and physical culture in China from their inception until the Communist takeover.

In this final chapter, dealing with the Republican period, we will treat in greater detail one area of Republican sports: the Far Eastern Championship Games series—a series which, perhaps more than any other single event before the Communists took control, sensitized the masses to sports. The existence of this series encouraged the development of a stronger domestic athletic program and, at times, provided the main rationale for the continuation of the National Athletic Meet series. As we have already seen, the Far Eastern Championship Games provided a convenient opportunity for China's physical education leaders to meet. It was during one of these meets that the idea of the China Amateur Athletic Union was born. Without a doubt, this series of meets was the most stable feature of Chinese athletics during the period.

The Far Eastern Championship Games (FECG) was a series of ten international athletic meets, conducted roughly according to the format of the Olympic Games, in which China, Japan, and the Philippines competed from 1913 to 1934. In the history of Far Eastern sports, these Games stand out as the first international games in which China competed, and, indeed, as the first international team competition in that part of the world. The Games must be regarded as one of the first links in the chain which today sees sports as a major area of interest for the Communist regime.

In looking at this series of Games, one must not fail to keep in mind that China underwent a period of internal unrest between 1913 and 1934. A glance at any chronology of the period will reveal such terms as: the Second Revolution against the rule of President Yüan Shih-k'ai of 1913; the Twenty-one Demands imposed by Japan on China in 1915; the Treaty of Versailles and the May Fourth Movement of 1919; the rise of the Chinese Communist Party in 1921; the first United Front between the Kuomintang and the Communists (1924-27); the Northern Expedition led by Chiang Kai-shek (1926-28); and the Mukden Incident in September, 1931. Clearly these games did not take place in ordinary times.

And yet, it is precisely the fact that they were able to continue regularly for more than twenty years—with Chinese participation in all of them—despite the fact that just about everything else in China was in upheaval, that causes us to marvel. It is not as important to note that the Games were terminated in 1934 because of political disputes, as that, somehow, they lasted until 1934.

THE INCEPTION OF THE FAR EASTERN CHAMPIONSHIP GAMES

As was the case with almost anything involving western sports in the Far East, the YMCA was instrumental in the inauguration of the Far Eastern Championship Games. For several years prior to 1913, it had been customary to hold international athletic events in conjunction with the annual Manila Carnival. Japanese baseball teams, groups of athletes from Hong Kong, and occasional contestants from Singapore had entered the events at various times.[1] In 1912, William Tutherly, Frank L. Crone, and Elwood S. Brown, all officers of the Philippine Amateur Athletic Association, announced that they would expand upon previous athletics at the Carnival and hold a formal international athletic meet in conjunction with the next carnival in February, 1913.[2]

The Philippine Amateur Athletic Association sent Brown to China and Japan to do promotional work for the meet and, as a result of his travels, the Far Eastern Athletic Association (FEAA) was formed with Dr. Wu Ting-fang of China, President, Elwood S. Brown, Secretary, and J. H. Crocker, Physical Director of the YMCA in China, as Treasurer; and China, Japan and the Philippines as competing nations.[3] Official formation of the Association and the adopting of its constitution didn't take place until February, 1913.

In the summer of 1912, in anticipation of the ensuing Games, the Far Eastern Athletic Committee for China was named—the first such national athletic organization in China—for the purpose of sending a team to the first FECG.[4] In 1919, the China Amateur Athletic Union took control of Chinese participation in these games. In 1924, the Union was reorganized as the China National Amateur Athletic Federation[5]—a group which controlled athletics on the Mainland until 1949.

From its outset, the FECG was not viewed by its organizers as a competitor of the Olympic Games. Its stated purpose was ". . . to supplement not to rival or intrude upon the programme of the International Olympic Committee which is to establish world-wide International contests. In this connection it is our object to develop Oriental athletes to the point where they may enter the International Olympic Contests and have as much chance of success as the athletes of the other nations of the world."[6]

According to the constitution of the FEAA adopted on February 10, 1913, the following events were to be contested at the Far Eastern Championship Games:[7]

TRACK AND FIELD	SWIMMING
100 yard dash	50 yard free style
220 yard dash	100 yard free style
440 yard dash	440 yard free style
880 yard run	mile free style
mile run	100 yard backstroke
120 yard high hurdles	220 yard breaststroke
running high jump	200 yard relay

TRACK AND FIELD	TEAM SPORTS
pole vault	tennis (singles and doubles)
discus throw	baseball
12 pound shot put	basketball
javelin throw	volleyball
five mile run	soccer
full marathon	
half-mile relay	
mile relay	
pentathlon (running broad jump, shot put, 220 yard dash, discus throw, mile run)	
decathlon (100 yard dash, running broad jump, shot put, running high jump, 440 yard dash, 220 yard low hurdles, discus throw, pole vault, hop-step and jump, mile run)	

The FIRST Far Eastern Championship Games[8] were held February 1-9, 1913, and proved to be a great success, as did all FECG meets through the years. Over 150,000 people paid their way into the carnival grounds, with the admission fee to the grounds also permitting entrance to the Games.[9] Of those attending, many must have been overseas Chinese, for the Chinese community in Manila rallied strongly behind the Chinese team, and, in fact, bore all of their transportation and hotel expenses. Spectators were treated to a great deal of pageantry during the Games, which were highlighted by the Olympic-style opening parade of athletes and elaborate closing ceremonies.[10]

The Philippines, with a team of about 80, was the only country to field a complete squad. The Japanese sent only a baseball team and several distance runners, while the Chinese team of about 40 (under the leadership of Alfred H. Swan— Physical Director of the Shanghai YMCA) competed in all events except baseball.[11] Most of the Chinese athletes (who had undergone three months of training under J. H. Crocker of the YMCA before leaving Shanghai) were products of China's colleges and universities—Nanyang, St. John's, Nanking, Tientsin, Tungchow, Peking, Tsinghua—and/or the YMCA.¹²

China's best performances in this inaugural event were in the decathlon (first and second places), 120 yard high hurdles (first and second), running broad jump (first), and running high jump (first).¹³ The Philippines, by virtue of their superior numbers, had been assured of the team title before the meet actually got under way.

The SECOND Far Eastern Championship Games, held in Shanghai May 15-22, 1915,¹⁴ can be called the first major international sports meet held in China, and thus, from a Chinese point of view, should be considered the most significant of the meets in this series. In every way this event had the complete support of Chinese officialdom. On the organizing committee (headed by J. H. Crocker of the YMCA) were such illustrious Chinese as Wu Ting-fang, onetime Chinese Minister to the United States; T'ang Shao-yi, Premier of the Republic of China; Chung Mun-yew, Director of the Shanghai-Nanking Railroad; C. C. Nieh; Yu Yah-ching; Chang Po-ling, President of the Nankai Middle School; and Chu Pao-san.¹⁵ Although it is highly probable that many of these people served merely in an advisory capacity, both E. S. Brown and A. H. Swan, in their reports on the Games, stress that the Chinese took a definite part in the running of these Games.¹⁶ The names of Chang Po-ling and C. T. Wang are referred to again and again in connection with these Games in subsequent years.

The attitude of the Chinese leaders toward the Second FECG and towards sports in general is no better illustrated than by the reply of several government ministers to the question posed by YMCA officials: "Can we count on your support for such a movement?" They replied [sic]: "It is not a question for us to decide. You are doing so much for the young men of China that it is our duty to help you. We want our men to have strong bodies, and your work will do more to make this possible than any plan that we could think of or carry out."¹⁷

Financial support from government officials was not lacking either. President Yüan Shih-k'ai donated $2,000 plus an additional $500 to bring a baseball team of overseas Chinese from Honolulu to compete for China. President Yüan also donated the trophy to be presented to the championship team. Vice-President Li Yüan-hung gave $1,000 and additional money was collected from other government officials. All other expenses were covered by ticket sales.

Despite all of this preparation, the Games almost didn't come off at all. Firstly, an influential group of Japanese were opposed to events of this type and refused to sanction the trip of the Japanese to Shanghai. Further, Japanese public opinion at the time (concurrent with the issuing of the Twenty-one Demands) apparently did not favor Japan's participation either. Only a last minute trip to Japan by J. H. Crocker was able to patch things up and bring the Japanese to Shanghai (though two days late).

The meet itself was held in the Hongkew Recreation Park, and in this too there is a story. The organizing committee of the Games had to ask special permission for the use of the park because the Municipal Council of Shanghai did not permit Chinese to use its public parks. To the surprise of everyone involved, this request was granted and a new quarter-mile cinder track as well as grandstands were built especially for the Games.[18]

Over 100,000 spectators filled the grounds during the eight days of the meet and they witnessed events in which 350 athletes competed. They were treated to a winning performance by the Chinese team which, with the aid of a superior number of athletes, was able to defeat the other two teams. Nevertheless, it was a Filipino by the name of Saavedra who stole the show with "firsts" in the 100 yard dash, high jump, and pole vault.

Immediately following the FECG events, a series of open events (with no restriction as to country of residence or amateur standing) was held in which British and American athletes also competed. As a part of these events, known as the Open International Games, the Chinese baseball team from Honolulu, which the $500 donation from President Yüan had helped bring to China (but which was unable to compete in the regular FECG because of professionalism), was victorious.[19] The Open International Games were a feature which regularly followed the FECG throughout their duration. Their original purpose was to give the best Oriental athletes a chance to compete against European and American athletes resident in the Far East. As the performance level of the Orientals grew, however, very few Westerners were able to overcome the lack of sufficient training and still compete with the Orientals on an equal footing. Thus the Open International events—originally a highlight of the FECG—gradually became an anticlimax to the FECG.[20]

In addition to the athletic competition, a boy scout competition, with several hundred boys from Wuchang, Canton, Tientsin, Peking, Soochow, and Nanking, took place during the Second Far Eastern Championship Games. Their demonstrations included gymnastic bridge-building, fire lighting, model airplane flying and tent pitching.[21] Demonstrations of a "mass" nature such as this one became a fixture during the history of the Games. Ten thousand participated in the demonstrations at the 1930 Games. Their visual effect might be compared to that received at the half-time show of an American football game.

The general reception that the people of Shanghai gave to the Second FECG can be judged from the following statement made by Elwood S. Brown, member of the Philippine delegation to the Second FECG:

> I have never seen such enthusiastic rooting and cheering in my life at any athletic event. The Chinese and Japanese cheer continuously. . . . [When the Chinese team scored a goal to tie the Filipino soccer team] instantly that whole Chinese crowd rushed from all four sides out into the field, thousands of hats sailed into the air, the Chinese players were lifted up. . . . It was fully ten minutes before the officials could clear the grounds and allow the contest to go on.[22]

Despite its immediate success, the Second Far Eastern Championship Games were most significant in China for their long range ramifications in the area of sports and physical education. People such as T'ang Shao-yi (who joined the physical education committee of the Shanghai YMCA) began to take an active role in Chinese sports which continued long after the Games themselves were completed. Interest stirred up by the Games helped bring about a great increase in the number of athletic meets at practically every school, and newspapers in Shanghai began to publish the results of the most obscure athletic contests.²³ In short, athletics began to make inroads into the lives of the average Chinese.

With the holding of the THIRD Far Eastern Championship Games in Tokyo, Japan, in May, 1917, the last of the three participant nations had all played host to the Games. (This order of the Philippines first, China second, and Japan third, as hosts, was to continue until the dissolution of the Games.) In the first two sets of games, Japan had never been represented by more than twenty athletes. Thus, the opportunity to field a complete team of 140 (as compared to 100 for the Philippines and 90 for China) ²⁴ gave her the first real chance to compete for the team championship (symbolized by a gold wreath presented to the FEAA by the International Olympic Committee).²⁵ Japan didn't waste this opportunity and her 120 points were 40 better than the total of the runner-up Philippines.²⁶

As had been the case in the Philippines and in China, government officials gave their full support to the Games. Because Tokyo had no athletic field with a sufficient seating capacity, a temporary stadium which could hold 20,000 fans was erected. Grace and dignity were added to the Games by the constant presence of Marquis Okuma, together with other elder statesmen and young princes.²⁷

F. H. Brown, who, with Dr. Jigoro Kano, Japanese member of the IOC, was the moving force behind the Games, summed up their impact as follows: "There have been many athletic meets which, for sheer size, surpass the Far Eastern Championships, but, with the exception of the International Olympics, there have been none which compare with this in influence upon international relations and the promotion of all around physical education."²⁸

The FOURTH Far Eastern Championship Games, held in Manila, in May, 1919, followed very closely the same pattern of those which preceded it. The Japanese, because of a reluctance on the part of school officials to give Japanese athletes time off to compete, were once again weakly represented, and China, with a complete contingent (with the exception of baseball) of about 100, supplied most of the competition for the victorious Philippines.²⁹

For the first time in the competition, no national team winner was declared. It had been decided instead to substitute separate championships in each sport instead of declaring one overall national champion. The practice of awarding points to each team in each event was similarly no longer followed. In this way, officials hoped to eliminate the disadvantage of the nations, which, because of a shortage of manpower, or climatic conditions which hampered their performance, were handicapped in certain events.[30]

The general success of the FIFTH FECG, held in Shanghai, in May, 1921, was summarized very accurately by J. H. Gray, National Physical Director of the YMCA in China, and in charge of all arrangements for the May, 1921 meet at Hongkew Park in Shanghai:

> In every way, I think it can be said that this set of games surpassed all of its predecessors. For in the number of athletes taking part, the interest shown by the countries participating, the attendance of the games, the amount of money involved, the difficult international political questions overcome, the spirit of sportsmanship displayed on the part of the athletes, the records that were broken and the realization of the principles for which the Far Eastern Athletic Association stands, all show a marked advance on previous contests covering a period of about ten years.

The basis of Gray's remarks is that in the 1921 competition, for the first time in the history of the Games, all three teams entered full squads of more than 100 athletes each. This undoubtedly contributed to the wave of athletic achievement which saw fourteen new records established and two old records tied.[31] As had been the case more often than not through the years, Filipino athletes again led all of their competitors in track and field, setting records in the 880 yard run, broad jump, pole vault, discus, and decathlon.[32] By taking "firsts" in basketball, volleyball, and soccer, China fared best in the team events. From an overall team-performance standpoint, the Philippines, with four championships (swimming, tennis, baseball, track and field) led, followed by China (with three championships), and the Japanese team (which won only the full marathon).³³ This marked the first time that the outstanding team performance was not registered by the host team.

China's failure to win the team championship might be attributed to the political unrest rampant in the country. Chaos in student life in 1919 and 1920, sparked by the May Fourth Incident, had made systematic coaching, training, and practice meets difficult to carry out. Indeed, many athletes involved in the student strikes of that period neglected their athletic training as well as their studies. Thus, it was not until a few weeks before the Games began that China's athletes went into serious training.³⁴

From the box office standpoint, the Fifth FECG was also a great success. About 155,000 people crowded into the Hongkew Park grounds, ignoring the rain which plagued the meet.³⁵ The organizing committee had initially been quite dubious about obtaining the $40,000 to $60,000 necessary to run the Games, and had scurried around making appeals to the Peking and Canton governments, as well as to some of the warlords who governed various provinces.³⁶ Although they were not always successful in gaining financial support from these sources, the extraordinary attendance enabled them to cover all expenses and realize a net profit of $14,000.³⁷

Part of the popularity of the 1921 Games can be attributed to the mass demonstrations traditionally presented as a part of the Games. In 1921, girls participated in these demonstrations for the first time. From 500 to 1000 girls, under the direction of the Physical Education Department of the YMCA, broke into small groups on the field and demonstrated various games and activities which could be adapted to popular use.³⁸

If the Fifth FECG were the best yet, the SIXTH were still better. Some 250,000 people (with many being turned away) streamed into the Osaka City Stadium for the May, 1923 Games. This stadium had been erected especially for the occasion, and was quite an improvement over the temporary structure which housed the Tokyo Games six years earlier. The total athletic contingent of 431 was made up of 177 from Japan, 141 from the Philippines, and 113 from China (with her delegation headed by F. K. Lau, L. K. Du, and J. H. Gray of the YMCA).

Again, chaotic internal conditions made training difficult

for the Chinese athletes. As a result, her athletes came in third. Nevertheless, the following statement by F. H. Brown, active in the organization of the meet, shows China's determination to be there:

> China's greatest victory lay in her success in bringing such a large team of athletes to Japan under difficult conditions. Certain elements in China saw in her participation in the games at Osaka a declaration of friendliness with Japan, and strongly opposed the sending of a delegation. The China athletic authorities, led by Dr. C. T. Wang, China's great Christian statesman, and Dr. J. H. Gray, National Y.M.C.A. Physical Director, held firmly to the position that political animosity should not be allowed to interfere with these international meetings.

Once again, the Games received enthusiastic government approval. Throughout their duration, Prince Chichibu, second son of the Emperor, acted as chief patron. In addition, trophies were presented by the Emperor and the Ministers of Education, Foreign Affairs, and Home Affairs.

On the athletic front, the quality of performance of the Asian athletes continued to rise. Of the seventeen events on the track and field program, new records were set in eleven, despite two days of hard rain. In swimming, the performance of the Japanese was nothing short of extraordinary. They won almost every place in every race and smashed all existing records. The tennis players from Japan were just as strong, coming out on top despite the fact that Japan's best players were in America at the time competing for the Davis Cup. The outstanding Chinese performance was registered in soccer, where China was victorious for the fifth consecutive year.

Going one step further than the Fifth Games, in which women participated in the mass demonstrations, the Sixth Games introduced actual competition for women for the first time. Chinese and Japanese women competed in volleyball and tennis. The results of the women's competition did not count in the team scoring.[39]

The SEVENTH FECG, held in Manila, in May, 1925, marks the beginning of a new period in the history of the Games. From the Seventh Games on, the metric system was adopted as the standard of measurement, in contrast to the English system which had been used until that time.⁴⁰ Although this required the discarding of all previous meet records, the new system did serve the purpose of making comparison with Olympic performance (always calculated according to the metric system) much easier.

For China, too, the Seventh Games marked a first. For the first time, she embarked on a systematic program to gather together her best athletes. Provincial meets were held, followed by sectional meets. The provincial and sectional meets were climaxed by a national tryout meet at the beginning of May. Among Chinese athletes who stood out at these preliminary meets were Ng Sze-kwong, tennis player from Hong Kong, Chu En-te, winner of the pentathlon and decathlon at the Fourth FECG, Tu Jung-t'ang, all around track and field standout at the Fifth FECG, and D. M. Wu, pentathlon winner at the Third National Athletic Meet (1924) and pentathlon winner-to-be at the Seventh Games.⁴¹

The delegation of athletes to the Seventh Games was of record size (China and Japan each sent about 150 athletes), the level of performance was generally quite high, and the attendance was certainly satisfactory. Nevertheless, it is a dispute which led to the withdrawal of several Japanese track and field athletes from the competition, for which this meet is most remembered. An official from the Philippines, present at the meet, describes the incident as follows:

> The unfortunate incident of the Japanese team withdrawing from the meet, was partially due to mistakes made by local officials, particularly by Mr. Quisumbing, the referee of the track and field meet. Nevertheless, the withdrawal of the team was mainly caused by the poor sportsmanship of the Japanese coach [Akabe], of the track and field athletes, and the captain of the team, Tani. The latter was defeated by two of our [Filipino] sprinters in the 100 meters. After this and other defeats by the Japanese runners, the coach evidently felt that there was little chance of victory, and of taking back to Japan the Emperor's Cup. He then allowed the purely human impulse to "save face" to get the best of him, and withdrew his team from the meet. . . .
> We postponed the running off of track and field events

for 24 hours. Franklin Brown and other Japanese delegates worked with the track athletes to bring about their return . . . but we were not successful. The other Japanese teams . . . refused to cooperate with the track and field strikers. The track team was almost ready to return the next day when Tani and the Coach succeeded in preventing them from coming back to the field. Some of the track coaches and other athletes participated in the track and field games to show that they were not in accord with the spirit of the leaders.[42]

The withdrawal of Japanese athletes raised quite a storm in Japan. The Japanese newspaper, *Asahi Shimbun* came out with an unequivocal censure of the athletes who withdrew, while *Hochi* sided with them. The immediate response of the Japanese Amateur Athletic Association was to ban Tani and his eleven striking teammates from future amateur athletics in Japan. They were also removed from their dormitories and put in private hotels.

This was not the only commotion at the Seventh Games. The Chinese volleyball team left the playing court for several minutes during their game with the Philippines over an alleged unfair decision by the Filipino referee. However, Dr. Sung, head of the Chinese delegation, was able to persuade them to return and the match was finished under protest.[43]

With all this "side-show" activity going on, one was almost tempted to ignore the winning performance of the Philippines, which, with championships in four events, left Japan and China trailing badly.[44]

The EIGHTH Far Eastern Championship Games were held in late August-early September, 1927, in Shanghai. This was a departure from the usual practice of holding the meet in May. Unlike many of the Games which were often marked by incidents or drastic changes in procedure of one type or another, the Eighth Games seem to have proceeded quite normally. This was due in part to the fact that Shanghai was now holding the Games for the third time, and as such, was experienced enough to know how to deal with most difficulties.

The year 1927 marked the continuation of Chinese dominance in the soccer event (winning it for the seventh time in succession).[45] It also marked the first time that the Chinese were able to win the team tennis championship. This was directly attributable to the return to China of tennis players Gordon Lum from Australia, and Khoo Hui-yi (Champion of Malaya), both of whom contributed to the defeat of Japan.[46]

With the completion of the Eighth Games, the practice of holding them at intervals of two years was terminated. The last two Games were held at intervals of three and four years respectively.

For the first time in the history of the FECG, a fourth nation sent athletes to compete in the NINTH Far Eastern Championship Games, held in Tokyo, in May, 1930. Although they did not compete as a team, three Indian athletes took part in several events.

The Ninth FECG were marked by the introduction of many new rules. After the 1925 Games, it had been decided unofficially to divide the track and field competition into two separate championships: one including the regular individual track and field events and the other (the *ch'üan neng chin piao*) including the decathlon and pentathlon, and two relay races (800 meters and 1600 meters). In this way, it was hoped to make the value of a championship in the various sports more nearly equal. (Under the system in effect, in which a track and field championship received the same credit in the team standings as one in basketball or volleyball, the far greater effort needed to win a track and field championship—because of its many events—was not reflected.) It was also intended, by adding one more championship, to decrease the possibility of a tie.

This proposal, however, was voted down by the Philippines, and it was not until the meeting preceding the Ninth FECG that all participants agreed to this change. Also voted on at this meeting were the proposals to substitute the 200-meter low hurdles with the 400-meter hurdles, to use a 16 pound shot-put instead of the 12 pounder that had been used (because of the smaller physiques of the Oriental athletes), and to have the scoring in the decathlon and pentathlon conform to the method of the International Amateur Athletic Federation. These latter changes were geared toward bringing the FECG more in line with the Olympic Games.

Once again, the more than 400,000 spectators who witnessed

the Games saw record breaking performances. Twelve new FECG records were set in track and field—highlighted by a high jump of 6' 6¾" by Toribio of the Philippines which surpassed the existing Olympic record—and four new ones in swimming. For the first time in the FECG, the sprints were not won by the Philippines.

Women's competition, on a non-team basis, was expanded. The delegation from the Philippines included women's volleyball and tennis teams, and China sent female athletes to compete in tennis, volleyball, swimming, and track and field. They competed against the Japanese women.[47]

The TENTH Far Eastern Championship Games, held in Manila in May, 1934, were marked by disputes on the athletic field, off the field, and in the conference room. The ultimate result was the termination of the Games.

The first incident occurred when the Chinese basketball team failed to reappear for the second half of their game with the Philippines because of what they claimed was an unplayable slippery floor. Their action was first met by forfeit, but later, their protest was upheld and the game ordered replayed.

Off the playing field, Filipino athletes, who had entered the baseball grounds to watch the Philippines-Japan game without tickets and had been ousted from the stadium, threatened not to compete. In still another incident, 5,000 Japanese spectators had to be dispersed by a riot squad when they were whipped into a frenzy over what they thought was favoritism in the awarding of a boxing decision to a Filipino over a Japanese by a Filipino referee.[48]

The biggest dispute took place, after the meet was concluded, in the conference room. The focus of the dispute was Rule 3 of the FEAA constitution which said that in order for a new nation to be admitted to the Games, the unanimous consent of all existing member nations had to be secured. As it read, Rule 3 would not allow the participation of Manchukuo (the puppet government which the Japanese had carved out of Manchuria) without the consent of China.[49]

In order to break this dispute, the Philippines and Japan managed (in a way which is not completely explained) to have the constitution changed so as to give the host country the unilateral power to invite any nation to compete in any particular meet. This decision brought about the hasty exit of Chinese delegate C. T. Wang. The next day, May 21, 1934, when the Chinese delegation did not appear, Japan and the Philippines dissolved the Far Eastern Athletic Association and decided to form the Amateur Athletic Association of the Orient which would admit Manchukuo and hold its first Games in 1938. Nothing ever came of this proposed meet because the International Olympic Committee, at its 1936 meeting in Berlin, failed to sanction it.[50]

It should be noted that China's stand in this matter was somewhat idealistic. Under the practice in effect at the time, under which the Games were held every fourth year, China was scheduled to hold the next Games in 1938. This would have ensured that Manchukuo would not have been able to compete (and, in doing so, humiliate China) until 1942. The Chinese, thus, had they wished to try to salvage the Games, could very well have attempted to do so from within the framework of the FEAA. In this way, they still would have had eight years (1934-42) to try to iron out the dispute.

LEVEL OF ATHLETIC PERFORMANCE AT THE FECG

In examining these Games, it is interesting to compare the level of performance at the FECG with the general level of performance of other athletes of the world at roughly the same time. The following data lists winning performances which can be measured qualitatively from the 1925 and 1930 FECG, and the 1924 and 1928 Olympic Games.[51] It is apparent that the level of performance in the Far East was considerably below the world-class level of those years. What is more significant, however, is the great improvement in the quality of Far Eastern performance between 1925 and 1930.

INDIRECT INFLUENCES OF THE FECG

To say that the entire world was eagerly awaiting the outcome of the FECG would be a gross exaggeration. Nevertheless, the Games did attract considerable attention and interest within sporting circles around the world. In 1920, the International Olympic Committee became interested in schemes to hasten the athletic development of "backward nations" which had

The Far Eastern Championship Games

EVENT	1925 FECG	1924 OLYMPICS
Track and Field		
100 meter dash	11.1 sec.	10.6 sec.
200 meter dash	22.5 sec.	21.6 sec.
400 meter dash	51.2 sec.	47.6 sec.
800 meter dash	2:01.7 min.	1:52.4 min.
1500 meters	4:07.8 min.	3:53.6 min.
10,000 meters	36:07.5 min.	30:23.2 min.
110 m. hurdles	15.9 sec.	15 sec.
high jump	6' 1/4"	6' 5 15/16"
pole vault	11' 2 1/2"	12' 11 1/2"
broad jump	22' 7 1/4"	24' 5 1/8"
hop-step-jump	46' 2"	50' 11 1/8"
discus	122' 8 1/2"	151' 5 1/4"
javelin	169' 7 3/4"	206' 6 3/4"
Swimming		
100 meter freestyle	1:04 m.	59 sec.
400 meter freestyle	5:16 min.	5:04.2 m.
1500 m. freestyle	22:10.5 m.	20:06.6 m.
100 m. backstroke	1:16.1 min.	1:13.2 m.
200 m. breaststroke	2:57.2 min.	2:56.6 m.

EVENT	1930 FECG	1928 OLYMPICS
Track and Field		
100 meter dash	10.8 sec.	10.8 sec.
200 meter dash	21.8 sec.	21.8 sec.
400 meter dash	49.2 sec.	47.8 sec.
800 meter dash	1:58.8 min.	1:58.8 min.
1500 meters	4:06. min.	3:53.2 min.
10,000 meters	32:42.6 min.	30:18.8 min.
110 m. hurdles	15.4 sec.	14.8 sec.
high jump	6' 6 3/4"	6' 4 3/8"
pole vault	13' 1 3/8"	13' 9 3/8"
hop-step-jump	48' 4 3/8"	49' 10 13/16"
discus	132' 1 3/8"	155' 2 101/128"
javelin	204' 3/8"	218' 6 1/8"
Swimming		
100 meter freestyle	1:00.8 min.	58.6 sec.
400 meter freestyle	5:04.6 min.	5:01.6 min.
1500 m. freestyle	20:03.4 min.	19:51.8 min.
100 m. backstroke	1:13.2 min.	1:08.2 min.
200 m. breaststroke	2:53.4 min.	2:48.8 sec.

been sending few or no athletes to the Olympic Games. The IOC regarded the Far East, South America, India, and the Balkan States as "backward areas" in this respect. Further, the IOC considered the FECG to be the type of development meet that could hasten the progress of these nations athletically. Elwood S. Brown, founder of the FECG, was asked to report on them to Baron Pierre de Coubertin (founder of the modern Olympic Games) in August, 1921, at Antwerp, Belgium, with a view toward the establishment of additional Games, on the model of the FECG, in various parts of the world, in non-Olympic years.[52]

Although there is no direct evidence that Brown's report to de Coubertin led to the immediate establishment of Games similar to the Far Eastern Championship Games, it seems reasonable to assume that the Games contributed, at least in part, toward the eventual establishment of many of the regional games being held today. To be readily cited as possibly bearing the legacy of the FECG are such events as the Pan American Games, the Caribbean Games, and the Asian Games.

The Far Eastern Championship Games were undoubtedly a strong factor in disposing many citizens of the participant nations toward sports and physical education. The Games accomplished this firstly by introducing western sports to people who had never known about them before. For those who were already familiar with them, it provided an incentive to train hard and long, with the hope of future personal participation. Further, the mass demonstrations and events for women showed the female population that physical education had much to offer them as well. This new awareness of sports in China (as well as in Japan and the Philippines) encouraged the development of school sports programs and local training programs and meets. In this way it helped to broaden the base of physical education in China.

By the same token, the strong involvement in the Far Eastern Athletic Association, and in the Far Eastern Championship Games, by such people of influence in government and education as C. T. Wang, Chang Po-ling, and T'ang Shao-yi shows that sports did not go unnoticed in official circles. In this respect, the fact that by 1932 national physical education laws and conferences were initiated, can, in part be attributed to the Far Eastern Championship Games.

Another influence of the Far Eastern Championship Games is that on nationalism. The Games originated at a time when China was little more than a loosely bound confederation of areas. By the time the series was halted in 1934, China was a nation, under unified, albeit ineffective, rule. This necessitated a transfer in allegiance by the Chinese from the local area to the nation. The assistance in this psychological shift made possible by the FECG was summed up by a leading Chinese educator as follows: "This is a great leveling force which cannot fail to be felt in future society. I have seen students cheering for their school and even for their city, but never before for China."[53]

As important as the FECG were in China, it would be a gross exaggeration to say that they caused interest in sports to sweep the entire country in a way that "World Series fever" infects the American public every October. For one thing, communications were not very good in China in those years, so that the possibility of reports of the Games ever being received in places other than the big cities was negligible. It must also be taken into consideration that while most of the burden for developing sports in China was handled by the YMCA, and later the universities, both of which were city-based, even in the cities, only a small proportion of the population was involved. Thus, the villages, where most of the people lived, were not yet given their first taste of western sports. As Mr. Charles Lo, active in sports in China in the 1930's has indicated to me in private conversation, it is highly probable that most of the people living in China at the time never even heard of the Far Eastern Championship Games.

It would be remiss to conclude this account without again stressing the role of the YMCA in the Far Eastern Championship Games. The names Crocker, Swan, and Gray (YMCA leaders whose names have been repeated so often in these pages) are big names in the history of physical education in China. Their involvement in the FECG, in many ways, parallels the involvement of the YMCA in sports in China. Initially, these YMCA people literally ran the entire show: arranging for the creation of a Chinese team, training the team, raising the money needed, accompanying the team overseas, and handling the administrative details.

Starting in the early 1920's, sports in China reached a stage of development whereby people trained directly by the YMCA, or in schools originally set up by the YMCA, were to a greater and greater extent able to take over the basic administrative tasks. At this point, the role of the YMCA became a more advisory one. In both the earlier and the later stages, however, their influence was unquestionable. It can be said with certainty that without the YMCA there never could have been Far Eastern Championship Games.

The Far Eastern Championship Games 71

TEAM PERFORMANCE IN THE FAR EASTERN CHAMPIONSHIP GAMES[54]

MEET	(1)	(2)	(3)	(4)	(5)
Place	Manila	Shanghai	Tokyo	Manila	Shanghai
Date	Feb. 1-9, 1913	May 15-22, 1915	May 8-12, 1917	May 12-17, 1919	May 30-June 4, 1921
Track & Field (team points)	P (65) C (40) J (11)	C (51) P (47) J (11)	J (48) P (47) C (20)	P C J	P J C
All-Around Championship (*ch'üan neng chin piao*) not held					
Swimming	P (49) C (2)	C (28) P (13) J (12)	J (47) P (3) C (3)	P J C	P J C
Baseball	J (3) P (0)	P (5) C (0) J (0)	J (10) P (0)	P	P J
Soccer	P (3) C (0)	C (5) J (0) P (0)	C (10) P (6) J (0)	C P	C P
Basketball	P (3) C (0)	P (5) C (0) J (0)	P (10) C (6) J (0)	P C	C P J
Volleyball	P (3) C (0)	C (5) J (0) P (0)	C (10) P (6) J (0)	P C	C P J
Tennis	P (8) C (0)	J (6) P (4) C (0)	J (10) P (7) C (0)	Singles—J Doubles—P	P J C
Cycling	P (6) C (0) 10 mile road race	J (3) C (3) P—disqualified 15 mile rd. race	J (5) P (1) C (0) 20 mile rd. race		
Team Championship	P (137) C (42) J (14)	C (92) P (74) J (32)	J (120) P (80) C (49)	P C J unofficial	P C J

MEET	(6)	(7)	(8)	(9)	(10)
Place	Osaka	Manila	Shanghai	Tokyo	Manila
Date	May 21-26 1923	May 16-24, 1925	Aug. 27-Sept. 5, 1927	May 24-31, 1930	May 12-19, 1934
Track and Field	J P C	P J C	J P C	J P C	J P C India
All-Around Championship				J P C	J P C I
Swimming	J P C	J P C	P J C	J P C	J P C
Baseball	P J C	P J C	J C P	J C P	P J C
Soccer	C P J	C P J	C J P	J & C Tie	C P J I
Basketball	P C J	P C J	P C J	P J C	P C J
Volleyball	P C J	P C J	C P J	C P J	P C J
Tennis	J P	J P	C P	J	J & P Tie
Cycling	not held				
Team Championship	J P C	P J C	J C P	J C P	

Part II
THE COMMUNIST PERIOD

4

The Chinese Communist Ideological View of Physical Culture

APPROACHED THEORETICALLY, the Chinese Communist system as a whole is a very tight one. Every activity in society is defined as to how it will be conducted and as to what its exact role is within the entire system. Thus, it comes as no surprise to us that sports has an integral place in Chinese Communist theory and practice, and has deep ideological roots in such areas as politics, health and economics.

We need not go much further than the Mainland interpretation of the Chinese word *t'i yü* to get our first sense of both the preciseness and the flexibility of the Chinese term which we translate as "sports." The word *t'i yü* literally means bodily cultivation and is sometimes used in this sense. But it means much more. It can mean physical exercise in the noncompetitive sense (the word *tuan lien* is also used here). It can, at times, refer to competitive athletics and ball games. It can also mean physical education within the school curriculum.

The problem that an American has in understanding the term *t'i yü* is a result of the difference between his conception of "sports" and the Chinese understanding of the same term. Americans generally make a strict distinction between the terms "physical education" and "sports," and see very little connection between the two. In fact, after an American completes his formal schooling, he is not very likely to have any personal contact with physical education. Physical education might very well connote to him something unpleasant or forced, far removed from "playing ball." Certainly U.S. physical education classes play very little part in the development of the athlete.

As will be seen in the coming chapters, all the various translations of the word *t'i yü* noted above come together rather neatly into one main concept for a Mainland Chinese.* The Chinese child, when he begins primary school, starts what is theoretically hoped will be the first step in a lifelong continuous process of physical culture. Every morning, like workers and students throughout the land, he will engage in "broadcast" exercises to radio music. He will participate in regular physical education classes plus "voluntary" after-school programs which expand upon the classtime work and pay more attention to games and athletics. Beginning with middle school, the "labor-defense system," participated in by men and women in all walks of life throughout China, will become his focus of attention. In place of the regular after-school sports program, the more qualified will be able to play on school teams or attend spare-time sports schools. If he has such inclinations, the student might qualify for a special sports high school or university-level physical culture training. The worker will often find a complete sports program at his place of employment as will the soldier on his army post, and it is fully possible that participation will not be voluntary. Since all of the programs are administered to a greater or lesser extent by the government Physical Culture and Sports Commission, uniformity is much more likely than it might be under other conditions, It is obvious, then, that the Chinese have no great need for the variety of terms which we use to define his all-inclusive *t'i yü*.

In this chapter we will try to do three things: 1) see how the Mainland Chinese view sports from a philosophical-ideological vantagepoint, 2) see what their pre-1949 experiences were in the realm of physical culture (as befits their view of

---

*It is for this reason that I so often use the somewhat pedantic phrase "physical culture" in these pages. This phrase, seeing little if any usage in the United States, leaves the reader more receptive to a new interpretation of a familiar concept.

practical experience contributing to future theory, and in turn to future practice), and 3) see what influence these experiences have exerted on contemporary behavior in this area.

MAO TSE-TUNG'S "A STUDY OF PHYSICAL CULTURE" OF 1917

The logical place to begin this discussion is with a presentation of Mao Tse-tung's April, 1917 article, "A Study of Physical Culture," (*T'i Yü chih Yen Chiu*) which appeared in the periodical *New Youth* (*Hsin Ch'ing Nien*). *New Youth* was clearly the most powerful organ of the intellectual "new breed" in China between 1915 and 1920, and, although physical culture was only rarely mentioned in its pages, the broader theme of strengthening China implied in Mao's article was certainly consonant with the ideas expressed in the publication.

The significance of this article is several-fold. In a country where "Maoism"—whether the term is subscribed to or not—has become the equivalent of a state religion, anything written by the Chairman is tantamount to canon. In such a context, "A Study of Physical Culture," the only article written by Mao before 1923 for which we have the entire authentic text, is of particular importance. For, although the specific theme of the article has not since been repeated in any of Mao's writings, the connection between a China able to defend her borders (about which he has had much to say) and a physically fit nation is easily drawn. From a strictly athletic point of view, this article represents the only extant Communist Chinese writing which approaches doctrine. Sports are certainly held to be important on the Mainland. There is no room for equivocation on this point. Yet, there is really little in writing which sets its general tone and which is held up as a model for study. Mao Tse-tung's article comes very close to serving this function. Lastly, this article shows the general consistency of thought of Communist Chinese leaders through the years with respect to athletics. The present Chinese course in physical culture is largely consistent with the principles laid down in 1917.

Mao Tse-tung's earliest acquaintance with physical culture can reasonably be dated no earlier than 1912 when he did his famous half-year stint at the Hunan Provincial Library in Changsha.[1] During this reading period he undoubtedly met up with occasional references to the need for physical training made by such people as Tseng Kuo-fan and Yen Fu. He was an avid reader of Liang Ch'i-ch'ao and probably read his article "The Bushido of China," which recalled the ancient Chinese military tradition, and called on China to strengthen herself physically to the point where she could stand up and defend herself.[2]

Mao spent the years 1913-1918 at the First Normal School in Hunan and it was here that his interest in physical culture crystallized. As did many students of his day, he digested, in their entirety, the pages of *New Youth* from its inception in 1915. Thus, he would have been struck by a statement by editor Ch'en Tu-hsiu in the periodical's very first issue that "half the youth of China had bodies of old men." In the second issue, Ch'en was even more forceful when he said: "I always see the young people of our country who have been educated: their hands haven't the power to choke a chicken and their hearts haven't the courage which is worthy of a man. They have pale countenances and slight builds; they're coquettish like young girls; they're afraid of the cold and the heat; they're weak like the sickly. How can people with hearts and bodies so powerless assume responsibility and act effectively?"[3]

Physical training at Chinese schools in those days was certainly no better than haphazard. In 1917, seven of Mao's classmates at the normal school died and he felt that the inadequate physical training program, which only consisted of ten minutes of physical exercise after school, was partially responsible. He took charge and developed a program of exercise which he formally presented in "A Study of Physical Culture." Exercise, he felt, must first of all be done regularly. To cultivate bravery, it must contain elements of the barbaric. Lastly, it must be as simple and of as short a duration as is possible.

During his school days he was quite resolute about his physical training. He went through the series of six exercises that he had developed, to be practiced after rising each morning and before retiring each evening. From Yang Chang-chih, also a contributor to *New Youth,* he picked up the habit of taking cold baths throughout the year. In summer and well into the fall he would swim in the Hsiang River. He was also fond of climbing mountains, hiking, and camping out. The diary of Chiang K'un-ti, a friend of those days, describes a 12 hour hike which they took in 1917 during which time they climbed mountains and forded rivers.[4] All this later proved to be unexpected preparation for the rigors of the Long March of 1934-35, and is noted here because it helped determine the future shape of physical culture on the Mainland.

In his introduction to "A Study of Physical Culture" Mao makes his purpose in writing the article very clear. China is militarily weak; physically her people are degenerating and cannot stand up to her enemies. A new system of physical exercise is urgently needed to contribute to the growth of the nation. Physical educators have failed to do their job properly. Though a lack of equipment and sound physical culture programs have contributed to this backwardness, it really stems from the fact that the Chinese people have not been properly alerted to its importance. "If one wishes for physical culture to be effective," he said, "one will not be able to attain this without tottering the subjectivity of the people and without promoting an attainment of [new] consciousness with respect to physical culture."[5]

To Mao, when one wishes to remould the outlook of a nation, he must start with one very basic question: What is physical culture? Mao Tse-tung replies that: "Physical Culture is the method employed by human beings in order to prolong their life and develop their bodies in a uniform manner."[6]

It is interesting to note here that Mao, in 1917, was content to treat physical culture as an entity in itself, for compared to his later style this essay is devoid of political flavor. He seems perfectly willing to consider the experiences of any people past or present regardless of the purity of their historical record and his personal feelings toward them. Mao is able to grasp the difference between the Oriental approach to physical culture and the Western emphasis on physiology and other sciences. He seems ready to borrow anything which may be of use to China.[7]

Mao recognized that if an individual is going to participate actively, and with enthusiasm, in physical culture, he has to understand its significance for his life. So he went about explaining the relationship between physical culture and other things in life: Physical culture, it had to be recognized, was the complement of virtue and wisdom. In terms of priorities, it is the body which contains knowledge (or wisdom), and knowledge is the seat of virtue. Thus, it follows, with a young child, first attention should be given to his physical needs (food, shelter, and bodily development). There is sufficient time later for the cultivation of morality and wisdom. Mao's quarrel with educators is that too many of them completely neglect the physical condition of their students. Education below the middle school level, he feels, should show more concern for physical growth than for discipline and accumulation of facts. At the middle school level a greater balance should be instituted.

He leaves no doubt about his faith in the power of physical culture: "The only misfortune of man is not to have a body. Otherwise, he has nothing to fear. If one finds a method to improve the body, the rest will improve automatically. To put the body in condition, there is nothing better than physical culture. Physical culture occupies a place of first priority in our life; when the body is strong one can advance rapidly in his studies and in his [level of] virtue and attain the potential of his great ability."[8]

Mao then attacks the greatest problem in dealing with reform: the breaking down of long-held, erroneous notions. The fact is, he maintains, man is an animal and as such needs to participate in activities involving motion. As a being of reason, his movement should be systematic. It is through systematic movement—a segment of physical culture—that the body is built up.

The old concept which contends that after age 25 man's body is unchangeable is incorrect, he says. The body never loses its capacity to be improved. One born weak can become strong through the proper exercise, and one born strong can deteriorate through inactivity. Further, there is no truth to the view that superior physical condition lessens one's mental capacity, or vice versa. History, both modern and ancient, is replete with people who advocated and practiced physical exercise without detriment to either their intellect or their life span. In fact, participation in physical activity serves not only to strengthen the body, but indirectly to increase one's knowledge by rendering healthy those organs of the body which are engaged in the absorption of knowledge.

But, perhaps the greatest value in physical culture is in strengthening one's will. For, the main practical consideration of physical culture is military heroism whose desired fearlessness, daring, tenaciousness, and courage cannot be achieved without the control over one's will developed through physical training.[9]

One who attempts to rectify indifference toward physical training must first isolate the origin of this indifference. In this section of his essay, Mao reveals a little of the philosophical flavor which is to characterize his future writings. Man, he says, cannot maintain an interest in physical training because he fails to grasp its relationship to himself. This is both the fault of the individual who has failed to delve into the subject in sufficient depth and of the physical culture instructor who has failed to attack the "why?" aspect of physical culture. Yet, neither the individual, nor the instructor are really to blame for their lack of sensitivity and knowledge about physical culture which is but a reflection of societal attitudes passed down through the ages. These attitudes favored "civil" activities, and approved of slow-flowing movement rather than the quick motion inherent in exercise. Such aphorisms as "a good man doesn't undertake the occupation of a soldier" had engrained themselves in the subconscious, and Mao recognized that acquired habits are very hard to break. Thus, he was not surprised that many people were ashamed of being seen exercising, and that some would only exercise in groups or in the privacy of their own homes where they would be spared the embarrassment of being seen without their flowing gowns.[10]

In the last two sections of the article Mao sets down his principles of physical training in concrete terms. Regularity is of the essence. One should exercise twice a day: after rising in the morning, and before retiring in the evening. The exercises should be performed either without clothing or with a minimum so as not to impede movement. By following a regular program of 30 minutes per day, the individual (provided that he has concentrated fully on what he is doing) will begin to derive pleasure from his perseverance and advancement, and will feel an inner urge to maintain the regimen. Mentioned briefly, and not expanded upon, is the necessity for elements of brutality in a program of exercise if a powerful person is to be developed. National defense physical culture programs stressed in the 1960's show the influence of this thought.

Mao's system of exercise is straightforward and consists of six larger categories:

1) exercises of the arms—sitting position: raising arms in various ways and stretching
2) exercises of the legs—sitting position: raising and lowering legs in various ways
3) exercises of the body—standing position: turning and bending trunk
4) exercises of the head—sitting position: rotating the head
5) slapping one's body to stimulate blood flow
6) exercises of balance: deep breathing and jumping[11]

What is especially noteworthy about these exercises is their mild nature. There is no great stress put on any of the muscles of the body, despite Mao's interest in the building of solid tough bodies. Similarly, they are not geared to developing any great amount of stamina. What these exercises do seem to do is to loosen the body and stimulate the blood flow which Mao considers their main purpose.

CHINESE COMMUNIST PHYSICAL CULTURE IN PRE-1949 CHINA

Before seeing how some of these ideas from 1917 have developed during the Communist regime, let us see how sports existed in the small pockets of Red society in the years before the official Communist takeover: 1) in the years spent in the Chingkanshan area on the border of Hunan and Kiangsi from 1927; 2) in the Kiangsi Soviet, 1931-34; 3) in Yenan, 1936-45. These were years of struggle for survival, in which objective physical conditions made formal sports programs difficult and the preservation of a contemporary written record about them virtually impossible. Nevertheless, fragmentary information from these years indicates that physical culture remained a priority item to be engaged in whenever possible.

Edgar Snow mentions that, among the Red soldiers in the Kiangsi Soviet, competition was encouraged in broad jumping, high jumping, running, wall-scaling, rope-climbing, rope-skipping, grenade throwing, and marksmanship. The outstanding units in group competition on levels from the squad up to the regiment were given pennants which were displayed in the Lenin Club—the social center of the unit. Table tennis as a favorite Chinese sport probably got its start during this period for it was reported that every Lenin Club had its ping pong table.[12]

The sports programs in the Red areas of China in the early '30's seemingly were well developed. Detailed descriptions of rules, court dimensions, training methods, and improvisation of equipment covering basketball, track and field events, volleyball, tennis, and table tennis are still available today. In 1933, a formal athletic meet was held in the Soviet Republic for Young Vanguards.[13] Further, the report of the Second National Chinese Soviet Congress of 1934 states that "A Red sports program has also been developing rapidly. Even remote villages have held track and field athletics and sports fields have been made in many places."[14]

After the Communists set up their base in the northwest Yenan area they were able to organize a somewhat more extensive physical culture program. In 1939, a Yenan Sports Committee *(Yenan T'i Yü Hui)*, sponsored and guided by the Youth Work Committee of the Central Committee of the Chinese Communist Party, was set up with Li Fu-ch'un as honorary director. This committee placed special emphasis on military sports events such as shooting, grenade-throwing, steeplechase running with full pack, and horseback riding.[15] On February 25, 1942, the committee was established on a more formal basis with representatives from government organs, the army, factories, and student groups attending the inaugural conference. The scope of the work of the committee was admittedly limited, but it received Party support from the Party organ *Liberation Daily (Chieh Fang Jih Pao)*, and was able to organize sports competition in government organs, schools, factories, and army units. In the summer, swimming competition predominated; in the winter, ice-skating; and in the spring and fall, ball games. There was usually endless sports activity on Saturday and Sunday and meets were customarily held to commemorate such dates as March 8th (International Working Women's Day), May 4th, and August 1st.

As early as 1937, before the establishment of the Yenan Sports Committee, physical training had become part of the regular routine of many people in the area. Troops went through calisthenics, running, and mountain-climbing daily. Chu Teh, who had been a physical training instructor before the 1911 Revolution, frequently rose early, climbed the hills around his home, engaged in calisthenics, and from time to time shot baskets. As time went on, activities were expanded with basketball, volleyball, swimming, and skating being very popular. By 1941, organized competition for girls was being held.[16] As can be readily imagined, sports equipment was not widely available and improvisation was the rule. Even ice skates were manufactured by attaching blades, made in the Yenan Iron Works, to slabs of wood. Boots captured from the Japanese often served as the skate shoes.

The largest sports meet during the Yenan Period in the Communist areas was the September 1st Meet, held in 1942. Some 1300 athletes participated in the six-day event. Entered were the Revolutionary Army Committee team, the Red Flag team of the Central Committee of the Chinese Communist Party (CCP), the Yenan Municipal team, the Shansi-Kansu-Ninghsia Border Government team, the Yenan Municipal School team, and a team from the Northwest Border Area. Chu Teh and Ho Lung, already important Communist officials, played leading roles in the administration of this meet. Competition was held in basketball, volleyball, track and field, swimming, and military events. Exhibitions were given in horsemanship, *wu shu* (traditional military arts), fording rivers with full pack, parallel bars, mass calisthenics, and wrestling.[18]

It was in Yenan, too, that the first Communist-conducted college level courses in physical culture were begun. In the spring of 1941, under the leadership of the CCP Central Committee Youth Work Committee, a physical culture training class was started at the Yenan Youth Cadre Training School. With the establishment of Yenan College (*Yenan Ta Hsüeh*) in August, 1941, the training class became the College's Department of Physical Education. With only one full-time cadre teaching in the Department, volunteers with sports backgrounds had to be relied upon. Courses were offered in dance, basketball, volleyball, track and field, gymnastics, anatomy, ice skating, swimming, and physical culture theory.[19] In 1942, the Yenan New Sports Institute was organized to study sports theory (including sports medicine and hygiene) and to aid in the general development of sports activities.[20]

It is thus clear that although sports activity during the Yenan Period was limited, before the end of this period the Communist leadership had decided in a general way the part which sports was eventually to play in Communist life. It will be seen that many of the currents which now exist on the Mainland sports scene can trace their origin to pre-1949 Communist areas.

Having outlined the pre-1949 Chinese Communist practical and theoretical background in physical culture, it is now our task to see how this experience manifested itself in the post-1949 Chinese view of sports. We will do this by looking at the most important statements found in Chinese Communist writings on sports. These will be of two types: 1) those which are frequently cited to provide sanction or justification for the need to implement a physical culture program, and 2) those which can be said to express general physical culture policy (which has remained relatively constant during the last 20 years).

SANCTION AND JUSTIFICATION

As in other spheres, the Russian influence in China up until the late 1950's was rather prominent in sports. The "labor-defense system" so visible on the Mainland scene was a 1931 innovation borrowed from the U.S.S.R. Early school physical education manuals were translations from the Russian, and some of Communist China's first international athletic contacts were with the Russians. Also reflecting Soviet influence were the creation of physical culture institutes, government financing and control of sports, and physical culture programs for women.[21] It is not surprising, therefore, that Communist China, which considers herself an orthodox socialist state, draws on the statements of the early communist theorists to justify her effort in physical culture.

Both Marx and Lenin saw physical culture as an integral part of the socialist system. Marx felt that: "Productive labor must be joined with education, and physical education. [For], this is not only one means of increasing socialist production, but is the one and only means for bringing forth man's complete development."[22] Physical education, according to Marx, stood on an equal footing with intellectual education, productive labor, and polytechnical education. His view of physical education was somewhat narrow, however, specifically meaning gymnastics and military exercises.[23]

Lenin stated that: "Just as the responsibility of completing the task of Communism stands before young people, just as the responsibility of struggling for the task of Communism stands before them; so they must have strong and healthy bodies, must have a steel will and torso to meet this responsibility."[24] Lenin interpreted physical culture in broader terms than Marx and felt that "healthful sport: gymnastics, swimming, excursions, physical exercise of every sort, and a variety of intellectual interests, study, analysis, and research should be combined as much as possible . . . [for] a healthy body houses a healthy spirit."[25]

Each of China's two constitutional documents makes a reference to physical culture. The Common Program—the legal guidelines of China before the setting up of a constitution in 1954—refers both directly and indirectly to physical culture. In article 41 it states that: "The cultural and educational* work of the People's Republic of China should elevate the people's cultural standard, and cultivate the nation's human talent for reconstruction; wipe out feudal comprador fascist thought; and should take as its principal duty the development of a thought which will serve the people." In article 48, the Program "advocates the people's physical culture." Article 94 of the Chinese People's Constitution of 1954 states that: "The nation is particularly interested in the development of the physical and mental strength of the youth."

Mao Tse-tung has been reported as having made four significant statements of the above nature on physical culture. In 1950, at the First National Middle School Education Conference, he said: "Let health be first" *(chien k'ang ti i)*.[26] In 1952, at the June inaugural meeting of the All-China Athletic Federation, he called on the Chinese people to "Develop physical culture and sports, and strengthen the physique of the people." In March, 1953, in a speech before the New Democratic Youth League, Mao coined the slogan "keep fit, study well, work well" *(shen t'i hao, hsüeh hsi hao, kung tso hao)*.[27] His most recent such statement came in the body of his February 27, 1957 speech "On the Correct Handling of Contradictions Among the People," when he stated: "Our educational policy must enable everyone who gets an education to develop

---

* Culture and education has been officially interpreted to include physical culture.

morally, intellectually, and physically, and become a cultured socialist-minded worker."[28] Although these statements are certainly terse, their significance lies in their constant citation, and in the fact that they, combined with Mao's 1917 essay, contain most of the substance of present-day Chinese Communist physical culture policy.

Other statements of this nature have been voiced by such leaders as Chu Teh, who has called on the PLA and the people at large to "extend the people's physical activity to serve production and national defense," to "train yourself so as to form an iron constitution and protect our most beloved fatherland," and to "strengthen the physical constitutions of staff and workers, so as to be able to serve the state's economic and defense construction much better." To Liu Shao-ch'i and Chou En-lai have been attributed such statements as "Develop physical culture and sports, and strengthen health so as to serve socialist construction," and "Develop staff and workers' physical culture and sports so as to advance the socialist enterprise." At the Eighth Party Congress in 1956, in a discussion about the Second "Five Year Plan," Chou stressed that "We should move a step forward in developing physical culture and sports among the broad masses, effectively strengthen the people's physical constitution and heighten our country's physical culture and sports level."[29]

Before proceeding to the present-day Chinese view of sports, it is appropriate that we portray briefly how they see sports in a historical context. Consistent with their general philosophical approach, they view physical culture as having a class nature and historically as having been a tool of the ruling people. According to this view, in the middle ages physical culture was used by the feudal nobility to train soldiers and oppress serfs. With the advent of capitalism, the privileged class used sports activities as a diversionary tactic so that the masses would ignore the "contradictions" in their society. More often than not, however, their monopoly over the wealth, and the leisure needed in order to participate in sports, completely cut off the masses from any type of physical culture activity. Likewise, the present-day imperialist phase has seen the imperialist countries monopolize international sports activities. The International Olympic Committee and other world sports organizations have thus become nothing more than another instrument of imperialist oppression.[30] This historical outlook helps point the main thrust of the Chinese athletic policy in its present direction: the people.

THE CHINESE COMMUNIST POLICY OF PHYSICAL CULTURE

As has already been stated here, because of the nature of the Chinese system, physical culture in China exists as an integral part of a larger whole and as such its principles and policies are very much controlled from above. Despite changes in emphasis which are inevitable in any society, the culture and education system, of which physical culture is a part, has been very consistent in its aims through the years. This basic direction was presented in the Common Program when it called for a culture and education of the New Democracy "that is nationalistic, scientific, and popular."[31] Feng Wen-pin, the inaugural President of the All-China Athletic Federation, spelled out the task of physical culture explicitly at the 1949 organizational meeting of the Federation. He stated concisely that the New Democratic physical culture's motto is "to develop sports for the people's health, New Democratic construction, and the people's national defense." Specifically, he defined New Democratic physical culture to be national (*min tsu te*), scientific (*k'e hsüeh te*), and mass (*ta chung te*).[32] The efforts that the Chinese have made in the area of physical culture in the last 20 years can be understood from Feng's words.

A physical culture which is *national* (or nationalistic) is one which pays careful attention to local conditions, to national conditions, and to national traditions. Thus, it opposes imperialism as a phenomenon which contradicts the right of a nation's sports program to reflect its national character by distorting the basic nature of the nation. The Chinese attitude toward traditional Chinese sports is that a nation cannot divorce itself from its historical past, of which sports are a very definite part. As a result, such pre-20th century sports activities as shadow boxing have actually enjoyed a rejuvenation during the past 20 years despite their association with the oppressive society of the past. On the other hand, western sports in no case have been rejected because of their point of origin.[33] It is somewhat ironical that two of the most popular sports on the Mainland today (basketball and table tennis) are U.S. inventions.

Inherent in the Chinese concept of a national physical culture is national organization of sports activities. This structure facilitates mass participation in meets and on teams from the most basic administrative level to the national level. National standards are set up as a goal for all (with awards of Master of Sport, 1st Degree Sportsman, 2nd Degree Sportsman, and 3rd Degree Sportsman), and this lure helps to push up the national level of attainment. It is rather interesting to find that on the Mainland, where one might expect to find a philosophy coinciding with that particular one in the U.S. which advocates doing away with the formal structure of intercollegiate athletics and "giving the game back to the students," there is such preoccupation with the level of athletic achievement. From almost the birth of the People's Republic, athletic records have received unceasing attention. The exact number of times national and world records have been broken has been constantly fed to the public and the *People's Handbook (Jen Min Shou Ts'e)* is replete with such information.

Very closely tied to this stress on records as a part of the concept of a national physical culture is the stress put on international athletics. There are no hidden meanings here. An athlete is asked to improve his technical level so as to be able to win glory for the fatherland.[34] An athlete who wins an international meet or surpasses a world record has brought glory to his country.

The term *scientific physical culture* implies that sports related activities must conform to the principles of science. Backwardness is intolerable as is haphazardness, and it is assumed that all programs will be well conceived according to the principles of physiology, hygiene, anatomy, physics, etc. Thus, for example, the scientifically aware physical educator will realize that although each school child goes through a set of physical exercises each morning, he still requires supplemental physical training. He will realize, on the other hand, that the septuagenarian profits most by such free flowing exercise as the traditional *wu shu*. It goes without saying that a close relationship must be maintained between physical culture and scientific research.[35] With this thought in mind, physical culture institutes (see chapter on school physical education) were initiated with solid science courses and special research divisions.

In addition to paying heed to the natural sciences, physical culture must pay attention to the social sciences. Exactly what the Chinese Communists mean by the term "social sciences" is unclear. For our purposes, the Chinese, when they call for attention to the social sciences in physical culture, mean: to view physical culture and its relationship to the rest of the world in an objective way. We can probably best come to grasp this concept by following the analysis given by Jung Kao-t'ang* in his article "Let Physical Culture Better Serve Socialist Construction." Jung's position in the realm of physical culture can be compared to that of the pre-Cultural Revolution Liu Shao-ch'i. As Liu was regarded as the chief CCP theorist, so Jung can be considered the chief theorist in the area of physical culture. Most of the main speeches and essays in this area, dating back to the early '50's, have been presented by him and he has been the top sports administrator during the 22 year history of the regime.

Jung lists four basic approaches of China in physical culture:

1) Dependence on the Party for leadership and adherence to the policy of politics takes command.

2) In conjunction with production and with militia training, physical culture must be made to serve productive labor and the building of national defense more satisfactorily.

3) Firm adherence to the mass line and the launching of

---

* Jung Kao-t'ang (1912-   ) has been the top name in the Chinese Communist sports bureaucracy, although he does not appear to have had a background in sports prior to 1949. From April, 1949 to May, 1957 he served as Secretary-General of the New Democratic Youth League and from August, 1957 to January, 1967 was a member of the Central Committee of the Communist Youth League. Jung's main involvement, though, has been with physical culture. From October, 1949 until January, 1967, he was a Vice-Chairman of the All-China Athletic Federation (concurrently Secretary-General, 1949-1956). He has also been a Vice-Chairman of the Physical Culture and Sports Commission from its establishment in November, 1954. Jung has taken an active part in the two National Athletic Meets in China (1959 and 1965) and in GANEFO. He has also accompanied many Chinese sports delegations abroad. In January, 1967, he was branded a counter-revolutionary revisionist during the Cultural Revolution.

mass campaigns on a large scale are fundamental means for unfolding physical culture and sports.

4) In developing physical culture and sports, one must "walk on two legs" and integrate popularization with advancement.[36]

An approach such as this is said to be based on a correct, objective use of the social sciences, and, if applied, will provide one with a valid view of the role which physical culture is to play. Let us now see what each of these points implies.

The slogan "politics takes command" has been a watchword in Communist China since 1958, and the pervasive spirit there throughout the 22 year history of the regime. In physical culture it means that political principles are to serve as the guideline for sports. Physical culture now has a purpose. Namely, to contribute to the attainment of the general aims of the state. Under this formula, the bourgeois approach of "physical culture for the sake of physical culture" becomes invalid. Accomplishments in the area of sports become proof of the viability of the Communist Chinese system.[37]

The starting point in the "politicization" of the athlete is the study of Mao Tse-tung's works. An athlete might study the phrase: "People who direct a war cannot strive for victories beyond the limit allowed by objective conditions, but within that limit they can and must strive for victories through their conscious activity."[38] From this phrase he is expected to derive that something more than technique is needed for success in sports. Correct diagnosis of the opponent's strengths and weaknesses, and adaptability to objective conditions can help overcome this technical deficiency. "Flexible study and application" (huo hsüeh huo yung) of Mao Tse-tung's thought is the training which puts the athlete in the frame of mind whereby he can make maximum use of his ability.[39]

This ideological training equips the athlete to see the dialectical relationships between various things in the world and thus react more positively to situations. Training progresses from the general to the specific. Appropriate slogans and phrases such as the "3-8 work style," the "four good" company, the "five good" soldier, and the "four firsts"* are learned.

---

* The "3-8 work style" refers to the three phrases and eight characters written by Mao to describe the working style that officers and men are exhorted to adopt. The three phrases are: correct political direction, simple and

The dialectical relationship implied in them is then brought out: a good body (*shen t'i hao*) and good work (*kung tso hao*) are inseparable. Good work is the aim, and a good body is the vehicle. Under ideal conditions each will become a precondition for the other so that neither will exist in isolation. Both the "tenseness" and the "liveliness" of the "3-8 work style" complement each other, for tension without release is an unbearable burden. Without proper living conditions, the other three "goods" of the "four good" company are impossible.[40]

Moving to the more specific, the swimmer will be taught to understand the relationship between attempting daring maneuvers and being reckless, between being cautious and being timid, between fearing water and belittling its might.[41] The table tennis player, who by being excessively defensive thinks that he is taking less risks, will be shown that he is doing just the opposite because his opponents will now be able to manipulate him. Even pre-match jitters are thought to be the possible result of an incorrect outlook. Nevertheless, despite their faith in the part that ideological training can play, the Chinese recognize the role of ability and chance. What they try to do is to get the maximum out of each individual's ability and thereby leave a minimum to chance.[42]

It is significant to note that contrary to what we might expect and to what seems to be the case in the Soviet Union, the study of politics by top athletes is not given to compromise. In tournaments, political guides have been reported to have been assigned to each team, and Party and YCL organizations

---

arduous working style, and flexible strategy and tactics. The eight characters are: *t'uan chieh* (unite), *chin chang* (tense), *yen su* (stern), *huo p'o* (lively).

The "four good" company is one whose soldiers are 1) good in political ideology, 2) good in "3-8 work style," 3) good in military training, 4) good in management of the living conditions of men.

The "five good" soldier is 1) good in political ideology, 2) good in military techniques, 3) good in "3-8 work style," 4) good in carrying out assigned tasks, 5) good in physical training.

The "four firsts" refer to a statement made in 1960 by Lin Piao regarding how to deal with the following four relationships: 1) between men and weapons, 2) between political and other work, 3) between all aspects of political work and ideological work, 4) between books and living ideas. The guideline to be used in this respect is that the human factor is first, political work is first, ideological work is first, living ideas are first.

Adapted from *A Glossary of Chinese Communist Terms and Phrases*, JPRS, 1966.

set up within them. Further, political articles have been made required reading for athletes during meets, and in at least one instance their spare-time during the meet was spent in performing public service in surrounding areas.[43] A comparatively recent returnee from the Mainland, active in their sports program, reports that real pressure is put on athletes who are adjudged inadequate politically and removal from the team for this reason is always a genuine possibility.

The theme that physical culture must be made to serve productive labor and the building of national defense is one which has methodically and continuously been stressed on the Mainland. It was voiced at the Preparatory Conference of the All-China Athletic Federation in 1949[44] and continued to be voiced into the '60's.[45] What should be stressed here is that in contrast to the theme "politics takes command," which has been dealt with above and which lends itself to much interpretation, the idea of physical culture contributing to national defense and production is easily arrived at and understood: A stronger, healthier worker will do a better, more efficient job. Thus, physical culture is the business of all interested in national advancement.

One of the philosophical debates which has arisen from time to time in this connection is whether or not physical labor can be considered a substitute for physical training. The official interpretation has always been that physical labor, though contributing to good physical condition, cannot serve as a substitute for it. Physical labor, by its very nature, does not give the body the variety of exercise that it needs, and often merely consists of repeated movements of restricted parts of the body. Hence, the worker who, in the course of his job, constantly puts stress on one part of his body, without supplemental physical exercises, is exposing himself to possible occupational injuries. The Chinese conclude their argument of this point with research findings that workers who engage in regular exercises are more productive.[46]

If we adopt Franz Schurmann's approach, we can rightfully view the phrase "politics takes command" as the guideline of *pure* Communist Chinese ideology (i.e. the theoretical basis). Likewise, the policy of "walking on two legs," the fourth point made by Jung (his third point—the mass nature of sports—will be treated below), may be taken as their practical ideology (i.e. their guide to action). "Walking on two legs," in sports, as in other areas of Mainland life, helps the Chinese decide where their priorities should be.

"Walking on two legs" in effect implies flexibility, variety, and openmindedness. Popularization of sports for the masses must exist alongside high level training for the few. Mass participation provides a large pool of potential experts, while advancement on the upper levels provides incentives for the masses and in turn raises the entire national level of performance. In terms of professional training, the phrase "walking on two legs" means that physical culture training courses should be offered on the highest planes in university level physical education institutes and normal universities for some, and on a spare-time or short-course basis for others. Athletic meets should be held on a local small-scale basis as well as on a grand national scale. Traditional sports should coexist with modern sports. The finest modern athletic equipment should be used when available, but when cash is short, or conventional equipment is in short supply, improvisation should take up the slack. In short, the policy of "walking on two legs" commits the Chinese to pursue a policy of sports for everybody.[47]

In addition to a national and a scientific physical culture, the Chinese have committed themselves to a *mass physical culture*. What the Chinese are saying, in essence, when they put their emphasis on mass sports is that physical culture has much to give to *each* person; and through the individual to society as a whole. The non-socialist societies have failed by severely restricting the scope of physical culture so that society-at-large has never really understood its benefits.[48]

In the school, physical education must reach every student. On the farm, physical culture must become a part of peasant life. In the city, it should become a part of the life of the worker. In the PLA (People's Liberation Army), it should be a part of army life.[49]

Physical Culture serves not only the people's health, national defense and production, but also inspires the collective work spirit necessary for the national unity which is a prerequisite to national construction.⁵⁰ It does this mostly by example. Participating in team sports teaches unity and cooperation. Going through a series of broadcast exercises day in and day out with fellow workers or students builds a sense of oneness. The widespread national sports bureaucratic structure which stretches from the basic to the national administrative level reflects this commitment to a broad based physical culture. How this concept of mass physical culture has been implemented on the Mainland, is discussed in detail in the following chapters.

From the above, it emerges that the burden put on the shoulders of the revolutionary athlete is a heavy one.

> He must study the latest techniques of other societies and must train himself well in basic skills. He must take hold of basic techniques and be good at making flexible use of them. He must learn humbly and dare to create things. He must look for the factor of success in defeat, and be able to perceive the defective aspects in success. He must, through practice and summing up things, continuously translate matter into spirit and spirit into matter, carrying out the revolution without interruption, and ceaselessly march forward.⁵¹

The Chinese, with their propensity for catch phrases, are able to express succinctly what they expect from the proletarian athlete. He should be "tough in five respects" (*wu kuo ying*) and have the "three no-fear spirit" (*san pu p'a ching shen*). The former demands that an athlete should be unwavering in ideology, keep up his physical fitness under all conditions, master the game, not spare himself in training, and go all out in competition. The latter requires that no athletic trainee should veer from his assigned task because of fatigue or injury. The glory that will come to China through such efforts will provide the compensation.⁵²

The athlete who wishes to join the CCP cannot do so on his athletic expertise alone. He must assume the proper attitude for joining the party and push away any thought of honor or material gain. He must realize that it is incorrect to hold the attitude that professional competence must be achieved while one's body is still youthful, with political competence to be acquired later on. For a potential Party member, politics should provide the incentive for advancing professional competence, while his profession should provide the vehicle for application of his political knowledge. He must overcome unacceptable class origin if necessary, but must realize that proper family class origin does not guarantee proper future conduct. His task is to publicize the physical culture movement and thereby lead the Chinese people toward national regeneration.[53]

We began this chapter by investigating Mao Tse-tung's earliest views on physical culture as expressed in "A Study of Physical Culture." In closing we can now see that the present-day Chinese Communist attitude toward sports follows very naturally from this early essay. The concern which he showed then over the degeneracy of the physical condition of the Chinese people, and the resulting sad state of the nation, has developed into the theme of *national* physical culture. His creation of a system of exercise and his insistence upon regular physical activity is very much in the spirit of *scientific* physical culture. His feeling that not just school children, but everyone should participate in sports activities is evidenced today in the concept of *popular* or *mass* physical culture.

5

The Organization and Administration of Physical Culture in Mainland China

TO AN AMERICAN, the notion of sports as a part of a formal political system is certainly a strange one. In recent years in the U.S. a President's Council on Physical Fitness has been created, but this has been mainly supervisory in nature with limited power and no network emanating from it which might carry out its programs. In general, it may be said that sports fits into the private sector of life in the United States.

Probably the first thing which strikes an American about physical culture in Mainland China is the major attention which it receives in the political system. One of the most direct ways of demonstrating its political nature is to show just how it fits into the general political organizational framework. In this chapter, I propose to do just this. The value of such an approach is threefold: 1) it provides a relatively quick grasp of the importance of physical culture in China, 2) it contributes to the general knowledge about the political system in the People's Republic, and 3) it helps us isolate some of those areas of Chinese Communist political organization about which we know little.

My attempt in this chapter will be to answer certain basic questions about the Chinese political system as it applies to sports. Namely, how is a mass organization formed? What are its functions? How does it complement the government commission or ministry working in the same area and how has this relationship evolved? How do such bureaucracies reach down to the lower administrative levels? Are the leaders of the sports bureaucracies professionals (defined here to be people who spend a preponderance of their time working in physical culture) or do they lend their names and status to the field without their talents?

A "mass organization" is commonly thought to be an organization of a particular interest group such as is indicated by the titles: All-China Federation of Democratic Women, All-China Students' Federation, or All-China Federation of Trade Unions. After a cursory study of this type of organization, however, it immediately becomes apparent that they differ considerably in their nature. Such an organization may be formed along sex lines (in the case of the Women's Federation), age (Youth Federation), employment (trade unions), etc. The All-China Athletic Federation is the mass organization involved with physical culture.

Notwithstanding the obvious chaos of reconstruction at the time of the establishment of the People's Republic of China, in October, 1949, provision for sports and physical culture was quickly made with the establishment of the All-China Athletic Federation (ACAF) Preparatory Committee on October 27, 1949. The only significance in the word "preparatory" is that, of necessity, a major portion of the time between the formation of the preparatory committee and the official establishment of the ACAF in June, 1952, was spent in setting up previously non-existent programs and in drawing up organizational rules. The Communists themselves number the preparatory congress of 1949 as the first congress of the ACAF and for all intents and purposes we may consider the organization to date from October, 1949.[1]

As it was structured in 1949, the Federation consisted of four committees which served under a secretariat. The secretariat served to handle day to day affairs, coordinate national and international liaison work, and publish the Federation's internal bulletin *Federation Affairs (Hui Wu T'ung Hsün)*. *The Draft Committee* dealt with the preparation of a set of draft rules for the national association as well as the branch associations on lower levels. The *Research Committee's* responsibilities involved looking into the entire realm of physical culture: school curricula, physical culture for society at large, physical culture for the military, equipment design, training of teachers. The *Propaganda and Translation Committee* published various booklets both on the instructional aspects of sports and the ideological (including booklets intended for study on the rationale for the development of a sports program). It also began publication of the Federation's journal, *Hsin T'i Yü (New Physical Culture)* which was published from 1950 until the Cultural Revolution. Most of its translations were from Russian writings on sports. The *National Sports Planning Committee* had departments dealing with physical education laws, development of national programs, and individual sports.[2]

The ACAF, in its first years, was clearly an active organization both on the national level and below. Branch organizations were formed in the six administrative districts as well as in provinces, municipalities, and counties. At the regional level only infrequent conferences were held, and it was the provincial, municipal and county level branches which were expected to go out among peasants, workers, schools, and government organizations to organize physical culture programs and recruit physical culture personnel. These latter organizations likewise had their own sports committees.[3] That the structure of the branches was as highly developed as that of the parent organization can be seen from the Canton branch which had a congress-elected executive committee, a standing committee, and a secretariat composed of a general affairs office, a financial office, an organization office, and an office of control *(pao kuan)*. There were also competition, propaganda and education, help and guidance, research, and welfare committees.[4]

From a political science point of view, the interesting feature of the early years of this mass organization is that it assumed the same functions which were later to be assumed by the government commission which was to deal with sports (the Physical Culture and Sports Commission). Evidence pointing in this direction is fairly clear. The Culture and Education Committee of the Government Administrative Council formed by the Chinese People's Political Consultative Conference in

1949 contained no Physical Culture and Sports Commission (PCSC).[5] It was only on November 15, 1952 that such a commission was included in the Government Administrative Council. Before this date, the Commission's functions were performed by the ACAF, for the regulations of the first two congresses of the ACAF (October, 1949, and June, 1952) both provided for departments which no longer exist once the PCSC is formed. The organization regulations passed at the inaugural ACAF congress held June 20-24, 1952 provided for the following:

1) organization department
2) propaganda department
3) international liaison department
4) secretariat
5) central national defense physical culture club
6) specialized committees dealing with individual sports[6]

The ACAF as it develops *after* the formation of the PCSC is completely different in character. It continues to maintain a general membership, standing committee, and secretariat. However, with the exception of the international liaison department and 22 specific sports organizations, all of its administrative departments have ceased to exist.

A look at the organization of the PCSC makes this more readily understandable. The PCSC at present contains 13 specific departments, which can roughly be divided into those which are more administrative and those more athletic.[7]

————GENERAL OFFICE————

ADMINISTRATIVE DEPTS.	ATHLETICALLY ORIENTED DEPTS.
Cadres Department	Aviation Department
International Liaison Department	Ball Games Department
	Land Sports Department
Political Department	Mountaineering Department
Propaganda Department	Navigation Department
	Traditional Chinese Boxing Department
	Mass Physical Culture Department
	Sports Competition Department

The *General Office* performs administrative tasks for the Commission as a whole and as such may be considered its backbone. It has custody of the official Commission seal, and thus all official outgoing communications go through its hands. All incoming correspondence goes through it before being passed along to the appropriate department. Another of its tasks is liaison work, both with other ministries and with physical culture and sports committees on lower levels of government. It is also responsible for maintenance of the Commission's physical plant.

The *Cadres Department* is equivalent to a personnel bureau. It keeps records of all physical culture workers and deals with their appointment, promotion, demotion, and transfer. It has alternately been called the Cadres Education Department which would indicate that it is involved in their training and holds periodic study meetings. It also makes periodic assessments of the work of cadres.[8]

The *Propaganda Department* of the PCSC is responsible for all types of public relations work. It does such things as advertise coming sports meets and exhibitions; speak out on the general value of physical culture; and produce films (such as the one dealing with the Games of the New Emerging Forces in 1963). It also maintains a publishing apparatus. The *T'i Yü Pao* Publishing House publishes *T'i Yü Pao*—a four page twice-weekly tabloid devoted to sports news which started publication in 1958. The People's Sports Publishing House handles all other publishing of sports material. It publishes two periodicals: *Hsin T'i Yü (New Physical Culture)*, the main physical culture journal which has come out since 1950, and *T'i Yü Wen Tsung (Sports Research Digest)*, a more scholarly journal. This press puts out many books and pamphlets on physical culture conferences and congresses, sports meets, sports instruction, and political subjects. It occasionally publishes material such as poetry which have nothing at all to do with sports.[9]

The *International Liaison Department* is the only administrative department which has a counterpart in the ACAF. It is responsible for organizing participation in international tournaments and dual meets both on Chinese soil and abroad.

The *Political Department,* as pointed out below, is a unit

which began to appear in government organs in 1964, but whose function has still not been satisfactorily explained.

The *Sports Competition Department* deals chiefly with arranging sports meets on the domestic front such as the National Athletic Meets held in 1959 and 1965 and the periodic national championships held in various sports.

The *Mass Physical Culture Department* is responsible for setting up sports programs for the public at large. Much of its work is in non-competitive athletics such as broadcast exercises, the labor defense system, and other mass sports movements (see chapter 7).

In addition to the above departments, references in the past have been made to a School Physical Education Department (*T'i Yü Hsüeh Hsiao Szu*) and a School Cadres Department (*Hsüeh Hsiao Kan Pu K'e*). Although these departments have not been referred to since 1960, participation of the PCSC in conferences dealing with school physical education in recent years seems to indicate that the PCSC has more than a passing involvement in this area.[10]

The other six departments of the PCSC deal with specific sports. It is probable that each one administers at least one of the national sports associations of the ACAF. The fact that ACAF consists almost solely of sports associations which can neatly be divided among the various athletic departments of the PCSC, as shown below, suggests, in effect, that the ACAF is subordinate to the PCSC.

Aviation Dept.: China Aviation Sports Association

Ball Games Dept.: China Table Tennis Association, China Basketball Association, China Volleyball Association, China Soccer Association, China Tennis Association, China Badminton Association

Land Sports Dept.: China Track and Field Association, China Weight-lifting Association, China Wrestling Association, China Cycling Association, China Gymnastics Association, China Wireless Sports Association, China Archery Sports Association, China Shooting Sports Association

Mountaineering Dept.: China Mountainclimbing Association

Navigation Dept.: China Maritime Sports Association, China Watersports Association

Traditional Chinese Boxing Dept.: China Wu Shu Association[11]

It can thus be seen that the Physical Culture and Sports Commission has generally assumed the functions that were carried out under the aegis of the All-China Athletic Federation before the establishment of the PCSC in 1952; and further, that the PCSC is organized in such a way as to incorporate the ACAF into it.

An analysis of the membership of the two organizations through the years gives some insight into the formation of a mass organization as well as into the relationship between the mass organization and the government commission in the case of sports.

The ACAF was in essence pieced together in 1949 from those elements in society which the Party and government thought should have an interest in physical culture. Delegates to the first congress in October, 1949, were allotted to each of the provinces (along the lines of the six administrative districts). These delegates were chiefly high provincial educational personnel, physical education personnel, or regional New Democratic Youth League Central Committee or Work Committee members. Also allotted representation were members of special interest groups: the All-China Federation of Labor, the All-China Federation of Democratic Women, the All-China Students' Federation, the All-China Federation of Democratic Youth, New Democratic Youth League National Central Committee, railroad labor personnel, Ministry of Education, the Ministry of Public Health, the army, and the national minority groups. The significance of including delegates from such a broad range of groups in the ACAF is the early definition of sports as an activity intended for the broad masses. Thus, it is not uncommon for many of the above groups to take an active part in the promulgation of a physical culture decree.[12]

A reasonable explanation to the question of why a ministry level Physical Culture and Sports Commission was not founded until November, 1952, is provided by an analysis of the make-up of the Standing Committee of the ACAF when the Federation was officially established in June, 1952. Of the 26 (of 31) members of the Standing Committee on whom some biographical information is available, about half were members of the

Communist Party or the Youth League at the time. Further, only five members of the Standing Committee can be labelled as physical educators or physical culture personnel. Only one of the six vice-chairmen can be called a specialist in physical culture, compared to three of four in 1949. This would tend to indicate that before the physical culture apparatus was allowed to obtain ministry status, the Party wanted to develop a corps of politically reliable physical culture administrators—versus those who were merely technically competent. Thus, the ACAF initially (in 1949) stressed technical competence. As the physical culture operation began to achieve more stability, the pure professional began to be phased out and a corps of both politically reliable and technically "promising" top physical culture administrators began to be developed. This is borne out by the fact that 24 of the 29 members elected to the rank of Standing Committee and above at the Fourth Congress of the ACAF in February, 1964 (when the political power in the sports field had already been transferred to the PCSC), spent most of their time as physical culture professionals. Yet, the corresponding proportion of PCSC members at this time (1964) who can be considered physical culture professionals is no more than half. In a government commission, apparently, political reliability is at least *as* important as technical competence.

In emphasizing this last item, we should point up the significance in the fact that the chairmen elected at the first two congresses of the ACAF—Feng Wen-pin of the New Democratic Youth League Central Committee and Ma Hsü-lun, Minister of Education (in 1949 and 1952, before the Federation became devoid of its political importance)—were non-physical culture personnel. In fact, such personnel *were* available in China at that time. For one, Ma Yüeh-han (also known as John Ma), Vice-Chairman of the Federation in 1949 and 1952, had been director of physical education at Tsinghua University since 1914 and was later to be called "the grand old man of sports" by the Chinese. Yet, he was not appointed as Federation Chairman until 1956, by which time the ACAF had changed its character. Also available was Tung Shou-yi, a member of the Chinese Olympic Committee before 1949 and a long-time top sports administrator and coach who has since played a significant role in Chinese Communist sports.[13]

The outstanding characteristic of the rosters of the two organizations in recent years has been their interlocking nature. Working with officials appointed in 1964, of the seven vice-chairmen of the PCSC, five are vice-chairmen of the ACAF. Of the 21 listed as members *(wei yüan)* or above, of the Commission, 12 are members of the Standing Committee of the ACAF. Of the nine who are not ACAF standing committee members only Lu Han seems to be a sports professional in any sense. Of the 12 who are high officials in both bureaucracies, 10 may be considered as spending a major part of their time in sports.

It would thus be expected, because of this interlocking directorate, that the ACAF and the PCSC would work closely together. The relative structure of the two organizations tends to imply that the ACAF is subordinate to the PCSC on the national level. In fact, the Commission at present seems to be responsible for broad policy and administrative work, while the Federation, befitting its status as a mass organization, is involved more directly with the people.[14]

As has been the case on the national level, the formal nature of the administration of sports below the national level has also changed during the course of the development of the People's Republic. At its inception, the ACAF had branches at the regional, provincial, municipal and county levels. The former two no longer seem to exist. The regional branch, which never did more than meet for yearly conferences, probably disappeared with the abolition of the regions in 1954, and did not reappear in 1961 when the regions were reinstituted.[15] It is not clear what exactly was the fate of the provincial branches, but it is possible that the Physical Culture and Sports Committee which is a part of every provincial government is identical with the branch ACAF. Such is the case at the municipal level where both the branch ACAF and the Physical Culture and Sports Committee of the municipal government maintain their separate identity in name but have almost identical leadership.[16]

The case of Shanghai illustrates well what is probably typical of the sports organizational structure of all municipalities. Although listings of the respective members of the Physical Culture and Sports Committee and the ACAF branch organization at a specific period in time are not readily obtainable, a check in the mid-60's in Shanghai shows that four out of six of the members of the government committee are members of the ACAF organization at that level. The intertwining of the two organizations is further exemplified by the representation, both in provinces and municipalities, of at least one Physical Culture and Sports Committee member in the national membership of the ACAF. If more concurrent lists were available, it is probable that the overlap would be shown to be both greater, as well as valid in other places.

The structures of both the government committees and the ACAF at the municipal level are similar to those at the national level. The municipal government sports committee has various administrative departments similar to those of the national commission, while the municipal ACAF branch, like its parent, has several specific sports organizations. Such organizations are only maintained, however, for those sports which are of interest locally. In Shanghai, badminton, track and field, soccer, gymnastics, swimming, tennis, and table tennis associations have been identified. In a municipality in the colder North, such associations as ice skating might be expected.[17]

At lower levels, the organization of physical culture becomes less complex. If county X in A. Doak Barnett's *Cadres, Bureaucracy and Political Power in Communist China* may be taken as typical, we can expect to find a physical culture and sports committee under the culture and education staff office of each county people's government. In the case of county X, four cadres were on this committee.[18] In earlier years reference was occasionally made to county level ACAF branches. Of late they have not been mentioned.

Below the county level, there appears to be no specific formal structure for the administration of physical culture. This function might be taken care of by a representative of the Culture, Education, and Health Department of the commune or its equivalent. The schools, the Young Communist League, and branches of the All-China Federation of Trade Unions provide other sources of physical culture leadership at this level. The YCL and the All-China Federation of Trade Unions are the only two other organizations which maintain departments in their bureaucracies which deal specifically with physical culture. The YCL Central Committee has a Department of Military Affairs and Physical Culture while the All-China Federation of Trade Unions has a Department of Physical Culture.[19]

Thus far in our discussion of the administration of sports, we have yet to deal with the role of the Party. Most writers on Chinese Communist bureaucratic structure, including Barnett and Schurmann, hold to the view that at every level, the Party oversees government operation at that particular level. In the words of the *People's Daily*:

> 1) the Party gives exact directives to the organs of state power on the nature and direction of their work; 2) the Party enforces Party policies through the organs of state power and other work departments and exercises supervision over their activities; and 3) the Party selects and promotes loyal capable cadres (party and non-party) for work in the organs of state power.[20]

That the structural apparatus to oversee physical culture authorities exists in the Chinese Communist Party (CCP) departments at each level is clear. The Propaganda Department of the Central Committee of the CCP contains an Office of Health and Physical Culture (*Wei Sheng T'i Yü Ch'u*). Similar offices probably exist in the Party committees under the Culture and Education, Propaganda and Education, or similar Party departments at the regional, provincial, municipal, and county levels. The question remains open as to whether or not this potential Party authority is in fact applied. My feeling is that less Party control might formally be applied than has heretofore popularly been conceded. One indication that the Physical Culture and Sports Committee at a particular level might be capable of making its own decisions without formal Party direction is provided by the case of Shanghai where the Deputy Director of the Shanghai Municipal CCP Public Health and Physical Culture Department, Chang Ch'ing-chi, doubles as Chairman of the government Physical Culture and Sports Committee. A further indication might be provided when the exact nature of the Political Department of the PCSC is uncovered. Chalmers Johnson and others seem to feel that the appearance of such political departments in government organs indicates an increased assertion of direct Party control in the government. If this is so, government organs might now be in a position to run their own affairs without a formal passing of command from Party department to government organ. Before this interpretation of the role of the Political Department may be accepted, however, the fate of the Party fractions, already known to be a part of all government organs, would have to be better understood. What also needs to be taken into account in the case of physical culture is the deep involvement of the Young Communist League (YCL) in this area, in light of the close relationship between the CCP and the YCL. It is not an unreasonable hypothesis that the YCL serves the Party control function in this specific area.

Since 1956, the Chinese People's National Defense Physical Culture Association has joined the ACAF and PCSC as administrators of sports on the national level. The National Defense Physical Culture Association is also a mass organization and probably has the same subordinate relationship to the Physical Culture and Sports Commission as does the ACAF. Its province, however, is the realm of defense sports (see chapter 7) in which the ACAF is less active.

The National Defense Physical Culture Association began as the Central National Defense Physical Culture Club (a part of the ACAF) in 1952. By 1956, organizations of this type existed in 50 cities with some 300,000 participants, thus making worth while the formation of the National Defense Physical Culture Association. The Association has branches in provinces, autonomous regions and municipalities. Most large cities maintain defense physical culture clubs which provide facilities for defense sports. It appears that the national association is mostly supervisory, for we know that it works closely with such groups as the YCL, the Ministry of Education, the Federation of Trade Unions, and the military. Many of the Defense Physical Culture Association personnel concurrently hold positions in the military.[21] More detailed information will be needed before it will be possible to ascertain whether the same cadres deal with both conventional physical culture and national defense physical culture in the more basic geographical units.

In concluding this analysis of bureaucratic structure in physical culture, a comment might be made as to the practical results of what is obviously a tightly knit system with far reaching authority. A recent returnee from the Mainland who participated in the sports program there both as a player and a referee has indicated that one of the outstanding features of Chinese Communist sports is its high degree of organization. His example was: If the Chinese claimed that there were 543,200 registered badminton players and they were called upon to do so, they would be able to produce all 543,200, and in short order.[22] The intricate bureaucratic system analyzed in this chapter is what stands behind this precision.

SUMMARY OF THE SPORTS BUREAUCRACY IN COMMUNIST CHINA

	PARTY	GOVERNMENT	MASS ORGANIZATIONS
National level	Office of Health & P.C. of Prop. Dept.	PCSC	ACAF Chinese Nat. Def. P.C. Assoc.
Regional level	P.C. Office of Dept. of Prop. & Educ. or Cul. & Ed.	Non-existent since 1954	Non-existent since 1954
Provincial level	P.C. Office of Cul. & Educ. Dept. or Equiv.	PC & S Cmte.	ACAF branch Defense Sports branch assoc.
Municipal level	Pub. Health & P.C. Office or Equiv. of Prop. or Cul. & Educ. Dept.	PC & S Cmte.	ACAF branch Nat'l Defense Sports branch assoc.
County level	P.C. Office of Prop. Dept.	PC & S Cmte.	ACAF
Commune level		Cul., Educ., & Health Dept. or equiv.	

6

Physical Education in Chinese Schools

AS NOTED ABOVE in the chapter on ideology, the Chinese make little formal distinction between school physical education and physical culture in the broader context. Early in their regime they let it be known that they wished to get away from the narrow confines of a physical culture defined solely as "school physical education."[1] Thus, the aims of physical education are those of physical culture as a whole which in turn are those of the entire culture and education system. It has been said: "There is, strictly speaking, very little in the Chinese Communist educational literature that can be regarded as educational literature per se. What the Chinese Communists have labelled educational theory is no more than the extension and application of certain aspects of dialectical materialism . . . to the direction of educational affairs."[2] Our aim in this chapter, then, will be to see how the Chinese physical culture program—national, scientific, and popular—is executed within the scope of the formal process of education.

THE PRIMARY AND MIDDLE SCHOOL PROGRAM

Forming the backbone of Chinese Communist physical education are the primary and middle school (more specifically, lower middle school—grades 7-9) programs. Because of the underdeveloped nature of the Chinese educational system, very few students advance past lower middle school. Thus Chinese physical educators have a relatively short period of time to cultivate the basic skills and attitudes with respect to physical education before the child passes from their control.

In organizing their school physical education program, the Chinese more or less had to start from the beginning. Although they had a significant amount of general experience in physical culture in pre-1949 China, most of this experience was of a less formal nature and was more useful as a guide for future programs among the population at large than for the formation of a program within the framework of formal education. Two basic questions which China therefore had to pose to herself in October, 1949, were: 1) Exactly what place is physical education to take in the curriculum? and 2) What can physical education reasonably be expected to contribute to the individual and to the nation?

To answer these questions and attain the goal of the "new physical education," Chinese educational authorities felt that the physical education apparatus built up in the old society had to be abolished.[3] In retrospect, we find it natural that they chose to depend largely on the Soviet Union for their model. To this day, despite the sharp about-face in Soviet Chinese relations, reading about the physical education system of the Soviet Union is still a valuable way to gain an insight into Chinese Communist physical education.

Immediately after the Chinese Communist takeover, a study of the Soviet experience in physical education began, and in 1954 the Soviet outline for the teaching of physical education to grades 1-4, 5-7, and 8-10 was translated so that all teachers could use it as a guide.[4] From their study of the Russian approach, the Chinese had come to view Communist education as consisting of five closely related component parts: intellectual education, physical education, moral education, art education, and comprehensive skills education (*tsung ho chi shu chao yü*).[5] To produce a complete, fully developed student along the Greek model, these five parts had to be coordinated.

The Soviet manuals which were studied, spelled out the Russian physical education program in detail: the aims and responsibilities of physical education (often adopted verbatim by the Chinese as their own aims); the different psychological and physiological traits of different age groups; basic methods and problems in physical education; organization of school physical education; testing and planning in physical education; materials for various grades; the special nature of girls' physical education; medical inspection; teaching the physically substandard student.[6] The scientific Soviet approach required the teacher to prepare a detailed analysis of each lesson including the specific effect that it would have on the student's body and character, keeping age, sex, and the student's capabilities in mind. Further, the precise steps in each exercise had to be spelled out in minute detail and their purposes explained.[7]

Through a detailed study of the Soviet experience, Chinese Communist educators came to the conclusion that physical education should be considered a subject on a par with others, the neglect of which would result in imperfect overall development and whose failure should be a factor in the promotion or non-promotion of the student.[8] In concrete terms, the responsibility of physical education should be to advance regular and systematic bodily growth of young people and to guard their good health; to promote bodily strength, stamina, speed, and dexterity; to teach students basic knowledge about physical culture and health; and to develop basic skills and habits.[9] Liu Ai-feng shows in the following statement the extent to which scientific awareness is a characteristic of Chinese Communist physical education:

> The object of middle school and primary school education is to guide the students to have regular and constant physical training and sports so as to promote the assimilation of the new and excretion of the old of the physical organs, develop the physiological function of the five senses, the four limbs as well as all members of the body and strengthen their muscles and physical strength in order to improve their health and physique. Simultaneously . . . we may carry out political and ideological education and communist moral education for the students.[10]

This passage hints at the close relationship in the school between the health program and the physical education program. Although the two programs generally function independently (one is ultimately responsible to the Physical Culture and

Sports Commission, and the other to the Ministry of Health), a well carried out physical education program is viewed as one of the contributing factors to a healthy student body. The health program in effect maintains a control function over physical education, and at the beginning of each school year, the school doctor examines each student and in consultation with the physical education instructor classifies the student in one of three categories: 1) may participate in the "labor-defense system," 2) may participate in a modified exercise program, 3) can only participate in light activities.[11]

Let us now proceed and see exactly what the mechanics of the physical education program are in Communist China. What is noteworthy at the outset is that the stress put on physical culture throughout the 12 years of elementary and middle school is relatively constant. From the first year of primary school on, two class hours are spent on physical training weekly in all grades, plus two more hours in extra-curricular sports activity.* The two hour segments might be split up or given together; instructors might be male or female; and emphasis might shift slightly depending upon age; but every schoolchild in China has this same basic program of four weekly hours of physical training[13] administered with a uniform purpose in mind. It is therefore possible for us to talk about the entire pre-university physical education program in more general terms than ordinarily would be possible.**

The Chinese recognize four basic aspects of any physical

---

* It is of interest to compare the number of hours spent per week on physical education with those spent on other subjects in the curriculum. According to the 1958-59 "Ministry of Education Middle School Teaching Plan" issued in Nanking, physical education received two hours per week in each of the six years of middle school, with the school year consisting of 34 weeks during the first five years and 32 weeks during the sixth year. In both cases approximately 30 hours per week are spent in class. This amounts to 404 hours of physical education in six years of middle school (excluding an equal number of after-school hours spent in sports activities). These 404 hours surpass the time spent on geography (306), biology (374), chemistry (334), music and drawing (both 102), and compare favorably with history (438), socialist education (404), physics (468), foreign languages (484), and productive labor (404). Only Chinese language (1,146) and mathematics (1,178) receive substantially more attention. When the 404 after-school hours spent on physical education are taken into account, timewise, physical education, with 808 hours, becomes the third most important subject.[12]

** Physical education on various levels is formally guided by the "Outline for Teaching Physical Education" (*T'i Yü Chiao Hsüeh Ta Kang*) first published in the fall term of 1956-57.

education program. The most basic is exercise—the core of the physical training program. Participation in a varied set of exercises is viewed as preparation for all other aspects of physical activity. What makes exercise so suitable is its adaptability. Older exercises can be modified and any two familiar exercises can be combined into new ones, to suit age groups, physical condition, and general purpose. The outline for middle school physical education published in 1959 included the following types of exercises: drill, synchronized group, general development and warm-up, climbing, jumping, throwing, and balance. Public displays are commonly given in Communist China in which dazzling visual effects are achieved by having thousands of colorfully-clad children perform the same exercise movements simultaneously. The main characteristics of exercise are non-competitiveness and utility. Constant repetition of them will give the student quickness, strength, toughness, courage, grace, and speed. If the exercises performed are sufficiently diversified, they will help develop all parts of the body.

The second aspect of Chinese Communist physical education involves both games and dance. Although both are included in the middle school program, these activities are held to be especially suitable for younger children. Dances are participated in most frequently during the October 1st independence day celebrations or on other similar occasions (e.g. May 4th, August 1st). Games essentially derive directly from the basic exercises. They play down the competitive aspect and at the same time combine some of the basic exercise movements into a pleasant pastime. They also begin to teach the younger child creativity, group consciousness, independence, flexibility, and discipline.[14]

Sports (the third aspect), like games and dance, are also seen as an extension of the basic exercises, but they add the ingredient of competition. Such sports as track and field, swimming, skating, and basketball are especially practiced in the middle school program where they tend to replace games and dance. Sports receive most of their attention during the after-school physical education periods. School teams in basketball, volleyball, and table tennis are relatively common, but, unlike the United States, acceptance to play on a school team depends on scholastic and political work as well as athletic ability. These interscholastic games are apparently well attended, with pressure brought upon students and teachers to this effect.[15] Sports competition for elementary and middle schools is generally held on non-school days or during holiday periods. From time to time national student games in various sports have been held with the first in 1954 in Port Arthur-Dairen.[16]

The final aspect of physical education involves training for labor and defense. Activities of this type are described in detail in chapter 7, and range from the 100 meter dash, to grenade throwing, to forced 10 kilometer marches. These activities, when they are performed as the "labor-defense system," as they are at the middle school level, form the main focus of the school physical education program, and have always had a military flavor. With the inauguration of the "Every Man a Soldier" campaign in 1958, the system began to wane in importance, to be replaced by the decidedly paramilitary concept of "sports for national defense" prevalent in the mid-'60's. This went so far as to involve elementary school children in activities which we would consider closer to military training than to sports.

The school "labor-defense system," during its heyday, was primarily intended for students of middle school age and above. The youth grade level (ages 13-15) was the youngest age group provided for in the system. Elementary school students, generally in the 7-12 age range, were thought to be physically insufficiently developed and psychologically unable to endure the stress and were thus excluded from the system. Facilities and personnel were also a consideration in excluding elementary schools from the "labor-defense system" for there were many instances where elementary school students were past the age of 12. Lack of equipment as well as medical and physical education personnel, however, made their participation impractical.[17] In 1958, this restriction was relaxed somewhat and physically able elementary school students occasionally participated in the system.[18]

Before proceeding, we should note one basic difference between American and Chinese physical education. Despite the differences in aims and programs that exist between the two systems, the majority of the activities found in a Chinese physical education class could conceivably be found in some form in its American counterpart. This does not apply to the physical facilities. The Chinese maintain no illusions about their paucity of equipment and the need for improvisation where equipment is concerned is a theme which has been sounded many times. Since school gymnasiums are all but unknown on the Mainland, the whims of the weather are something which must be taken account of in program planning. For one thing, alternate activities which can be held indoors, often in very limited space, must always be available in case of inclement weather. Further, a stretch of unseasonably harsh weather can play havoc with the physical education schedule which in China depends greatly on meeting certain standards by appointed dates. Careful programming is thus essential, and detailed schedules of three types are prepared: 1) showing the general areas of stress for the year, 2) detailing the activities for each month, 3) apportioning the time within each class period.[19] In light of this unpredictable element, it is not surprising that Chinese physical education leaders have, from time to time, stressed the need for a flexible approach to physical education, taking into account differences in climate, physical resources, and student health.[20]

The backbone of the school physical education program is the school-time physical education class held twice a week for one hour (or occasionally for two hours once a week). It is during these sessions that the students learn the basic knowledge, undergo fundamental training, and master the basic techniques and skills for their age group. The instructor makes out a formal lesson plan in consideration of the age, sex, bodily development, and physical education background of the student. A typical period is broken down as follows:

> *Opening stage*—3 to 5 minutes. Students line up, attendance is taken, and the teacher explains the contents and aims of the day's lesson. Students then get into troop formation and go through marching and double-time (running march) drills. The primary purpose here is to loosen up the body.
>
> *Preparatory stage*—8 to 15 minutes. This stage includes empty-handed exercises (*t'u shou ts'ao*), rope-jumping, dance steps, and games. It aims to further warm up the body for the main activity of the day as well as cultivate general bodily harmony and precision.

Main stage—20 to 30 minutes. It is during this segment that the instructor introduces and explains new techniques and movements. Activities here include jumping, running, throwing, scaling, climbing, balance maneuvers, weight lifting, and games. At this point in the period, the student is sufficiently loosened up to put forth his maximum effort in acquiring movement skills, practical skills, and athletic skills. Included among the practical skills are such paramilitary activities as are listed in the "labor-defense system." During this stage, the teacher is aiming to cultivate a spirit of daring, determination, quickness, and resoluteness, as well as a collective outlook.

Concluding stage—3 to 5 minutes. The lesson is tapered off so as to give the students a chance to cool off while the teacher summarizes the day's work.

Like other courses, physical education has the responsibility of advancing "thought development" (or in layman's terms, to infuse the Communist way of thinking into the child) from the day of his entrance into primary school. This wasn't always the case. In the early and mid-50's, the physical education class wasn't thought to be as good a place as other classes for teaching thought education. The "Socialist Education Campaign" of 1957 and the "Great Leap Forward" of 1958 doubtless had a part in this change. The physical education teacher has since been required to inject thought cultivation into his lesson, whenever at all possible. The exploits of the People's Liberation Army serve as examples of how physical culture prepares one to sacrifice for the nation's sake. Through team games, group awareness and mutual aid are cultivated, and by naming squads and teams after well known communes, current events are tied into the lesson. Likewise, discipline and organization can be instilled through marching routines and drill formation. The teacher is expected to gain further insight into the child's thought processes by taking an interest in his private life and by mingling among the students after class.[21] What the instructor is basically called on to realize is that merely trying to pass along abstract thoughts to students will not achieve the desired results. The teacher must make every effort to link the more abstract with that which the student can readily identify.²²

The second aspect of school physical education, and which might be called its staple, is the early morning exercise period. These "early morning exercises" (*tsao ts'ao*) or "broadcast exercises" are done to radio music by everyone in school, usually before the first class period. During the winter season they are sometimes advanced to the second or third period (or between periods) because of the low temperatures.²³ They have also been reported to serve as an aid to warming up on cold mornings in those schools without heat.²⁴ This set of exercises has been a major part of the athletic scene in China since 1951. The most recent set (the fourth) was issued in 1963. Generally speaking, this exercise program, supervised by the physical education instructor, provides about four minutes of exercise designed to tone up the student's body and prepare him for a productive day.²⁵

The third aspect of elementary and middle school physical education is the extracurricular two hour weekly sports program. This program is closely coordinated with the classroom physical education program. Skills and techniques learned in class are practiced here, and once again emphasis is put on the all-around development of the student's body through regular training. The after-school program puts particular emphasis on preparing for the "labor-defense system" and on competitive athletics. This is the only part of the school physical education program which gives the child any opportunity to participate in activities of his own choice.²⁶

The middle school extracurricular program caters to four types of students: 1) those who have not mastered the basic skills well and have no real interest in them—who participate in group training and for whom an effort is made to improve their interest; 2) those already having the basic skills as well as an interest in sports—who participate in group training one session per week and in items of their own choice during the other session; 3) those especially good at sports—who represent the school at matches and train at other times (as of 1964 there were school teams in track and field, gymnastics, basketball, volleyball, table tennis, and marksmanship); 4) those who are physically unfit and must do light exercises (e.g. shadow boxing) adapted to their condition.[27]

The organizational unit of the after-school program is the small squad (*hsiao tsu*). In lower elementary school, the squad is based purely on skills. In the upper elementary and middle school grades, division is by sex as well as by ability. During the course of the lesson, the physical culture instructor circulates among the different groups assisted by Young Pioneers, Young Communist League members, and sports activists. The athletically superior student is generally excused from formal participation in this program to participate on school athletic teams and in "spare-time" physical culture schools.[28]

In theory, after-school physical education classes are strictly voluntary. In fact, however, hidden pressures leave the student no choice but to volunteer. Chinese officials in general prefer to use less coercive measures and basing the after-school program on friendship groups has proven to be a successful means of stirring up enthusiasm. But, more than anything else, it has been the "labor-defense system" which has stimulated participation in the program. This results from the fact that successful participation in the system is imperative for the student's future; and that these two hours per week offer the only opportunity for supervised practice of the system's events. Regardless of the student's motivation for participating in the system, it is made explicitly clear to him that extracurricular dance groups and singing groups are of a lower priority than the after-school sports program.[29]

To enable students and teachers to continually grasp the significance of physical education and to carry it out properly, each school's program is subject to re-evaluation three times per term. At the beginning of each term, students and teachers are assembled to study the Party's educational guidelines, discuss physical culture work for the term, and plan the part to be played in this work by the classmaster, the Youth League, and the Young Pioneers. In the middle of each term a review of physical education work to date is carried out. The term is concluded with a summary of all work.[30]

One question which remains open regarding elementary and middle school physical education is exactly who administers it. What emerges from all the available documentation is somewhat hazy. The Physical Culture and Sports Commission seems to be its overseer and inspector. The "Simplified Regulations" of the Physical Culture and Sports Commission (approved March 23, 1956) holds the Commission responsible for guiding the entire physical culture program of the nation. As part of this responsibility, the Commission reviews and approves all physical education teaching outlines, teaching materials, and texts in cooperation with the Ministry of Education and other concerned ministries.[31] The actual implementation of policies and the initiation of local programs must tentatively be accredited to the physical education section of the local branch of the Ministry of Education. What is more than possible is that at the grassroots levels physical culture personnel attached to either of these organizations are one and the same individuals bearing two titles.[32]

THE GENERAL EDUCATION PHYSICAL EDUCATION PROGRAM IN SCHOOLS OF HIGHER EDUCATION

Unlike the middle school level and below, physical education as a part of general education on the university level (excluding professional physical culture training schools) does not receive a great deal of attention in Communist Chinese writing. We do know that physical education in universities (which consists of two hours per week for the first two years) has been noted in the past for having been conducted in an unsatisfactory manner.

The "Joint Directive of the Ministry of Higher Education, the Ministry of Health, and the Central Committee of the New Democratic Youth League Concerning Strengthening Physical Education in Institutions of Higher Education" sketches what is expected of university physical education programs. All institutions of higher education are required to maintain physical education programs geared to develop the basic skills and attain the basic aims of physical culture. Even more than at lower educational levels, the "labor-defense system" is to receive most of the stress at this level. In addition, students are asked to develop competence in one sport so as to help develop a program of intercollegiate athletics which should involve 9% of the student body as players and 1% as referees and coaches.

The head of each institution should take the lead in the implementation of such a program. He should appoint a deputy who in turn will organize a physical education department, a staff of teachers, and a student athletic association. The department is to administer the overall program and carry out instruction and research. The athletic association—mainly supervised by the Young Communist League—is responsible for organizing mass sports activities for the bulk of the students and for discovering talented athletes for school teams. Overseeing the total program should be the provincial, autonomous region, or municipal level Physical Culture and Sports Committee.[33]

The Hofei Mining Institute of Anhwei (designated the "National Sports Red Flag Institute" of 1958) and Tsinghua University provide two examples of what are considered model programs. In 1953, small sports training groups were organized throughout the Hofei Mining Institute and in 1954 the "labor-defense system" was incorporated into the regular physical education classroom curriculum. To halt fading interest in sports, a student sports association was formed in 1956 which succeeded in encouraging mass sports participation and "labor-defense" training. Under the influence of the physical education faculty and the association, and with the close cooperation of the provincial Physical Culture and Sports Committee, standards were raised to the point where 63% of Hofei students passed the 1st Class "labor-defense" standards in 1956 and 100% passed 2nd Class (the higher ranking) standards in 1958.[34]

Tsinghua, with a gymnasium, two track and field facilities, 50 basketball courts (outdoors), and indoor and outdoor swimming pools (as of 1959), has one of the top sports facilities in China. Ever since 1949, sports activities there have received considerable attention. In 1953, when the "labor-defense system" first appeared on the campus, numerous small training squads were organized to prepare for the system's events. As a result, in 1958, 70% of the students had attained at least the 1st Class standards and 40% the 2nd Class standards. Sports meets have been held at Tsinghua at the departmental, interdepartmental, and university-wide levels and 20% of Tsinghua's students engage in special training for individual events or school teams (which compete in 22 events). In 1959, there were four Masters of Sport, 30 athletes of 1st Class rank, and

200 of 2nd Class rank (this ranking differs from the "labor-defense" ranking).[35]

SPECIALIZED PHYSICAL CULTURE SCHOOLS

From the outset, the greatest hindrance to the successful development of the large-scale physical culture to which the Communists had committed themselves, was a lack of manpower. As a first step in alleviating this shortage, the Chinese had no choice but to institute emergency short-term training programs (two weeks to a month) for potential cadres among workers and students who were physical culture enthusiasts. In 1950, about 700 cadres in Peking went through a program geared to train individuals in specific sports and return them to their schools and factories as directors of the physical culture program there.[36] These courses were the forerunners of spare-time cadre training courses of longer duration, and of the present-day network of physical culture training schools which now train athletes, teachers, trainers, researchers, coaches, and administrators on levels from elementary to post-university. Despite a constant increase in physical culture training programs, however, the shortage of adequately trained manpower remains a major concern. In 1954, there was a reported shortage of 30,000 physical education instructors at the middle school level and above.[37] The availability of only 369 physical education teachers for about 600 jobs in 312 middle schools in Hupei Province in the mid-'50's caused one half of the Hupei physical education staff to hold a second position and the average teacher load to be 532 students. The situation in elementary schools was even worse.[38] In 1958, only 40% of middle school physical education teachers had special physical culture training.[39]

University Level Training in Physical Culture

At the top of the system of training centers for physical culture workers are the post-secondary (implying graduation from upper middle school or the equivalent) or university level schools. These can be divided into two categories: 1) physical culture institutes, and 2) physical culture departments in the normal schools of higher education (*kao teng shih fan hsüeh hsiao*). The latter breaks down into normal universities (*shih fan ta hsüeh* or *shih fan hsüeh hsiao*) and normal technical schools (*shih fan chuan k'e hsüeh hsiao*).[40]

Of the above, the most prestigious are the institutes of physical culture. These schools aim to develop high level athletes, specialists in physical culture theory, top level administrators, instructors for middle schools and schools of higher education, coaches, referees, and researchers.[41] They differ basically from American professional schools of physical education in that their programs are geared to train sports personnel (and especially athletes) for work *outside* of educational circles as well as inside.

The first such institute was established in Shanghai as the East China Physical Culture Institute (since renamed the Shanghai P.C. Institute) in 1952. The Peking P.C. Institute—the largest in China—was opened in November, 1953. Since 1953, eight more such schools have been opened in Wuhan, Chengtu, Shenyang, Sian, Nanking, Kwangchow, Tientsin, and Harbin; for a present total of ten which by 1964 had graduated 19,000 students.[42]

Applicants to the institutes take the regular higher education entrance examinations in Chinese language, general politics, chemistry, and physics, in addition to special physical culture skills tests for those not having the 2nd Class "labor-defense" certificate. Men are required to show their proficiency in the 100 meter dash, the high jump, the shotput, and in chin-ups; and women in the 100 meter dash, the high jump, and in push-ups.[43] Academic competence does not, however, seem to be as important an admissions criterion as sports ability. Tall students with special competence in one sport and political soundness are reportedly given preferential treatment. The latter trait is treated seriously, for the institutes are major breeding grounds for top athletes and the Party wants assurances that athletes who might be called upon to represent China in international competition will behave as expected.[44]

When the physical culture institutes first began operation in 1952, the original aim was to provide a four year course of study. However, owing to the pressures of national reconstruction, the course was trimmed to two years and designated a technical course (*chuan hsiu k'e*). Upon completion of the two year program, the better students were permitted one additional year of research.⁴⁵ Beginning with the summer of 1957, the two year course was dropped in the institutes and retained only in the higher normal schools.⁴⁶

The curriculum at the institutes stresses general education and scientific training, as well as physical culture training. In the first category, courses are required in Marxism-Leninism, dialectical materialism and historical materialism, Chinese revolutionary history, economics, educational theory, and a foreign language (usually English for purposes of international travel).⁴⁷ Science content courses are offered in human physiology, human anatomy, psychology, hygiene, and medical supervision. All students in the institutes receive general professional training in physical culture theory, track and field, gymnastics, swimming, and various ball games. Electives are available in such areas as boxing, wrestling, and traditional Chinese sports. To encourage specialization in the skills and theory of a particular sport, beginning in his third year, a student is permitted to pick one sport for special emphasis.

This is especially true at the Peking and Shanghai Institutes which have established "sports departments" (*yün tung hsi*) to produce coaches, instructors, and athletes highly competent in one sport. The Shanghai P.C. Institute Sports Department offers training in three specialties: track and field, gymnastics, and ball games (soccer, volleyball, and basketball). In addition to what is offered at Shanghai, the Peking P.C. Institute Sports Department offers table tennis and swimming. To enter these special departments of the institutes, a student must attain a special level of competence. As he advances in the department, the number of hours of instruction in his specialty are increased.⁴⁸

Another area of stress in the institute program is that of scientific research in physical culture. Since 1956 each institute has had a unit dealing with the scientific approach to physical culture. Topics investigated vary, from the best way for an athlete to keep in good physical condition, to the effect of Chinese traditional calisthenics on certain illnesses. In addition to the science research units at the ten institutes, at least two independent sports science institutes exist in Peking and Shanghai,⁴⁹ as well as departments of sports medicine in various medical schools. The first medical class of 41, specializing in sports medicine,* graduated in June, 1956 from Peking Medical College.[50] In April, 1959, the first independent sports medical institute was opened in Peking to investigate the relationship between good health and sports as well as the treatment of sports injuries.[51] The interest in sports medicine has spurred a growing number of conferences on the topic.**

A glance at the Peking P.C. Institute gives an idea of the best that China has to offer in this area. The institute was first established in November, 1953 (as the Central P.C. Institute), as a continuation of the Physical Culture Department of the Peking Teachers University. This department had 14 teachers and 51 students in 1953, and from 1919 to 1948 had only graduated 440 students. From a modest beginning in 1953, at which time Russian instructors were an important part of the faculty, the institute developed to the point where in 1963 it had 1,600 students (including 400 women) engaged in eight branches of study. In its first 10 years, 2,800 students graduated from the institute including former world table tennis champion Chuang Tse-tung and other world class athletes.[53]

The facilities at the Peking P.C. Institute are the best of all the institutes. The school covers 600,000 square meters complete with indoor and outdoor swimming pools, an indoor track, three gymnasiums measuring 75 x 20 meters, two indoor basketball-volleyball courts, and a weight lifting hall. It also has five soccer fields, three track and field areas, and 20 outdoor basketball courts.[54]***

A notch below the physical culture institutes in prestige, and geared mainly toward training teachers rather than coaches or athletes, are the physical culture departments of the normal universities and the normal technical schools. These depart-

---

* Sports medicine specializes in the treatment of athletic injuries and does research on the effects of sports activities on the body.
** The 1st Physical Culture Scientific Conference was held at the Peking P.C. Institute Feb. 1-7, 1956. In March, 1960, the 1st National Physical Culture Science Work Conference was held. In November, 1964, the 1st National Symposium on Sports Science was held.[52]
*** Worthy of mention, although not specifically fitting into the university institute category, is the Physical Culture Institute of the People's Liberation Army which opened in January, 1961, in Canton. This school is very much like the other institutes and offers 10 courses including basketball, soccer, track and field, gymnastics, swimming and military sports. It trains physical culture cadres for the army's sports program and also carries on research.[55]

ments are just one of many in their respective schools. The normal university offers a four year course intended mainly to produce middle school teachers in such areas as school and pre-school education, Chinese language and literature, minority peoples' languages, foreign languages, history, political education, mathematics, physical education, and the sciences. The normal technical school ordinarily offers the same courses, but its program only extends for two years and is intended for prospective lower middle school teachers. Generally speaking, the normal universities all have technical departments (*chuan hsiu k'e*) whose two year program is equivalent to that of the normal technical school.[56]

The higher normal school physical culture student is required to acquire the basic knowledge required of the students in every other higher normal school department. With the exception of a foreign language, the general education courses correspond to those given in the physical culture institutes. In addition, in the area of pedagogy, the student is required to take courses in educational psychology, educational theory, teaching methods, and teaching practice. In his professional content courses, the higher normal school student takes the same science and physical culture program as his counterpart at the institutes, but spends more time on educational theory pertaining to physical education and teaching methods of physical education, and does not have the opportunity for close specialization in a specific area.

Numerically speaking, there are more physical culture departments in higher normal schools than physical culture institutes. By 1965, 23 of 28 provinces, autonomous regions, and major cities had at least one institute or higher normal school department of physical culture, with a total of 10 institutes, and 17 departments within teachers training colleges.[57]

Physical Culture in Middle School Level Normal Schools

Within the overall framework of the normal middle school, special physical culture middle schools were organized in 1956 for lower middle school graduates. Specifically, the "specialized physical culture middle school" was one of 22 types of "specialized middle schools" (*chung teng chuan yeh hsüeh hsiao*) geared toward special professions and trades. The course generally lasts three years (sometimes ranging from two to four years) and trains students to be lower middle school physical education teachers, physical culture cadres in government organs, factories, and mines, and youth group leaders.[58] To gain admission, entrance exams are required in Chinese language, mathematics, politics, and physical skills.[59] The course of study in these schools mirrors (although on a more basic level) the physical culture course offered at the higher normal schools. Courses are taken in the theory of teaching physical education, pedagogy, psychology, human anatomy, human physiology, hygiene, gymnastics, track and field, ball games, swimming, and children's games. At least 14 of this type of school are known to exist, and in several cases they are affiliated and share facilities with a full-fledged physical culture institute.[60]

Spare-Time Athletic Schools

Of all the schools specializing in sports in Communist China, the most widespread and most interesting is the spare-time athletic school. For one thing, it is the only sports school that most Chinese will ever have a chance of coming to know personally. Most Chinese children do not reach upper middle school, hence the probability that a Chinese child will be among the select to reach one of the 50 special physical culture schools on the middle school level or above, is remote. On the other hand, there are thousands of spare-time sports schools and acceptance into one of them is a realistic goal for a Chinese child. This type of school is also significant because it serves as the basic-level training ground for China's future athletes; a place where future competitors in national and international meets can be discovered and trained. In its first nine years, the spare-time program produced over 3,200 athletes who participated on provincial, autonomous region, municipal, or national teams.[61]

The spare-time athletic school is further noteworthy for its longevity. Until the culmination of the Cultural Revolution, it existed in relatively full vigor for 12 years, making it one of the Chinese Communist physical culture's most enduring institutions.

Spare-time athletic schools were first set up in 1955 in

Peking, Tientsin, and Shanghai on a limited basis. As it was originally conceived, this type of school included two age groups: 13-17 (*shao nien*), and 17-23 (*ch'ing nien*). Within each age group there were two types of school: 1) those teaching one particular sport (e.g. swimming, gymnastics, track and field), and 2) those teaching several sports. These tuition free schools were run by the Physical Culture and Sports Commission with the cooperation of the YCL, labor unions, educational authorities, and health authorities. Each student attends two-hour sessions two to four days per week. The schools are run formally with examinations and promotion, and, at the completion of the three year course, students who meet the Physical Culture and Sports Commission standards for their sports are awarded certificates according to their achievements.[62]

These schools were originally intended to be selective and in 1957 there were only 73 of them in all of China with 7,000 students.[63] With the rapid expansion of makeshift education in China, spurred on by the "Great Leap Forward," the spare-time sports schools underwent an inevitable expansion in numbers (with an equally inevitable reduction in quality). In October, 1958, it was announced that these schools would be set up in large numbers throughout the country for youngsters, ages 8 to 18—13 had been the previous minimum age—in both urban and rural areas. To provide facilities, use would be made of primary schools, secondary schools, and institutions of higher learning, as well as public stadia and sports grounds. The schools would be staffed by sportsmen among primary school teachers, government workers, demobilized army veterans, and peasants. Initially, courses in the 8 to 18 age group would be offered in basketball, table tennis, swimming, track and field, and marksmanship.[64] On the other hand, very little was said about the senior spare-time school after this date and it is probable that it was phased out.

Paralleling other innovations which emerged during the "Great Leap" there was an instant explosion in the establishment of these schools which quickly subsided. By the end of 1957, there were 105 of this type of school with 10,000 students.[65] In 1958, there were suddenly more than 4,500 spare-time athletic schools catering to more than 200,000 children functioning in Chungshan County of Kwangtung Province alone.[66] As of 1959, Peking registered 700 such schools with 70,000 middle and primary school students attending.[67] By 1960, normality began to reappear and the count in Peking read 310 schools with 28,427 students.[68] As in other areas which saw a retreat from "Great Leap" levels, the retreat was not total. The spare-time schools maintained their increased vigor relative to the situation before 1958, and the new age categorization was maintained.

In establishing the spare-time athletic school, the Chinese left no doubt as to its major purpose: the cultivation of a reserve strength of top-grade athletes so that there would be a perpetual source of athletic talent. Thus, selectivity is of the essence. There must be enough students to maintain a pool of quality athletes. Yet, if the school is to develop an elite, it can only defeat its own purposes by fully opening its doors to the masses. By putting the prospective athlete in such a selective environment, he can progress as fast as possible without the constraint of classes or semesters. Further, by concentrating the best talent in these schools, maximum usage can be made of expert teachers and scarce equipment.

The Chinese, like other nations striving for athletic excellence, have learned that youth is the key. This was undoubtedly their principal motivation in lowering the entering age in the spare-time sports schools from 13 to 8. This thought is expressed concisely in the following slogan: "Cultivate from an early age, train for many years, establish a good foundation." In concrete terms this is translated to mean that sports such as ice skating and swimming should be begun at ages 8 or 9; track and field, gymnastics, table tennis, and diving at 10 or 11; soccer, volleyball, basketball, badminton, tennis, ice hockey, water polo, and speed skating at 12 or 13; and marksmanship and cycling at 13 or 14. Only by beginning at an early age and practicing uninterruptedly for many years can mastery be attained.

In carrying out this program, general bodily development is to receive first priority, especially with the younger students. As the body becomes more developed, the focus then switches to the acquisition of specific skills. Thought training and military arts training also are included in the program, but the Chinese apparently feel that these aspects can be dealt with elsewhere and should be of secondary priority to the goal of producing a reserve force of future athletes.

Although this school focuses mainly on the cultivation of athletic talent, it does not lose cognizance of the fact that the simultaneous development of the moral, intellectual, and physical capabilities of the child are the broader goals of education. Thus, the regular school course remains the chief objective for the student and satisfactory performance there is a prerequisite to continued enrollment in the spare-time school. Sports instructors are expected to keep abreast of the student's scholastic progress, reduce sports training at exam time, and, if necessary, consult with the student during free evenings.[69]

Mainland China has never been known for the uniformity of her schools, and it is more than likely that there has been a great deal of variation among spare-time athletic schools. Nevertheless, perhaps the best way to gain an appreciation of the general nature of this type of school is to present a brief portrait of one of them.

In 1959, the Shihchahai Junior Spare-time Athletic School was one of the best equipped in Peking, with a gymnasium, eight basketball courts, and three swimming pools. It had 346 students (ages 8-18) in three grades, 23 classes, and eight instructors. Most of its students came from middle schools. They were chosen by virtue of their special talent for sports, good grades, and good health as certified by a doctor. The students at Shihchahai attended classes two to four times per week in sessions of from two to three hours, starting at 4:30 P.M.

Being a student at Shihchahai seems to have carried some special status, but it also represented an added burden. Examinations had to be passed both at the regular school and at the sports school. For example, a gymnastics student was required to pass a sportsman's test plus the "labor-defense" test before progressing to the second grade at Shihchahai. To graduate, he had to meet the standards of a 1st Class gymnast as well as pass the "labor-defense" test at the 1st Class level.[70]

IN-SERVICE TRAINING OF PHYSICAL EDUCATION TEACHERS

As already noted, the major stumbling block in the way of the development of physical education in Chinese schools has been the critical lack of qualified teachers. This problem was first attacked by giving "hurry-up" courses to people with some background or interest in sports. A further attempt came in the mid-'50's when the Chinese began to institute programs of in-service training (i.e. while employed in a profession) geared to raise the standards of teachers already employed in physical education.

In 1956, the Physical Culture and Sports Commission, Ministry of Education, and Ministry of Higher Education issued a directive for the organization of in-service training programs for physical culture instructors. The programs stipulated, varied for different levels of education, but, in general, they required teachers to study the general directives for their grade level as well as the appropriate Soviet physical culture literature. In addition to in-service classroom work given during the school year, special vacation-time courses would be run in both physical culture theory and sports skills. The vehicle for carrying out this program was the "seminar" (*chiao yen tsu*). Regular study sessions would be organized for the physical education staff in the school (or several schools) during which time professional and ideological problems would be reviewed.[71]

It is not at all clear that the in-service program was a success or that it was carried into the '60's. Chinese literature on the subject, while being skimpy, does hint that universal implementation of the program was never attained. Despite our lack of information in this area, the in-service program is mentioned here as an example of one attempt made by the Chinese to solve what continues to be a major problem in all of her education.

In this chapter we have shown how the Chinese have established physical education as a major component of general education, and further how they have stretched the scope of the physical education system to include the training of athletes and other physical culture personnel not ordinarily catered to in programs run by education authorities. In the process, they have established institutions which remain true to the cultivation of a physical culture which is national, scientific and popular.

It goes without saying that the development of school physical education is dependent on the overall educational situation. Education has as yet not been made available on a high quality level for the bulk of the population in China, and in recent years has been all but non-existent. Under such circumstances, physical education cannot help but suffer. What we may conclude as a result of our study of Chinese Communist physical education is that the Mainland Chinese have given every indication that as education progresses, as it inevitably must, physical education will be given a priority position within its framework.

7

Mass Sports and the Concept of National Defense Physical Culture

IN THIS CHAPTER we will attempt to get to the heart of sports and physical education in Mainland China. Available evidence indicates that the term "national defense physical culture" (*kuo fang t'i yü*), when extended sufficiently, gives one an adequate understanding and feeling of what the Chinese see as the dominant purpose in their promotion of physical education. The effort here, then, will be to present Chinese sports and physical education as attempting to follow the theme of "sports for national defense." It will become clear that I am discussing sports for national defense on three levels:

1. On the broadest level, the Communists view participation in sports in general, as having value for national defense. The term "mass sports" seems to carry this connotation.

2. In a more limited sense, we will deal with various selected sports (some of which are definitely paramilitary events, having only a slight connection with sports in the western sense), which the Communists see as being more particularly germane to national defense.

3. In the most limited sense, we will deal with a program known as the "labor-defense system" (*lao wei chih*) which is a scheme to promote physical fitness among the masses with a view towards national defense.

Old-time Communist Party member Hsü Te-li playing table tennis before some young admirers.

I must point out, that it is not my intention to give the impression that the Chinese see the goal of all sports to be in the interest of national defense. Significantly, table tennis, the most publicized sport on the Mainland, is rarely mentioned in this connection. I also do not intend to give the impression that the Chinese are opposed to fun or enjoyment through sports. Here, one most pointedly runs into the difference between official pronouncement and actuality. The Chinese only rarely, in their official pronouncements, give the impression that receiving enjoyment from sports is important (though the term *yu hsi*—play or games—sometimes does appear). We can, nevertheless, be sure that the people of the Mainland are no different from those who live in other countries, and that deriving pleasure from sports is a universal characteristic.

It seems clear that when the Chinese Communists came to power in 1949, they knew very definitely the function and purpose that sports was to occupy within their society. There is evidence that as early as 1942 a sports meet was held in Yenan which included some of the sports later associated with national defense sports programs (e.g. swimming with equipment). We also know that a sports program existed in Red Soviet areas in the early 1930's.[1] Finally, the fact that a national sports association was set up on the Mainland only months after the Communist takeover,[2] indicates that a great deal of planning must have been done prior to October, 1949.

THE "LABOR-DEFENSE SYSTEM"—1951-1958

The concept of sports for national defense in China can be traced back to 1951 when the local branch physical culture organization in Peking, together with the municipal Democratic Youth League committee, worked out a set of "physical culture training standards" for school youth, based on:

1) the "labor-defense system" first developed in 1931 by the Russian Communist Youth League in order to raise the level of the people's health quickly, and

2) local conditions in China.[3]

This system of 1951 was followed, in the spring of 1952, by a complete draft of regulations for the trial implementation of the "Ready for Labor and Defend the Fatherland" Physical Culture System, (*Chun-pei Lao-tung yü Pao-wei Tsu Kuo T'i*

Yü Chih-tu Shih-hsing T'iao-lieh). These regulations (accompanied by a set of standards for time, weight, and distance) provided for the division of men and women into three groups of male and three groups of female, according to age: for men, 15-17, 18-28, 29 and over; for women, 14-15, 16-23, 24 and over, with varying standards according to age. There was further subdivision into first and second classes among adult groups within each category.[4]

The decision to make the "labor-defense system" a formal program ratified by law, was apparently reached during the first plenary session of the Central People's Government Commission on Physical Culture held January 16-21, 1954, in Peking. This meeting included all members of the Commission, members of the Physical Culture Committees of the six administrative regions, and representatives of the Political Departments of various military regions.

At this meeting, Vice-Chairman Chu Teh, representing the government, stated the connection between national defense and physical culture rather clearly, when he said: "In the field of national defense, powerful and skillful arms are needed by the country. Because of this, the young people must be strong in physique and bright and lively, courageous and sharp, tough and unyielding."[5]

The meeting decided, as part of the central task for physical education in 1954, to require all schools above the middle school level (which had suitable facilities) to plan for the experimental stage of the "Physical Culture System to Prepare for Labor and National Defense." Physical culture for labor and national defense was also to be promoted among the armed forces.

The plenary session also endorsed the dissemination of propaganda specifically designed to let the people know the scientific value of physical culture for work, study, production, and national defense. This would be accomplished via newspapers, movies, radio, etc. To train cadres for this program, short-term, physical training classes would be held during spare-time in factories, mines, government organizations, armed forces, and schools. Holidays and vacations would be made use of, and in some cases, cadres would be removed from their appointed tasks to receive full-time training.

On May 4, 1954, the Physical Culture and Sports Commission of the People's Government officially ratified the regulations and standards for the "labor-defense system." The system, which was only meant to be experimental, was initially intended to be carried out in specific locations where conditions were suitable. In practice, this limited the initial stages of the program to schools above the middle school level.[6]

An examination of the "Joint Directive for Launching the Mass Sports Movement in Institutions of Learning Above the Middle School Standard," promulgated in May, 1954,* is helpful in understanding the intended purpose of physical culture in schools, and the place of the labor-defense system in both schools and society at large. It states in part that 1) sport is a vital component of overall education; 2) physical culture work in schools has as yet not come close to meeting demands; 3) schools should launch various sports activities liked by students (including the training of teams and the organizing of tournaments) ; 4) the physical culture system of the Soviet Union should be studied with an eye toward reform; 5) student societies and selected Youth League members should help in popularizing the movement; 6) the labor-defense system is the basic system for carrying out physical culture among the masses; 7) the system is essential for the unification of the physical education curriculum, outdoor sports activities, sports competition, and morning drills.[7]

The labor-defense system, as it evolved into the 1954 law, bore many and pronounced resemblances to the original 1952 system mentioned above. One major difference, however, was the establishment of the ages of 13-15 as the youth stage (*shiao nien chi*) for both boys and girls, and the establishment of first and second grade categories (with further subdivision) for both men and women above 16. The following statement, which appeared in the periodical *Railroad Construction* (*T'ieh Tao Chien She*), offers a good answer to the question: "What is the labor-defense system?"

> The labor-defense system is an abbreviation for "labor and defense of the fatherland." Why do we have to organize labor-defense system training? Its aim is to advance the health of the bodies of working people, to fully develop

---

* Promulgated by the Physical Culture and Sports Commission, Ministry of Higher Education, Ministry of Education, Ministry of Public Health, Central Committee of the China New Democratic Youth League, and the All-China Students' Federation.

their physical abilities, and to enable them to be able to participate much more significantly in socialist construction.

The labor-defense system is divided into the labor-defense system youth stage, the labor-defense system first class stage, and the labor-defense system second class stage; they [in turn] are divided into several groups according to age, and sex. . . . They go through tests (according to their age and sex), and, if successful, are awarded badges and certificates.

The content of the labor-defense system for those in the youth stage is: labor-defense exercise, rope climbing, 60 meter dash, 500 meter run, high jump or long jump, hand grenade or softball throw, 25 meter swim or 60 meter obstable course run, and calisthenics, etc. Nine events in all. For the first class: 1) labor-defense exercise; 2) rope climb, or [a choice of] pull-ups or pushups; 3) 100 meter dash; 4) 800 meter run or 1500 meter run; 5) high jump or long jump; 6) hand grenade throw, or [a choice of] shot put or weight lifting; 7) gymnastics; 8) shooting, or [a choice of] 10 kilometer march, day-long march, 10 kilometer cross-country bicycle trip, or five kilometer cross-country bicycle trip; 9) 100 meter swim or 50 meter swim. For the second class: 1) labor-defense exercise; 2) rope climb, or [a choice of] pull-ups or push-ups; 3) 100 meter or 200 meter dash; 4) 800 meter run or 3000 meter run; 5) high jump or long jump; 6) hand grenade throw, or [a choice of] shot put, discus, javelin, or weight lifting; 7) gymnastics; 8) shooting, or [a choice of] 10 kilometer march or day-long march; 9) swimming, skating, or obstacle course run.[8]

From a physical education standpoint, it is significant that this series of activities is quite complete in that every person who participates in it is required to demonstrate ability in just about every physical skill of which the human body is capable: speed, stamina, strength, coordination, and grace. Also worthy of note is the fact that the labor-defense system standards were not attainable by an athletic elite alone. Theoretically, anyone, through conscientious, regular training, was capable of attaining the standards of the first class level.[9]

If the labor-defense system was sound from a physical education standpoint, from an organizational standpoint it apparently left much to be desired in its early years. As has already been mentioned, in its first few years of existence (1951-56), the labor-defense system was largely confined to schools above the middle school level. The feelings of the students involved indicate that the system was far from well run.

The foremost complaint was that students did not have sufficient time to train in the manner which was required. Some students felt that too much time was taken away from their studies. Students were either faced with the need to give up their recesses in order to train properly, or to run the risk of taking the test without sufficient preparation. The problem was especially acute for students being tested in the 10 kilometer hike. For this event, each practice session demanded well over an hour of time.[10] By not training properly for the tests, students took risks on two counts. First of all, they endangered their chances of graduation, since it was the rule in some schools to require as many as 80% of their students to meet the standards of the second class level as a criterion for graduation. Secondly, students who took the tests without proper training, took risks with their health. The collapse and subsequent death of Li Yüan-hua, a student at the Peking Russian Language Institute, after a 10 kilometer full-pack march, dramatized this point for the students.

Other criticisms of the system attacked the shortage and, sometimes, complete absence of trained physical culture personnel. Equipment was often inadequate. Schools often demanded that students attain the standards in only a fraction of the time allowed by the Physical Culture and Sports Commission. In addition, individual physical differences of students were often glossed over as schools stressed the attainment of record performances at the expense of the objectives of physical culture. This was sometimes carried to such an extreme that schools lied about the performances of its students in order to improve its image.[11]

In the relatively few middle schools which undertook the labor-defense system, similar complaints were heard. Physical education teachers were accused of taking the system out of its proper context by placing total emphasis on it. Time allocated for extra-curricular sports of particular interest to the students was, instead, sometimes used for labor-defense training. Teachers were also accused of neglecting the gradual approach for the sake of the speedy attainment of labor-defense standards.[12]

Despite the rather heavy barrage of criticism, the ultimate

validity of the system was upheld by sports officials who continued to maintain:

1) that many of the criticisms were unsubstantiated,
2) that many of the seeming faults of the system were the result of directives carried out incorrectly, and
3) that the standards were obtainable with normal training.[13]

It is difficult to assess whether it was the system itself which was at fault or the manner in which it was administered locally. At first glance, judging from the nature of the criticism, one is inclined to blame local administration. It is also possible, however, that either the actions of local school authorities were heavily influenced by pressures passed down through the chain of command, or that the system itself was unadministrable.

THE LABOR-DEFENSE SYSTEM IN 1958

It was in 1958 that the labor-defense system reached full maturity. Throughout the middle months of 1958 it flourished like never before. Strangely, or perhaps expectedly—in view of the rocky course of the "Great Leap Forward"—by 1959, the term "labor-defense system" had practically vanished from the vocabulary of physical culture.

It often seems to be the case in Mainland China that a campaign reaches its peak before the official pronouncements regarding it are delivered. This appears to be what happened to the labor-defense system in 1958. It is quite likely that *unofficial* directives regarding the modification of the 1954 system were handed down months before the official decree was proclaimed in October, 1958. Let us deal first with the official decree, though chronologically it was made at the end of the 1958 campaign.

On October 20, 1958, the State Council, at its 81st session, ratified regulations regarding the "ready for labor and defense" program.[14] Five days later, the Physical Culture and Sports Commission of the People's Government promulgated the new decree. Its chief points of emphasis were the following:

ARTICLE 1
    The labor and defense system intends to encourage participation in physical training, to promote extensive development of physical culture and sports, to raise the technical standard of sports, and to give participants a stronger

physique and will power in order to better serve socialism and the defense of the fatherland. . . .

ARTICLE 3
The first and second grades in the labor defense system engage in six items of training, with items 1-5 specified by the Physical Culture and Sports Commission, and the sixth locally. The five items for the teenage youth grade are all specified by the Physical Culture and Sports Commission.

ARTICLE 4
The Physical Culture and Sports Commission and its local committees are generally given control to promote the system throughout the country. Educational establishments and trade unions supervise industrial workers and schools. The health establishments are responsible for the medical supervision of the labor-defense system. The Young Communist League is to take a leading part in this work. . . .

ARTICLE 7
In order to insure uniformity and quality in labor and national defense system work, local Physical Culture and Sports Commission units have the power to conduct exams.

ARTICLE 8
Badges and certificates are to be given to encourage participation.[15]

From an athletic point of view, the chief change inserted into the 1958 version of the labor-defense system was a reduction in the number of events. The 1954 version had demanded that standards be met in nine events. As was pointed out above, the excessive time required to train properly was one of the chief complaints about the 1954 version. Accordingly, the number of events was reduced to five for young people (boys and girls 13-15) and to six for men and women above 15.[16] For the 13-15 age group the events were: 1) 60 meter dash, 2) 400 meter dash, 3) long jump or high jump, 4) grenade throw or softball throw, 5) rope climb or pole climb (with both hands and feet).[17]

For men and women, five types of events were specified. A sixth event was to be added according to local conditions (e.g. areas with natural water facilities would stress swimming, areas in the North such as Harbin would stress ice skating). The specific events varied according to the age of the participant.

For men and women 16 and above the events were: 1) 100 meter, 60 meter, or* 200 meter dash, 2) 800 meter run, 1500 meter run, or 3000 meter run, 3) long jump or high jump; weight lifting or pull-ups, 4) pushups or rope climb, 5) shooting, hand grenade throw, or marching with full pack (six kilometers for men, four kilometers for women), and 6) an event chosen according to local conditions.[18]

It is significant to note that the 1958 version does not exhibit the variety of skills required in the 1954 version. The 10 kilometer march, the event apparently most criticized, was modified, swimming was stressed less, and the gymnastics event was removed, leaving no test of dexterity.

In spite of the fact that the 1958 labor-defense system did not receive its legal sanction until October, 1958, most of its effect had already been heavily felt by the summer of 1958. Its chief point of emphasis was the rural areas of China which had not been affected to any great extent by the 1954 system. The connection between the emphasis on the countryside and the general nature of the times in China in summer, 1958, is apparent enough. The "Great Leap Forward" put a great deal of stress on the rural areas, especially in the formation of communes. As a result, large numbers of cadres, formerly based in urban areas, were dispatched to the countryside. It can be assumed that, along with other types of cadres, a great many more physical culture workers were in the countryside than had ever been there before, thus facilitating its rapid expansion. The formation of the communes along *hsiang* (expanded village) lines, rather than *ts'un* (local village) lines, undoubtedly also contributed to the efficiency of the implementation of the labor-defense system.

Although, as is usually the case for Mainland China, statistics regarding the labor-defense system are inconsistent, enough of them do exist to show that the system received thorough attention during the first nine months of 1958. In considering these statistics, it is advisable to keep in mind the great exaggeration which was later found to be characteristic of "Great Leap" figures.

During the first nine months of 1958, 5,000,000 people were reported to have attained the criteria of the system as compared

---

* The choice indicated in this listing usually refers to events assigned to a specific age group and/or sex.

to the 1,700,000 who attained the standards from the summer of 1954—when it was first launched—through 1957. During these nine months, 730 universities, middle schools, and primary schools, and various government organs reported that nearly 100% of their membership had met the standards.[19] Available information indicates that the system was promoted with equal thoroughness in many parts of China. In Paitou *hsiang*, Hsiangtan *hsien*, Hunan, 1,020 (62.6%) of all able bodied young men were said to have passed the standards. Agricultural workers there usually trained during their rest hours. In Kaot'ang *hsien*, Shantung, 60,000 (60% of all able bodied men) trained under the system, and 16,000 passed. In Peipiao *hsien*, Liaoning, 75,000 passed.[20] In Inner Mongolia, 150,000 people passed.[21]

The sudden sputtering of the labor-defense system in the fall of 1958 can be simply viewed as another result of the failure of the "Great Leap." Quite understandably, under the pressure of having to muster all available energy to get the economy back on the right track, physical culture became an expendable item. When we consider that many people in China had been working extended work days for several months, it appears reasonable to expect that by the fall, 1958, the people of China were generally physically exhausted. These two points appear relatively clear. Later, however, we will deal with a question which is not so simply answered, namely: Why was the labor-defense system not reinstituted in the early 1960's when things once again became more normal in Communist China?

During the years preceding and following 1958, the term "national defense physical culture" was used in its broadest sense, and it is at this time that the term "mass sports" takes on the connotation of sports for national defense.[22] During this period, more so than at any other time in the history of the People's Republic, participation in sports in almost any form, by as many people as possible, was held to be in the national interest. Thus, during this period, although the labor-defense system remained the focal point, substantial consideration was given to the organization of sports groups in factories, communes, and spare-time sports schools. All were encouraged on the grounds that they further the national good. The Party Central Committee stressed one aspect of the value of sports when, in 1958, it said: "In order to meet the demand of the broad masses of the toiling people for a stronger physique [and thus] to bring about a great leap in production, physical culture and sports must be energetically promoted among the masses."[23] An apt slogan put it more directly: "Take physical exercise ten minutes a day and you will be able to give ten more years to the building of socialism."[24]

One of the characteristics of this period is the emergence of spare-time sports schools discussed in the previous chapter. Athletic schools for children were first set up in 1955 in Peking, Tientsin, and Shanghai on a limited basis. They continued in existence until the Cultural Revolution began in the fall of 1966.

SPORTS IN FACTORIES

By having a large number of people as captive participants, factories provided a natural place for the encouragement of sports activities. Although the following description of the sports program at the Tientsin Wool and Feather Factory is undoubtedly atypical, it does give some indication of how a sports program was intended to function in a factory.

> The Tientsin Wool and Feather Factory has 900 workers, mostly old and middle-aged. In this factory 700 of the 900 workers do daily exercises during the morning and afternoon breaks. Since 1956 an amateur athletic association has been in operation. The program includes basketball, football (soccer), track and field, gymnastics, cycling, motorcycling, weightlifting, wrestling, *wu shu* (traditional boxing and exercise), relay races, swimming, canoeing, and ice skating. Whenever there is free time during the day, some workers are usually practicing. At noon the daily contests take place.
>
> The aged and weak in the factory are encouraged to climb stairs as a conditioner. Other remedial exercises are also available for those chronically disabled. Everyone in the factory takes part in the exercises to some extent, and the directors and most active members of the athletic association spend much time after working hours as referees, coaches, etc. Thirty-seven of the workers have passed the labor-defense system test at third class level and two at second.[25]

SPORTS IN COMMUNES

Sports first began to blossom in the countryside in 1956, as the movement to encourage individual farms to become part of larger cooperatives, gained momentum. Physical culture and sports committees mushroomed in the basic level People's Committees.[26] Sports teams were organized among production brigades and teams. Special attempts were made to organize sports activities according to peasant work schedules. Thus, much sporting activity took place during rest periods, before work, and especially during slack seasons.[27] Generally, the nature of the program in communes coincided with that of the factory.

Through this concerted effort, mass sports made great headway—especially in the rural areas. By September, 1958, a reported 1,800,000 sports teams and physical training groups were actively engaged in various programs in the countryside. In the short span of time, from June, 1958, through September, approximately 100,000 peasants successfully participated in the "ready for labor and defense" program.[28] All told in 1958, 130,000,000 people regularly took part in sports activities.[29]

EQUIPMENT

In a country as fundamentally poor as Mainland China, the acquisition of suitable athletic equipment was often a serious obstacle to the implementation of a mass sports program. Improvisation thus became a necessity. It was not uncommon to use old doors for basketball backboards, flat stones for the discus, round stones for shot puts, and a piece of wood between two trees as a horizontal bar or a high jump standard.[30]

BROADCAST EXERCISES

At the heart of the mass sports movement were the physical exercises broadcast over the radio and set to music. These exercises have been a part of the Chinese Communist sports scene since the inception of the republic. Sets of these exercises were published in 1951, 1954, 1957, and 1963. The following is an official description of the set published in April, 1963:

> This set of physical exercises comprises altogether nine parts. Namely, extension movement, chest expansion move-

A Chinese family goes through its daily exercises.

ment, leg kicking movement, abdominal and back movement, sideward and bodily movement, rotation movement, whole body movement, jumping, and readjustment. . . . These exercises give balanced training to all parts of the body, and are more profitable to people who do mental work or desk work. . . . There are two climaxes in these exercises, at the end of which the rhythm slows down gradually. The whole set of physical exercises requires a little more than four minutes to do.[31]

SPORTS FOR NATIONAL DEFENSE

Thus far in this chapter we have dealt with 1) the labor-defense system, and 2) the "mass sports" concept—the idea that sports can contribute to the health of the individual and to the general welfare of the nation. To be sure, the Chinese *do* see a connection between the above two categories and national defense. Nevertheless, the connection is mainly semantic, for general exercise of various kinds is really no more vital to national defense than proper diet, adequate medical care, or personal hygiene.

But the Chinese do more than talk about sports for national defense; they practice it as well. During the discussion that follows, it will become apparent why, after the rebound from the "Great Leap" was concluded, the Chinese did not renew the theme of the labor-defense system which was so abruptly dropped in 1958, and, instead, moved closer and closer in the direction of military sports; and then, practically speaking, allowed military training and physical training to fuse.

"National defense physical culture" (*kuo-fang t'i yü*), like the "labor-defense system" and the concept of "mass sports" can be traced to the beginning of the People's Republic. The movement started with the formation of the Central National Defense Physical Culture Club (*Chung Yang Kuo-fang T'i Yü Chü-le-pu*) in 1952.[32] The scope of the activities of the club ranged from water sports, to parachuting, radio operation, and flying. The club expanded gradually until 1956 when there were organizations of this type in some 50 cities with some 300,000 participants.[33] In 1956, the Central National Defense Physical Culture Club became a mass organization under the title of the Chinese People's National Defense Physical Culture Association (*Chung Kuo Jen Min Kuo-fang T'i Yü Hsieh Hui*).[34]

The association began to show increased vigor and purpose at its work conference in February, 1957, attended by representatives from the Federation of Trade Unions, the Physical Culture and Sports Commission, the Ministry of Education, and the Youth League.[35] It remained, however, for the beginning of the campaign to make "everyone a soldier" (*ch'uan min chieh ping*), in September, 1958, for the National Defense Physical Culture Association to begin to gain in importance.

The "everyone a soldier" campaign followed the revival of the People's Militia and the Quemoy-Matsu crisis of August, 1958.[36] The Chinese saw the national defense physical culture movement as a means of training people for the People's Militia. It seems to have been, at least in part, the Quemoy-Matsu crisis which was responsible for the transformation of physical training into military training and, in the process, the relegation of the labor-defense system proper to a very minor role. It will subsequently be seen that there is a high correlation between the *nature* of the activities stressed with respect to national defense physical culture, and the degree to which the Chinese feel that there is a threat of war.

Before going any further with this discussion, it seems advisable to describe in detail those sports which the Chinese have in mind when they use the term "national defense physical culture." Along with this we shall discuss the specific significance that each sport has in the national defense scheme. These sports can conveniently be divided into three categories: 1) land activities, 2) aviation activities, 3) navigation activities. It must be strongly stressed that although many of these activities seem to have little relation to what we understand by the term "sports," and would be classified as paramilitary activities by us, the Chinese quite definitely consider them to be an integral part of sports. They are fully included in the scope of the term *t'i yü*.

MILITARY CAMPING

Gulfing the boundaries of the three categories mentioned above (though it is certainly more a land activity than anything else) is military camping. Military camping is actually a very broad term which includes many other activities which are a part of it. In our society, military camping might be called ROTC or basic training adapted to Chinese use. The stated aims of military camping make this quite clear. They are: 1) to promote regular military training, 2) to develop military consciousness (through study of politics, anti-U.S. propaganda, and absorbing such themes as "kill the enemy" and "learn from the PLA"), 3) to help production.[37] Camping of this sort was first practised on a large scale with the inauguration of the campaign to make "everyone a soldier," in the summer of 1958. The basic purpose of this campaign was to give as many able bodied men and women as possible fundamental military training so that they would be ready to defend against foreign attack.[38]

Administratively, the system of military camping was carried out in a variety of forms. Students in universities and secondary schools were the backbone of the program administered jointly by such groups as the People's Militia athletic authorities, the People's Liberation Army, and the Young Communist League.[39] Factory workers also participated actively. The program was generally run in the summer, and, until the Cultural Revolution, only the year 1961 seems to have been missed.[40]

The exact form that military camping takes also has varied greatly: from a period as short as one hour, held on a plot of land or in an armory adjacent to a factory, to a 10 day training period, held in the country, and involving anti-aircraft defense and anti-chemical warfare. In its mildest form, military camping was held from one hour to half a day, and was known as "on the spot camping" or "camping on a nearby ground." This type of camping has the advantage of being inexpensive, timesaving, and not hindering production. During these abbreviated sessions militiamen could participate in simple marching drills, practice shooting, undergo physical training, and listen to lectures. A drill lasting an entire day gave militiamen an opportunity to go through maneuvers in the field itself.

The above forms of military camping were likely intended to serve as interim training between more intensive sessions lasting three days, seven days, or ten days. These latter sessions quite often began in the middle of the night with the militiamen being awakened, and required to pack their knapsacks quickly for a forced march.[41] Once the march began, the militiamen (both men and women) might be called on to perform just about any of the activities described below (with greater emphasis on land and water activities).

LAND ACTIVITIES

As might be expected, *marksmanship* receives considerable attention among the various defense sports. It was reported in 1958 that shooting was the most popular of all the events in the program of defense sports, with 500 towns and 1,660,000 participants involved in shooting groups in colleges, middle schools, and factories. At that time, more titles of Master of Sport (*Chien Chiang*) had been conferred in shooting than in any other defense sport.[42]

In carrying out their marksmanship program, the Chinese

ran into their perpetual problem of a shortage of instructors and a shortage of equipment. The latter was solved by working in shifts and by having some participants use air guns. The former was often dealt with through methods reminiscent of the "mass education" methods of James Yen. For example, at the Tientsin No. 90 Middle School, three of the best shooters among the students were selected for special training. These three in turn trained a class of 43 from which the six best were chosen to be squad leaders.[43]

The training that novice shooters had to go through was quite thorough. The Young Communist League "Guidelines for Theoretical Shooting Study" called for a knowledge of 1) the six principal parts of a gun and their functions, 2) the three main factors involved in shooting: aiming, holding one's breath, pulling the trigger, and 3) maintaining and cleaning a gun. In addition, intensive ideological training was called for, as well as rigorous physical training for those too weak to shoot.[44]

In addition to the obvious military value of shooting skill, expert marksmen also served domestic, non-military functions. One group of marksmen was reported to have shot 10,000 rodents in Inner Mongolia that had been playing havoc with herds by spreading germs in the grasslands.[45] In Kweichow, a team of shooters was called on to deal with a bunch of wild pigs that were ravaging the crops.[46]

Mountaineering is another sport widely advocated for its value in connection with national defense. It is said to foster perseverance, increase courage, and develop stamina.[47] Although a national association for mountaineering was formed in June, 1958, it first received widespread national attention in July, 1959, when the scaling of 7,546 meter Mount Muztagh Ata in the Pamir range (Tibet) by 33 climbers, received extensive coverage in the Chinese press.[48] When the periodic skirmishes which the Chinese have had with India in mountainous Tibet are taken into account, the value of mountaineering for national defense becomes more understandable.

The third significant category of land-based events, widely practiced in connection with national defense, is *communications*—a vital part of any war effort. Communications activities —stressed more after July, 1964—take the following forms: 1) simple sound signals: whistle, drum, and gong, 2) visual:

Telegraphy as a defense sport.

semaphore (flag), and fire, 3) wireless Morse code sending and receiving, and 4) telegraphic.[49]

Among the other land-based activities practiced (either independently or as a part of military camping) are: bayonet-charge, first aid, rank and file marching, grenade throwing, emergency assembly, running obstacle courses (with or without full equipment), shadow boxing for the purpose of capturing the enemy, and the use of daggers.[50]

AVIATION ACTIVITIES

Activities involving flight through the air in various forms have long been widely publicized in Communist China. One is led to believe, by the frequent attention that such sports have been given in the press through the years, that they are widely practiced. It is more likely, however, that, because of the obvious cost of any sport involving aircraft, the number of people actually involved has been rather limited.

Aviation activities are of four general types: 1) flying in standard planes (which need not be treated here), 2) gliding, 3) flying model airplanes, and 4) parachuting.

*Gliding** began as a sport in China in 1953 when several gliding clubs sprang up. By 1955, the first gliding school had been started[51] and in September, 1958, the first national gliding competition was held.[52]

The Chinese see gliding as an economical, effective means for conducting elementary flight training and, in the process, testing a person's aptitude for flying. Since a glider basically operates on the same principles as does an airplane, a prospective pilot can be trained in a glider and, if sufficiently skillful, can later be transferred to a regular plane. Those not sufficiently skillful are not advanced to the next stage of training. In this way, China feels that a maximum amount of funds can be spent on her best pilots.[53]

Gliders also find use in insecticide spraying, afforestation, and transportation.[54]

Building and flying *model airplanes* is definitely not child-play, as the term might connote. Such planes, operated by re-

---

* Gliding essentially is flying without an engine. The craft gains lift either by being towed down the runway by a vehicle, or by being attached to a plane which takes off while tugging the glider. After the glider is airborn, it is able to remain aloft for several hours.

mote control, have been reported to have flown higher than three miles and to have remained airborne for more than six hours.[55] The exact contribution that the flying of model airplanes makes to national defense is not too clear. They may serve some purpose in research.

Parachuting, of all the aviation sports, is the one most adaptable to mass participation. Further, since it is so closely connected with paratrooping, it has indisputable military sig-

Chinese women parachutists in training.

nificance. Parachuting clubs were widely in evidence in China by September, 1958, when the first National Gliding and Parachuting Contest was held. Parachuting clubs provide training which starts with instruction in the scientific principles of the sport, and then progresses to jumping from a tower and, finally, from a plane. In competition, the object is for the team or individual to see how close he can come to landing on a spot marked on the ground. Separate competitions are held for men and women (both singles and in teams of three) at heights of 600, 1,000, 1,500, and 2,000 meters.[56]

Before concluding this section on aviation sports, it might be of interest to present a brief portrait of the Aviation Club of Peking—China's largest club of this type as of 1962—so as to get an idea of the scope of the operation.

The club is based at Lianghsiang Airport, southwest of Peking. Among its facilities are an aerodrome, Chinese built Yak-18 and An-2 trainer planes, a 45 meter concrete parachute training tower, laboratories, and lecture halls. Participants in the club's activities come from among local workers, students, teachers, office employees, and peasants. They take short term courses in parachuting, model aircraft flying, gliding, and flying. An all-around physical training program is provided, as is training in physics, math and meteorology. On several occasions members of the club have flown insecticide spraying missions to help peasants in Hopei, Honan, and Shantung.[57]

NAVIGATION ACTIVITIES

Chinese interest in activities involving water stem largely from the experience of the Chinese leaders during the Long March. Edgar Snow points out how often the Communists came up against water obstacles during the course of their yearlong trek to Shensi Province in 1934-35.[58] Long Marchers were often called on to swim with full gear across rivers such as the Wuchiang, the Chinsha, and the Tatu. The Communists had similar experiences during the War of Resistance against Japan. In addition to practical experience, indicating its use, wide-scale swimming activity is also implied by Mao Tse-tung's statement that "freedom of action is the lifeline of an army."[59]

The principal aim of water-based sports from a national defense point of view, then, is to provide increased mobility for Chinese soldiers by making water obstacles their ally rather than their enemy. Basic to navigation activities is proficiency in swimming. Swimming has been popular in China ever since Mao was reported to have swum across the Yangtse River for the first time near Wuhan in June, 1956.[60] Other reports credited Mao with swimming feats in 1961, 1964, and 1966.[61] Although swimming was popular earlier,[62] it was not until 1964 that swimming was officially included among those sports considered vital for national defense. By 1965, the swimming movement had built up tremendous momentum, and in 1966 reports of huge throngs swimming in natural bodies of water were commonplace.[63] This will be dealt with more thoroughly below, as will another aspect of swimming which is of particular significance to defense sports: soldiers swimming with their equipment.

As is the case with model aircraft, competition involving *model naval vessels* is held on a very sophisticated level. The first such competition was held in Peking in August, 1958. Entered in the competition were model boats operated from the shore, which performed signaling, smoke camouflage, and rocket-launching. Also seen were model merchant ships and model racers with internal combustion engines.[64]

Numerous other water-based events have been held for both men and women including rowing, sailing, shooting from boats, driving motorboats, and navigating warships.

The nature of the sporting events which the Chinese stress in connection with national defense is of definite significance. Unmistakably, these activities show the commitment which the Chinese still have to guerilla warfare. Most of their emphasis is on skills which provide mobility, without reliance on advanced technology. Hence, the extreme emphasis on physical fitness, marching, mountain climbing, and swimming. This is not to say that their national defense sports program has remained oblivious to modern developments in warfare. Antiaircraft training, aviation, navigation, and chemical warfare all receive some measure of treatment. Nevertheless, the Chinese continue to expend most of their energy on cultivating those skills that proved so useful for them in the 1930's and 1940's. It seems clear that, at least for the present, the Chinese Communists remain resolved to steer clear of military conflicts which will make heavy demands on ultra-modern equipment. They will fight on terms acceptable to themselves, or not at all.

THE PERIOD AFTER 1958

Following the peak period of national defense sports activities in the summer of 1958, the movement seems to have subsided, and entered a state of suspended animation.[65] The foremost indication of this is a reduction in the number of articles on defense sports appearing in the Communist press. Undoubtedly, many subtle reasons can be found for downgrading the sports campaign at this time. But, actually, there is no need to speculate or to search too deeply for reasons for the decline. The programs of the "Great Leap Forward" were withdrawn. Belts were being tightened, priority lists were being drawn up, and physical culture was no longer of the highest priority.

Despite the downgrading of sports activities at this time, it is significant that we find that a conscious effort was made in some quarters to keep the concept of sports for national defense alive. For example, the first National Athletic Meet held under Communist auspices, in September, 1959, included competition in riflery, parachuting, and model airplanes.[66] Spare-time sports schools for children continued,[67] and periodic exhortations were made by the Physical Culture and Sports Commission and Young Communist League as to the virtues of national defense physical culture.[68] Even if these exhortations and programs were not followed up by the usual reports of mass activity, it is quite clear that this type of activity remained alive.

The first sign of rejuvenation seems to have come with the publication of the fourth set of radio broadcast exercises in April, 1963. The last previous publication had been made in 1957.[69] A month before, Chao Cheng-hung, Vice-Chairman of both the Physical Culture and Sports Commission and the Chinese People's National Defense Sports Association,[70] had issued one of the few substantial directives of those years, in an article entitled: "Do a Still Better Job of Physical Culture for National Defense." In it he emphasized: 1) the need to keep in close touch with the military departments, YCL units, labor units, education departments, as well as to develop training classes, sports groups, and spare-time athletic teams in combination with military training and student extra-curricular activities, 2) organization of small and simple athletic competitions at the basic organizational levels, 3) active attempts by groups, already organized and possessing high skill levels, to help spread sports for national defense activity at the basic organizational levels, and 4) the need for political activists to take a greater part in the sports program.[71]

It was not until 1964, however, that the real revival of "mass sports" occurred. In the spring, the YCL put forth the slogan: "Let the whole league do physical culture work," in which it called for 1) focusing attention on young people (for young girls emphasis would be on table tennis, and for young boys on miniature soccer), 2) more attention to specific national defense sports (such as shooting and camping), and 3) a greater stress on sports emphasizing local character (e.g. horse racing for Mongolian nationalities).[72]

The strategic directive, however, was delivered in July of that year when the Physical Culture and Sports Commission called for the mass launching of swimming, shooting, communications, and mountaineering activities as part of this campaign. The emphasis on swimming was to strengthen the people's physique in every way, and militiamen were to receive special instruction in swimming with their equipment. The marksmanship campaign would be geared toward ordinary shooters and children (who would be instructed through the use of air rifles). Communications activities would involve mechanical and manual means (telegraphy, fire, sound, semaphore), and would be carried out not only during militia training, but in mines and factories as well. Mountaineering (which here apparently implies military camping as well) would be directed toward developing courage, stamina, and perseverance.[73]

In compliance with this directive, there was a marked increase in defense sports activity. In primary and middle schools, general military training and shooting practice was stressed more than ever before.[74]

In 1964, we begin to see a change in the tone of the drive for military sports. The 1964 campaign mentions the "three precautions" against: air raids, poisoning, and secret agents; and the "five know hows": how to shoot, how to throw grenades, how to conduct air defense, how to apply topography and utilize ground objects, and how to stand watch and scout. Themes such as "kill the enemy," and "learn from the PLA" (People's Liberation Army) became commonplace, as did such PLA phrases as the "3-8 work style," the "four good" company, and the "five good" soldier (see chapter 4). The frequent appearance of this type of language in connection with national defense physical culture seems to indicate, at the very least, a psychological prepartion for war.[75]

In March, 1965, *T'i Yü Pao* reported active participation in mass athletic activities for the first two months of 1965. It attached particular significance to the fact that military camping (which for all intents and purposes was basic training) was being carried out widely in the winter months for the first time. The direct cause of this intensification is explicitly spelled out by the Chinese. At a national Young Communist League work conference on military sports, held in February, 1965, in Changsha, a call went out for "extraordinary stress . . . [in] conducting military sports which directly serve national defense." Delegates were warned that the U.S. ". . . plans to expand the war in Indochina, and gravely threatens the security of our country and world peace."[76]

In April, 1965, the *Chung Kuo Ch'ing Nien Pao* (the thrice-weekly newspaper of the Youth League), in calling on the people to join in military physical culture activities, stated that: "The Chinese people are resolved to support the people of Vietnam and to struggle through to the end to defeat U.S. imperialism."

"In these circumstances," it continued, "it is more important and significant to join in military sports activities. We must be well prepared for taking up our weapons and fighting shoulder to shoulder with the youth of Vietnam in order to annihilate the U.S. aggressors when we are called upon to do so."[77]

These goals were implemented in the spring months of 1965 by the greatest stress on military sports since the inauguration of the People's Republic. The target of this emphasis was, clearly, the youth. Every effort was made to give children the feeling of preparing for war. Reports exist of primary school children, ages 9-12, engaging in shooting, bayonet-charge, and signaling. One "game" involved two teams of children cutting through barbed wire, crossing trenches, climbing ropes, and destroying the "enemy fortress." In Changsha, Hunan, all of the children in the 147 primary schools were involved in various types of military sports.[78]

Other reports from Tientsin credited 41% of the middle schools and 39% of the primary schools with having pursued national defense sports activities. The most widely taught activities were shooting (with either air guns or small bore rifles), wireless radio sending and receiving, and semaphore signaling. A popular means of practicing marksmanship was shooting at pictures of Chiang Kai-shek and Lyndon Johnson.[79]

At Tsinghua University, U.S. aggression in Vietnam was credited with heightening students' interest in defense sports in 1965. Every student at Tsinghua was required to undergo marksmanship training with military rifles. Shooting squads were formed in each of the 11 departments of the university. In this way, every Tsinghua graduate theoretically possessed the basic rifle skills. The Tsinghua program also included running barbed wire obstacle courses, and navigation activities in a pond artificially built on the campus.[80]

Primary school students involved in military sports.

In the light of the heated nature of the campaign to develop defense sports in the spring, 1965, the unusually practical view that the YCL took of this training is noteworthy. They asked physical education workers "to unfold the activities gradually in the light of reality; to adopt means appropriate to region, time, and human factors; to develop the activities from one item to many items, from among a few people to many people, and from being simple to being complicated; to set different requirements according to different participants, and to refrain from setting uniform requirements; and to integrate labor with rest."[81]

The spirited campaign for defense sports and war preparation in the spring, 1965, is as noteworthy for its rapid shift in emphasis as for its intensity. Most of the activity (associated with preparation for war), mentioned in the last few paragraphs, seems to have been crowded into the months of March, April and May. After May, periodic directives calling for the continued cultivation of the more militant aspects of sports continued to be issued and mass activity again took place in the winter months of 1965-66.[82] Yet, for the most part, land-based military sports were eclipsed by the directives for mass swimming that were issued in May, 1965. Swimming held the spotlight in military physical education until the coming of the Cultural Revolution.

The official directive calling for widespread "efforts to enable servicemen and civilians, and particularly the youth and children, throughout China to learn to swim," was issued on May 14, by the Physical Culture and Sports Commission, the Headquarters of the General Staff of the People's Liberation Army, and the YCL. Swimming was cited as having special significance with respect to "physical fitness for national defense," because of its value as an all-around conditioner. To further the campaign, it was proposed that propaganda was to be issued on the value of swimming. Army units, as well as government offices, schools, factories, mines, rural people's communes, and militia organizations were ordered to map out plans to organize swimming lessons for the masses. Cadres were to encourage mass participation in cross-river swimming, and swimming fully armed, as well as engage in training swimming instructors. In all cases, efforts were to be made to swim in natural bodies of water (ponds, lakes, rivers, and seas), in addition to artificial pools, for which safety instruction and safety personnel were to be provided.[83]

Strangely enough, the highlight of the 1965 swimming campaign took place in 1964. In June, 1964—but not played up in the press until May 27, 1965, when every front page in China carried the story—Mao and Liu Shao-ch'i allegedly swam in the Ming Tombs Reservoir on the outskirts of Peking.[84] They reportedly swam for two hours. While swimming, they chatted with young people and encouraged them to practice swimming.[85] This feat was repeatedly publicized in 1965, and, together with Mao's previous crossings of the Yangtse, held up as an example for the youth of China to practice swimming in rivers, lakes, seas, and other natural bodies of water.

The May 14 pronouncement was followed by the usual flood of reports of compliance. On May 23, over 8,000 people ranging in age from 9 to 63 (including steelworkers, soldiers, military personnel, doctors, engineers, teachers, peasants, and members of national minorities) took part in a 900 meter swim

A mass swimming scene in Changchou, Fukien. Sign calls for the liberation of Taiwan.

across the Yangtse at Chungking, Szechuan.[86] Two days later, 10,700 people crossed the Chialingkiang River (a tributary of the Yangtse).[87] In Canton, a group of militiamen (including one woman) swam over 100 kilometers. In Harbin, the swimming season was officially opened 10 days earlier than usual.[88] Similar reports of activity flowed out of Wuhan, Nanchang, and Tientsin.[89]

In an effort to hasten the development of swimming, schools in Peking held physical training classes in pools, and militiamen from factories, communes, and government offices swam in natural waterways as a part of their regular routine. All the standard propaganda media were mobilized in the campaign with radio broadcasts, newspapers, and movie houses devoting substantial time and space to it. The *People's Daily* ran articles on swimming technique and the history of swimming. In Peking, a film entitled: "Swimming for Beginners" was concurrently being shown at seven movie houses.[90]

In contrast to the reckless march forward of sports at the time of the "Great Leap," the swimming campaign did not press for achievement at the expense of practicality. Although the PLA added swimming as the sixth "big technique" in the training of soldiers, it recognized the need to learn to swim in a gradual, thorough manner. Safety training was provided, lifeguards, apparently, were available, and swimming areas were pre-checked for currents, whirlpools and sharks. Those not fit to swim were not allowed to do so.[91]

The mass swimming campaign did not slacken in the summer of 1966 (and to an extent continued through the winter). In most places, in 1966, the swimming season began earlier than usual. For example, in Shanghai, public pools opened on April 1—a month earlier than usual—with swimming taking place from 6:00 A.M. to well after dark.[92]

Once again the campaign received its chief impetus from the exploits of Chairman Mao, and once again mystery shrouded his feats. According to a concensus of reports, on July 16, 1966, Mao swam down the Yangtse, near Wuhan, covering 30 li (about 10 miles) in 65 minutes.[93] This purported feat has been well publicized, especially through films seen on U.S. television in which several heads were seen resting above the water, one of them belonging to Chairman Mao. Without going into a detailed analysis of this controversy, there appears to be some error in either the amount of time Mao was in the water, or the distance that he covered.*

The 1966 swimming campaign theme closely paralleled that of 1965: "To swim in big rivers and the sea and toughen . . . [yourself] in strong wind and high waves." The mood, clearly, was serious. Swimming solely for relief from hot weather was frowned upon, and each swimmer was expected to grasp clearly the concept of "swimming for the sake of revolution."[95]

As with other national defense sports, swimming activity all

---

* The winning time for the four-mile swimming event in the 1966 AAU Long Distance Swimming Championships was 1:27:36.7 hours.[94]

but came to a halt after August, 1966, when the Eleventh Plenary Session of the Eighth Central Committee unfolded the Cultural Revolution.

The campaign for national defense physical culture stands out most for the gradual union that apparently took place between physical training and military training (excluding the professional training of soldiers for the PLA). Determining the exact time that this union took place is an impossible task. We are led to believe that there was a *gradual* transfer of emphasis. We know that by 1960 many communes had already made physical training a part of military training. Reinforcing this feeling are indications that at about this time the leadership of physical culture, and that of the military, began to overlap in certain respects.[96]

A study of the background of the leadership of the Chinese People's National Defense Physical Culture Association sheds some interesting, though inconclusive, light on this last point. Four names frequently appeared in the early and mid-1960's as prominent in this organization: 1) Li Ta—Chairman from June, 1959, 2) Chao Chün-yi—Vice-Chairman from October, 1960, 3) Lin K'ai—Vice-Chairman from October, 1960, and 4) Chao Cheng-hung—Vice-Chairman from May 16, 1961. Of the four, at least two (Li, and Chao Cheng-hung)[97] received their first experience as sports officials, in *military* sports, and only afterwards became active in the Physical Culture and Sports Commission or the All-China Athletic Federation (the organizations which control sports in a more general sense in China). Li—a member of the Communist Party from 1921—brought a strong military background into his post as chairman. He was made a full fledged general in 1954 and, at various times in the 1950's, held posts dealing with the training of the military. Chao Cheng-hung brings a background which includes the former directorship of the Political Department of the Liaotung military district.[98] The chief point here is that both Li and Chao Cheng-hung brought non-athletic (and in the case of Li, distinctly military) backgrounds into their roles as chief administrators of, first, the defense sports association, and then, the non-military national sports associations. This infusion into sporting circles of non-sports personnel indicates somewhat strongly that in the late 1950's and early 1960's, a shift of emphasis was taking place, whose goal was the union of what might be called *pure* sports with military sports.

Also pointing toward the gradual consolidation of physical culture and military training is the inclusion of distinctly military sports in the two national sports meets held in Communist China. The first such meet was held in 1959, and only a limited number of distinctly military sports were included in the program (riflery, parachuting and model airplanes).[99] In 1965, the number was increased markedly to include bona fide competition in marksmanship, wireless radio sending and receiving, parachuting, flying model planes and model boats, and motorcycling.[100] In all cases, these events were considered full-parity sports, with no attempts being made to differentiate between them and the more conventional sports (such as basketball or swimming). This co-existence, of what we would view as markedly different types of activities, has contributed greatly towards the blurring of the distinction between paramilitary events (and, by extension, military training) and what we would call sports.

A final indication of this transfer in stress is given by a slight change in emphasis regarding terminology. In the late 1960's the term "military sports" (*chün-shih t'i yü*) seems to have come more into usage. Even though the term *kuo fang t'i yü* (national defense sports) remains in use, the shift in emphasis is apparent.

POSTSCRIPT

Exactly what happened to mass sports and defense sports during the Cultural Revolution as well as the rationale behind such action is still somewhat of a mystery. We do know that sports too came under the torrent of the Red Guard apparatus. Specifically, Ho Lung—Chairman of the Physical Culture and Sports Commission—was an important target of the Red Guards. In general his charge was the not unfamiliar one of being unfaithful to Chairman Mao's thought. Of particular relevance to this chapter is the charge that he mishandled the administration of national defense physical culture:

> . . . For the past ten years, he has paid attention not to mass physical education, but to forming professional teams and highly-developed activities. In 1962, he openly

advocated that: "The National Physical Education Committee only pay attention to athletic teams and that the provincial and municipal levels take care of mass physical education and national defense physical education."

When Chairman Mao issued the great call that the party embrace military affairs to bring about the policy that all people be soldiers, Ho Lung refused to carry through the Chairman's instructions. He repeatedly restricted and stifled national defense physical education work, which contributes greatly toward the policy that all men become soldiers. He only allowed national defense physical education to be carried out in the big cities, and only let the person in charge of national defense physical education take care of gliding. He even cut 50% of the personnel from the national defense physical education workforce, and proposed to dissolve motorcycling, radio, and other clubs in an attempt to stifle the cause of national defense physical education. . . .[101]

8

Sports and International Relations, A Case Study: China, the Olympic Games, and the Games of the New Emerging Forces

WITHIN THE GENERAL topic of sports and international relations there are many questions which a lack of data makes unanswerable. However, by focusing on one particular aspect of Chinese Communist international sports policy on which comparatively abundant material is available, we are able to gain an insight into the area of sports and foreign policy as a whole. In this chapter, then, we will first give a general sketch of what is known about the subject. We will then give a case study which will portray Communist China's relationship with the International Olympic Committee in the 1950's, and the ensuing organization of the Games of the New Emerging Forces in the 1960's.

The most notable fact which sticks out with regard to China's international sports policy is that from the establishment of the regime in 1949 until the Cultural Revolution which began in 1966, at least one Chinese team has toured abroad in each calendar year. The following tables give the trend for the first nine years.[1]

Though exact figures are not available after 1957, a survey of the *People's Handbook (Jen Min Shou Ts'e), Survey of the China Mainland Press,* and other sources indicates that activity

DELEGATIONS LEAVING CHINA

	1949	1950	1951	1952	1953	1954	1955	1956	1957 (approx.)
No. of Delegations	1	3	3	3	6	15	17	49	50
No. of athletes	9	41	46	72	53	374	620	493	—

DELEGATIONS COMING TO CHINA

	1949	1950	1951	1952	1953	1954	1955	1956	1957 (approx.)
No. of Delegations	—	1	—	2	1	4	13	23	40
No. of athletes	—	25	—	43	30	70	411	323	—

was abundant in 1958, during which time the Chinese posted a record of 221 wins, 171 losses, and 17 ties in 409 contests.[2] After a lull in international competition during the recovery from the Great Leap Forward in 1959, 1960, and 1961, activity seems to have returned to, if not surpassed, the peaks of the 1950's.

Despite limited information, Chinese motives for participation in international athletics are readily discernible. In the 1950's they were most concerned with learning from other nations. It is probably this desire to advance in skills level as quickly as possible, which encouraged them in the early and mid-1950's to compete largely with Eastern European countries (U.S.S.R., Poland, Hungary, Czechoslovakia, Rumania) most of whom had much stronger athletic traditions than the geographically closer South or East Asian nations with which closer athletic relations were later established. The fact that the Chinese often lost 90% or sometimes all of the games on a tour in those years was doubtless considered the price of rapid advancement.[3]

In addition to improving athletically, the Chinese naturally saw foreign visits as an opportunity to enhance their image abroad. As such, though apparently rarely mixing with foreign athletes socially on trips abroad, the Chinese have made it their custom to host dinners in honor of other delegations when at overseas meets involving several countries. This custom probably started during their abortive trip to Helsinki for the 1952 Olympic Games.[4] In 1954, at the 12th World University Games

Liu Shao-ch'i greets the leader of a Guinean basketball team touring China in 1965.

in Hungary, they again hosted a series of banquets: one for the Indian and Indonesian delegations and another for the English, Scottish, Irish, and Australian groups.[5]

Another Chinese characteristic in athletics, probably intended to enhance their image, is their general refrain from gloating over attainments or deriding their opponents. This is a difficult thing to document, but Chinese accounts of international events in which they compete are unusually free of self-praise, and it is not at all unusual to find long accounts of a particular event without the slightest mention that China was the victor. Phrases such as "friendly competition" fall into heavy usage.

A scanning of the nations with which China has competed through the years, both confirms prior expectations and offers surprises. The watchword here seems to be flexibility. In dual meet competition (i.e. with one other nation), China—especially in the 1950's—has preferred Communist Bloc countries, and underdeveloped Asian nations such as Burma, Cambodia, and Ceylon. Those countries most often involved in this connection have been the U.S.S.R., Yugoslavia, Rumania, Czechoslovakia, Hungary, Poland, and East Germany; as well as North Vietnam, North Korea, and Mongolia in Asia. Nevertheless, the Chinese have also sent teams to France, and in 1957 received a British swimming team. In international tournament play (i.e. with several other nations at one time), however, the Chinese meet teams they ordinarily would not have contact with. Among the competitors at the 1961 World Table Tennis Championships held in Peking were West Germany and Denmark. U.S. and Chinese players had met in international play even before the spring, 1971 visit of the U.S. table tennis team to China (e.g. at the 23rd World Table Tennis Championships in 1956 in Tokyo). Though falling outside of their general pattern, the Chinese have also sent teams to Africa and Latin America. It should be noted that despite the Sino-Soviet split, as late as 1963, Chinese teams appeared on Soviet soil and vice versa.

Increasingly before the Cultural Revolution, the Chinese had been holding international athletic contests in China designed to counter what they consider the imperialist controlled meets of the West. The first championship international athletic competition held on the Mainland since 1949 took place in November, 1955, when China hosted the International Friendly Shooting Competition. In October, 1958, an international volleyball tournament was held. In April, 1961, the 26th World Table Tennis Championships were held in China. In August, 1963, there were the Basketball Championships of Friendly Countries, and in 1965 an invitational international table tennis tournament. All of these events were held in Peking and limited largely to Eastern European or Asian Communist nations.

In closing out these introductory remarks, a few words should be said about what has become the most famous Chinese sport: table tennis. The Chinese first competed in the World Table Tennis Championships (the 20th) in 1953 in Bucharest, Rumania, with the men coming in tenth (of 15 nations) and the women second. At the 23rd Championships in April, 1956, in Japan, the men came in sixth and the women eleventh. In Stockholm, in 1957 (the 24th Championships), the men's team was fourth and the women third. Both Chinese teams finished first in the 26th event held in Peking in April, 1961. The men won the Swaythling Cup and the women the Corbillon Cup. The men repeated in 1963 in Prague at the 27th Championships, where the women were runner-ups. Both teams prevailed in the 1965 competition (28th) held in Japan. Despite their string of successes, the Chinese did not compete in the April, 1967 competition (29th) held in Stockholm owing to the Cultural Revolution and Mao's dictum to "concern yourself with the affairs of state and carry the Great Proletarian Cultural Revolution through to the very end."[6] It should be noted here that the two periods during which the Chinese have missed world championship tournaments in table tennis were both times of internal havoc—the Great Leap Forward in 1959, and the Great Proletarian Cultural Revolution 1966-70. With the 1971 31st World Table Tennis Championships in Japan, the Chinese returned to the international scene.

We now turn to a detailed discussion of one episode in Chinese international athletics: her involvement with the Olympic Games and the resulting development of the Games of the New Emerging Forces. Such an examination should give us a greater insight into the way in which China conducts her international athletic policy.

BACKGROUND

Although the first Olympic Games of the modern age began in Athens in 1896, China first participated in them in 1932. Like all other nations which have ever had any association with the International Olympic Committee (IOC), China had its own national Olympic Committee. Among those who fled to Taiwan in 1949 after the revolution, were most of the pre-

Communist representatives to the International Olympic Committee.[7] Because the policy of the Olympics is to keep politics separate from sports, the Chinese members of the International Olympic Committee were not stripped of their positions when they left the Mainland. Theoretically, they retained control of Chinese Olympic affairs both on the Mainland and on Taiwan. Actually, the IOC had no reason to consider the People's Republic of China because from 1949 to 1952 the Communists had no communication with the IOC.

THE 1952 OLYMPIC GAMES

The 1952 Olympic Games were scheduled for July 19-August 4, 1952, at Helsinki, Finland. Apparently, without any prior indication, the Communist Chinese All-China Athletic Federation (ACAF) informed the International Olympic Committee on or about February 13, 1952[8] that she wished to participate in the Helsinki Games.[9] This first communication between the Mainland and the IOC brought forth a flurry of rumors which implied that the Communists had already been barred from participation. On Feb. 18, 1952, Avery Brundage of Chicago (a high IOC official) issued a statement which denied reports emanating from Moscow that the Communist Chinese had already been barred from the 1952 Games. He explained that since Nationalist China already had three members on the International Olympic Committee, the situation was a complicated one, and required further study.[10]

Nothing further developed until June 16, 1952, when Sigfried Edstrom, President of the International Olympic Committee announced that neither Nationalist China nor Communist China would be able to compete in the 1952 Games. The situation, however, appears to have been somewhat fluid since sources close to the IOC at that time indicated that this problem probably could be resolved when the IOC executive committee met prior to the opening of the Helsinki Games in July.[11] But a statement issued on June 25 by IOC Chancellor Otto Mayer confirmed the decision that neither of the two Chinas would be admitted to the 1952 Games. The reason given for turning down Communist China's application was that she was not a member of a sufficient number of international sports organizations, and that this was a pre-requisite for competing in the Olympics. At that time her only affiliations were with the International Basketball Federation and the International Swimming Federation.[12] Later events tend to indicate that this reason was only an excuse.

The situation was complicated somewhat by a statement emanating from Taiwan on July 3, by Hoh Gun-sun, head of Nationalist China's Amateur Athletic Federation in which he protested the exclusion of Nationalist athletes from the 1952 Games. Hoh Gun-sun made a hurried visit to the U.S. and then to Finland,[13] and, as a result of his visit, on July 17, 1952, by a 33-20 vote, the IOC authorized athletes from both Chinas to take part in the Games.[14] Although no specific names or details are available, it appears that some people attributed this turn of events to a partial attempt to placate the Communists after they were refused admission to the United Nations.[15] This change of policy by the IOC did not satisfy Nationalist China, however. She resented the acceptance of Communist China and immediately announced her refusal to participate in the Finland competition. In addition, the Nationalist Chinese newspapers announced a boycott of all news about the Games.[16]

Though she never actually competed in the 1952 Games, Communist China was involved in a great deal of confusion and conflict. Before the July 17 decision of the IOC, which allowed both Chinas to compete, Jung Kao-t'ang of the All-China Athletic Federation had already sent (on July 14) a message of protest against the "inclusion of the so-called question of recognizing the All-China Athletic Federation as the Chinese Olympic Committee for discussion at the 47th IOC meeting, and its invitation of the reactionary KMT [Kuomintang] bloc in Taiwan to send athletes to participate in the 15th Olympic Games to be opened on the 19th."[17]

Once it was decided that the Mainland Chinese were coming to the Games, their exact date of arrival became the first item of confusion. On July 23, Sheng Chih-pai announced that a swimming team and a basketball team were enroute. On July 25, Peking radio announced that a plane had left on that date. Eventually, a team of 41 athletes (two girl swimmers, basketball players, and soccer players) arrived on July 29, including Tung Shou-yi (a member of the IOC) and Jung Kao-t'ang (Vice-President and Secretary-General of the All-China Athletic Federation).[18] This delayed arrival on the part of the

Communist Chinese was possibly planned so that the Communists could make sure that Taiwan would not be coming to Finland.

Aside from random accusations which charged that the Chinese were violating the spirit of the Olympics by spreading Communist propaganda through a "World League of Democratic Youth" camp (being held concurrently with the Games in Helsinki),[19] things went relatively smoothly for the Communists, once they arrived in Finland. The Finnish newspaper *Tyokansan Sanomat* devoted a four-column headline story to them, and a housing problem, that the Olympic Committee had feared, did not materialize. In addition, on August 2, as a goodwill gesture, the Communist Chinese hosted a reception for 100 athletes from 16 countries: Finland, Austria, Australia, Canada, Ceylon, Great Britain, New Zealand, South Africa, Sweden, Switzerland, the United States, the U.S.S.R., Poland, Czechoslovakia, Rumania, and the German Democratic Republic.[20]

Because of the late arrival of the Chinese delegation (the Games began on July 19), they were unable to participate in any of the official Olympic events. Since participation in the Olympic soccer tournament required participation in pre-Olympic qualifying matches, it is difficult to see why the Chinese sent a soccer team to Helsinki at all. The Chinese, however, were able to engage in exhibition soccer matches and a swimming meet (both of which were not official Olympic contests) before the Games closed on August 4th.[21]

Future difficulties for Mainland China were forecast when, during the Olympic Games, the International Amateur Athletic Federation shelved for two years Communist China's request for membership in the IAAF. (Membership in this federation is necessary for participation in Olympic track and field events—such events as running, jumping, and weight throwing.) This move by the International Amateur Athletic Federation was a direct result of U.S. intervention. A statement by Avery Brundage* of the U.S. delegation seems to shed some light on the U.S. position at that time. He indicated that the official group that had sent Chinese athletes to the Olympics since 1936 was now based on Taiwan, and that "you will be

---

* Brundage's views may be considered even to the right of the orthodox anti-Communist government views prevalent in the 1950's and 1960's.

unjust to an old member—the Formosa body—if you take in the people from Peiping."²² The U.S. at that juncture could not have been expected to do anything that would hurt the prestige of Taiwan.

DEVELOPMENTS BETWEEN THE 1952 GAMES AND THE 1956 GAMES

The years between the Helsinki Games and the 1956 Olympic Games in Melbourne saw many crucial developments concerning China. On August 3, 1952, Jung Kao-t'ang, of the Communist All-China Athletic Federation, lodged a protest with Otto Mayer of the International Olympic Committee over the IOC's refusal to grant complete jurisdiction over Chinese athletics (both on the Mainland and on Formosa) to the All-China Athletic Federation.²³ At its April 20, 1953 meeting in Mexico City, the Communist Chinese membership application was tabled by the IOC for the third straight year. (The Communists had been granted permission to compete in 1952 but were not formally voted into the IOC at that time.) In preparation for the 1954 meeting in Athens (where the committee was expected to take up the question once again), IOC President Avery Brundage instructed Constantin Adrianov (Soviet delegate) to collect data on the "national sports unit" of Communist China.²⁴

By a vote of 23-21 at the Athens meeting on May 14, 1954, the IOC voted Communist China into the International Olympic Committee.²⁵ No sooner had Communist China been admitted when Nationalist Chinese delegate Hoh Gun-sun stated that Taiwan would never compete should the Communists be allowed to do so.²⁶ But, the IOC paid little attention to this threat, and on November 2, 1954, formal invitations were extended to both Chinas. This immediately brought forth a demand by Taiwan (on Dec. 21) for Mainland China's ouster.²⁷

As the end of 1954 approached, and with the Melbourne Games just two years away, developments began to foreshadow the controversy that was to come in 1956. Communist China formally accepted her invitation to participate in the 16th Olympiad on December 20, 1954. In February, 1955, the Mainland Chinese Olympic Committee filed a protest over the invitation that had been extended to Taiwan. The grounds cited

Sports and International Relations, A Case Study 175

中 國 奥 林 匹 克 委 員 會
(中 華 全 國 體 育 總 會)
ОЛИМПИЙСКИЙ КОММИТЕТ КИТАЯ
(ВСЕКИТАЙСКОЕ ОБЩЕСТВО ФИЗКУЛЬТУРЫ И СПОРТА)
CHINESE OLYMPIC COMMITTEE
(ALL-CHINA ATHLETIC FEDERATION)
COMITÉ OLYMPIQUE CHINOIS
(FEDERATION NATIONALE ATHLETIQUE DE CHINE)

16 TUNG CHANG AN STREET, PEKING, CHINA   TELEGRA: ATHLECHINE, PEKING

Mr. Avery Brundage, President of the I.O.C.
Mr. Otto Mayer, Chancellor of the I.O.C.
C/O Olympic Committee of the Soviet Union

April 9, 1954.

Dear Sirs,

    I have been directed by the Chairman of the Chinese Olympic Committee (All-China Athletic Federation) to convey you our request that the International Olympic Committee, at its forthcoming 49th Session in Athens on May 14, 1954, settle the question of uninterrupted recognition of our status on the International Olympic Committee.

    As you will recall, the Chinese Olympic Committee has been in existence for a long time and has several times participated in the Olympic Games. In 1952 it also sent Chinese teams to take part in the XV Olympic Games. At present it is actively making preparations to participate in the XVI Olympic Games to be held in Melbourne in 1956.

    The Chinese Olympic Committee has been in contact with the International Olympic Committee since December 1951 regarding our request for continued recognition. Very regrettably, no solution of this question has as yet been forthcoming.

    We are asking the Olympic Committee of the Soviet Union to forward to you a copy of our Constitution, together with an English translation, and a list of the leading officers on our Committee, since we are of the opinion that the question of continued recognition of the Chinese Olympic Committee should be solved satisfactorily without any further delay. The Chinese athletes are looking forward to opportunities for common endeavour with athletes of all the countries in the world to further promote the traditions of the Olympic Games and friendship among all peoples.

With greetings,   Faithfully yours,

                                        Jung Kao-tang
                             Vice President and General Secretary

---

Communist Chinese request that the IOC deal with the question of the status of China at its May 14, 1954 meeting.

```
Telegramm - Télégramme - Telegramma
```

= LT = IOC CHANCELLOR
OTTO MAYER AND IOC MEMBERS
CARE OTTO MAYER CIO LAUSANNE

= CHINESE OLYMPIC COMMITTEE QUOTE ALLCHINA ATHLETIC FEDERATION UNQUOTE IN REPLY TO MELBOURNE ORGANISING COMMITTEE DECEMBER TWENTIETH 1954 FORMALLY ACCEPTS OFFICIAL INVITATION TO PARTICIPATE IN SIXTEENTH OLYMPIAD MELBOURNE 1956 STOP BUT IT IS REPORTED THAT MELBOURNE ORGANISING COMMITTEE ALSO EXTENDED INVITATION TO SOCALLED SPORTS ORGANISATION OF TRAITOROUS CHIANGKAISHEK CLIQUE CHA CLIQUE LONG REPUDIATED BY SIX HUNDRED MILLION CHINESE PEOPLE STOP AGAINST THIS UNREASONABLE MEASURE WE PROTEST PARAGRAPH CHINESE OLYMPIC COMMITTEE QUOTE ALLCHINA ATHLETIC FEDERATION UNQUOTE IS SOLE LEGAL OLYMPIC ORGANISATION IN CHINA STOP CHINESE PEOPLE AND ATHLETES WILL NEVER RECOGNISE SOCALLED SPORTS ORGANISATION OF TRAITOROUS CHIANGKAISHEK CLIQUE AND IT IS NO LONGER QUALIFIED TO TAKE PART IN ANY INTERNATIONAL SPORTS ACTIVITIES STOP INVITATION TO SOCALLED SPORTS ORGANISATION OF TRAITOROUS CHIANGKAISHEK CLIQUE TO PARTICIPATE IN SIXTEENTH OLYMPIC GAMES THEREFORE CONSTITUTES GROSS VIOLATION OF OLYMPIC RULES STOP IT IS ALSO HARMFUL TO HEALTHY DEVELOPMENT OF INTERNATIONAL SPORTS ACTIVITIES STOP THEREBY WE REQUEST IOC TO WITHDRAW MELBOURNE ORGANISING COMMITTEE'S INVITATION TO SOCALLED SPORTS ORGANISATION OF TRAITOROUS CHIANGKAISHEK CLIQUE ATOLECHINE PEKING +

Text of Mainland Chinese acceptance to participate in the 1956 Olympic Games (dated February 19, 1955).

were that since Taiwan did not represent the entire Chinese people (Taiwan merely being a province) the invitation was a "gross violation of Olympic rules," which provided for only one Olympic committee from each country. These actions by the IOC, it was therefore claimed, were "harmful to [the] healthy development of international sports activities."[28] This type of statement was to be repeated many times in the years that followed.

In June, 1955, the Communists sent a delegation consisting of Tung Shou-yi (member of the IOC, and Vice-Chairman and Secretary-General of the ACAF) and Chang Lien-hua (member of the Chinese Olympic Committee) to the 50th IOC meeting in Paris. The main purpose of this meeting was to discuss preparations for the 16th Olympiad (to be held in Melbourne in the fall of 1956) and the 7th Winter Olympic Games (to be held in Cortina D'Ampezzio, Italy, in the Winter of 1956). Jung Kao-t'ang, however, used the occasion to point out that by listing the Chinese Nationalist Amateur Athletic Federation as a bona fide Olympic committee, the Olympic rules requiring only one committee from each country were being violated. He attempted to show that, at its 1954 Athens meeting, the IOC had given the Chinese Olympic Committee (Mainland) the designation of "official Chinese committee."[29] The fact is, however, that the committee had merely admitted the Communists to the IOC at that time, and had said nothing about jurisdiction over *all* Chinese athletics (the Mainland and Formosa). When Avery Brundage refused to consider this question, Jung demanded that it be put on the next agenda.[30] The Communist press branded the IOC action as an example of U.S. hostility toward China.[31]

In spite of these periodic outbursts by the Communists, no indication was ever given by them that they would not compete in the Olympics if their demands concerning Taiwan were not met. On November 29, 1955, Jung Kao-t'ang proved that China was very eager to participate. He sent a letter to the Philippine Amateur Athletic Federation regarding the qualifying soccer match that had to be arranged between Communist China and the Philippines in order to determine which nation would be able to compete in the official Olympic soccer tournament.[32] (This was necessary because when more than 16 nations file applications to participate in the Olympic soccer tournament, the 16 participants are determined by pre-Olympic qualifying matches. This limitation is set so that the tournament will be completed in a reasonable length of time during the Games.)

On Nov. 21, 1955, the Nationalist Chinese announced a change in their policy. They had formerly stated that they would not take part in the Olympic Games if the Communists participated. They now said that they would participate in the Games regardless of what the Communists did. The Nationalist Chinese Olympic Committee indicated that the desire of Chinese athletes at home, as well as that of foreign organizations, was responsible for this policy change.[33]

In the early months of 1956, Communist Chinese participation in the Melbourne Games seemed a certainty despite the Nationalist announcement that Formosa would definitely compete. This feeling prevailed even though the Chinese delegation (Tung Shou-yi and Chang Lien-hua) had again asked that recognition of the Chinese Nationalist Amateur Athletic Federation on Taiwan be withdrawn. This request was made at the 51st IOC meeting held in conjunction with the Winter Games at Cortina D'Ampezzo, Italy, January 24-25, 1956. But the committee failed to deal with the question because it was not on the agenda,[34] and a similar protest filed on March 18, met with the same fate.[35] Nevertheless, plans were completed for Communist China to compete in a two game pre-Olympic qualifying match in India with the Philippines on June 3 and June 5.[36] Communist China eventually qualified for the official Olympic soccer tournament in Melbourne when the Philippine team failed to show up in India. This canceled soccer match was the closest that the Communists have come to engaging in any international competition which had any direct connection with the Olympics.

CHINA'S PREPARATION FOR THE 1956 GAMES

If there were any indications that the Communists might not take part in the Melbourne Games, they were certainly veiled. The coming Games were discussed openly in the press, and, although Chinese officials were relatively candid in acknowledging that success in any event in Olympic competition would not come easy for them, they did cite several areas in which the Chinese could hope to do well: weightlifting, women's track and field, and swimming. In addition to these events, they also planned to compete at Melbourne in soccer, basketball, gymnastics, marksmanship, and men's track and field.[37]

In early September, Jung Kao-t'ang announced that from October 7-16, Communist Chinese athletes could compete for spots on the Olympic team, in trials (tryouts) to be held in Peking. He stressed that athletes from Taiwan and Macao were also eligible, and said that "all traveling expenses, lodging and board would be paid for by the All-China Athletic Federation for entrants from Taiwan." In addition, government permission for free entry and exit to and from the Mainland was guaranteed. In answer to a question raised at the news conference, Jung stated that "we have always been against professionalism in sports. . . . Sports are promoted in China in the interests of the people's health."[38] A month later, Nationalist China requested that Communist China be barred from the Olympics on grounds that her athletes were state subsidized (i.e. professionalism).[39]

A particularly emotional statement appeared in the *Jen Min Jih Pao (People's Daily)*, as an editorial, soon after Jung's announcement. It called on athletes from Taiwan to participate in the trials by asking them to "respond to this patriotic call and overcome all difficulties and obstructions in their struggle to proceed to Peking to take part in the contest for the sake of the glory of the fatherland and the cause of sports, as well as the prospects of going to Melbourne."[40]

The Olympic trials held in Peking were undoubtedly a pageantry-filled affair. Approximately 2,000 athletes poured into Peking to compete, including a contingent of approximately 100 from Hong Kong and Macao. A Chinese spokesman labeled the trials "the biggest sporting event in China to date," and the contingent of athletes was called "the largest and most powerful" group of athletes China ever assembled together.[41] When the trials were completed, it was announced that a team of 92 athletes (including two from Hong Kong and one from Macao) would be sent to Melbourne. They were to leave for Melbourne after completing a two week training period (the maximum period permitted by Olympic rules) in Canton. The Chinese Olympic Committee delegation consisting of Ts'ai Shu-fan, Ma Yüeh-han (also known as John Ma), Jung Kao-t'ang, and Tung Shou-yi left for Melbourne on October 23—earlier than the contingent of athletes. They were accompanied by news correspondents, cameramen, motion picture photographers, and radio commentators.[42]

As Olympic excitement within China heightened, political developments began to take on new significance. On October 22, 1956, Jung Kao-t'ang held a press conference at which time he again asked for immediate withdrawal of the permission that had been granted to Taiwan to send a separate team to Melbourne. He also objected to a step that the IOC was planning to take whereby Taiwan would be designated "Formosa China" and the Mainland delegation "Peking China." He called this an "offense to China's self-respect and an attempt at artificially splitting up China." After once again stating that to accept the Formosan delegation would be a violation of Olympic rules, he expressed indignation at the recent acceptance by the IOC of a protest from Taiwan which called the invitation by the Communists, to Taiwan athletes, to participate in trials on the Mainland, a "political maneuver." At the end of this news conference, Jung hedged on a question posed to him as to whether or not China would still send a team to Melbourne if the invitation to Taiwan were not rescinded.[43] This represents the first time that the question of non-participation on the part of the Communists was ever mentioned in any Communist Chinese news release.

This news conference evoked an immediate, long response in *Jen Min Jih Pao*. In addition to a repetition of many of the old arguments, the separate invitation to compete in Melbourne which was issued to Taiwan was referred to as part of the intrigue to create two Chinas in which the United States was said to have played a major part. Further, Chiang Kai-shek was held responsible for preventing Taiwan athletes from participating in the Mainland trials contrary to their wishes.[44] Despite this editorial harangue, no hint was given that Communist China would withdraw in the event that the International Olympic Committee did not comply with their wishes.

THE WITHDRAWAL

In view of the displeasure that the Communists often expressed with the Olympic Committee's handling of the China

Sports and International Relations, A Case Study 181

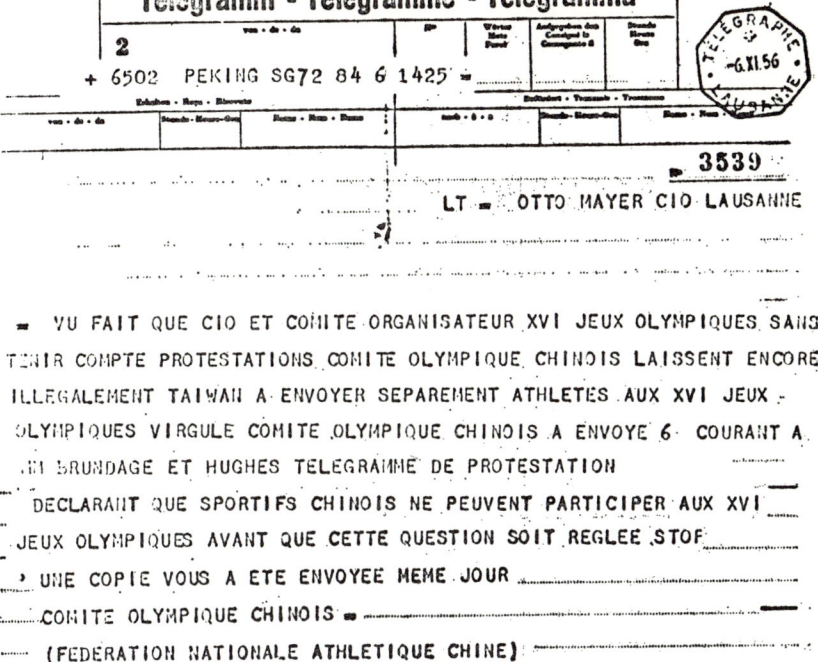

Telegram of November 6, 1956 that Communist China would not participate in 1956 Olympic Games.

situation since 1952, it is not surprising that they eventually chose not to participate in the 1956 Games. Nevertheless, the suddenness of their decision was certainly surprising.

The Communist Chinese administrative delegation (not including athletes) arrived in Melbourne on November 4, 1956.[45] On November 6, Jung Kao-t'ang cabled Avery Brundage that the Mainland would not participate in the Melbourne Games. Many of the previous charges were repeated and special displeasure was taken with the use of the terms "Formosa China" and "Peking China" in IOC literature.[46]

One is hard put to find an immediate cause for the turnabout in the Communist position. The only reasonable hint as to a direct cause for the sudden withdrawal of Communist China two days after their arrival is provided by their reaction upon seeing the Nationalist flag flying in the Olympic village.

Since Jung mentioned this in his cable to Brundage, we may assume that it was a very important offense to the Communists. (An interesting sidelight with respect to the raising of the nationalist flag: on October 29, before the arrival of the Mainland delegation, the Chinese flag was raised when the Nationalist team arrived. However, by mistake, the Communist Chinese flag was hoisted. The Nationalist officials immediately hauled down the Red flag and raised their own.[47])

On the same day that Jung sent his statement to Brundage (November 6), another statement by the Chinese Olympic Committee (Communist) was issued to explain its stand. In this explanation, the Communists stated that they would not participate in the 16th Olympiad "unless there is a satisfactory settlement of the question arising from the IOC's persistence in inviting Taiwan to send athletes separately to take part in the Olympic Games."[48] In all other statements on this issue, the Communists had asked for an out-and-out rescinding of the invitation to Taiwan. The use of the phrase "satisfactory settlement" seems to indicate that the Communist delegation was authorized to work out a compromise. The phrase, "athletes separately," seems to be hinting at a joint team consisting of athletes from both Chinas along the lines of the team which later represented the two Germanys. No attempts at compromise, however, were ever initiated.

One wonders, as he studies the above statement, to what extent the decision not to participate was decided upon prior to the arrival of the Chinese Communist delegation in Melbourne on November 4. It is not difficult to believe that the Communists were prepared to compromise; and would not insist upon the expulsion of Taiwan. The fact is that the Communists went to considerable expense to prepare for the Games —something that most probably would not have been done unless they arrived in Melbourne with every intention of participating. Further, on November 3, the Communist Olympic soccer team was reported to be training on Yifsaton Island, Canton,[49] thus indicating that as late as three days before the withdrawal, the Chinese athletes, if not the officials, were still very much expecting to compete.

The question arises as to the mental letdown of the Chinese athletes after going through selective trials in Peking, and a feverish training period in Canton. In addition, the public had been primed for China's announced participation in the Olympic Games through the media, and they too could be expected to be somewhat disappointed by the withdrawal. Apparently, the All-China Athletic Federation recognized this problem (which they probably felt might create difficulty in arousing interest in future international competition) and made an attempt to keep China's athletes together as a team for a while after the withdrawal. For this reason, on November 18, the *New China News Agency* announced the breaking of the world bantamweight clean and jerk weight-lifting mark by Chen Ching-kai (137.5 kgs.) "at a sports performance by the Chinese Olympic team"[50] (although this meet had nothing to do with the Olympics).

Communist China's refusal to participate in the 1956 Olympic Games in no way led her to curtail her participation in other international sporting events (as long as the question of Taiwan was not an issue). The 1957 schedule of athletic events, released in January of that year, listed approximately 50 proposed excursions abroad for Communist Chinese teams with about 40 foreign nations expected to visit Communist China. Some of the countries involved were: Soviet Russia, Egypt, Japan, Britain, Burma, Brazil, and Indonesia, in addition to other countries from the Middle East, Southeast Asia, and Africa. The types of sports the various countries were to compete in were quite varied, and included, table tennis, soccer, basketball, badminton, swimming, ice hockey, weightlifting, boxing, speed skating and tennis.[51]

Apparently, Communist China's misadventure with regard to the 1956 Olympics in no way lessened her desire to take part in the 1960 Games at Rome. On September 18, 1957, Tung Shou-yi of the All-China Athletic Federation left for a meeting at Sophia, Italy, where the 1960 Games were to be discussed.[52]

At approximately the same time that Tung was on his way to Italy, interesting developments were going on in the United States. The 1960 Winter Olympic Games were to be held at Squaw Valley, California. With indications being that the Communists might very well want to compete in these Games, the question of whether athletics and politics could be kept separate was a very real issue. On September 10, Secretary of State Dulles said that he hoped that a way could be found to admit the Communist Chinese athletes to the United States for the

Squaw Valley Games. He added that the Eisenhower administration was very much in favor of keeping politics out of the Olympics.[53]

A week later, the State Department announced that all bona fide athletes, including those from Communist China, would be admitted to the U.S. for the 1960 Winter Games. In order to create a minimum of friction, the usual fingerprinting procedure would be waived, although the normal health checks would be made. Dulles insisted that there were "no gimmicks" attached and that only those Chinese who were found to have a definite record of espionage would be barred from the country.[54] The U.S. policy never reached the point where it could be tested, for in 1958 Communist China severed all connection with the International Olympic Committee.

THE EVENTS OF 1958

It was in 1958 that the Communists made a more or less complete break with the established international sports community.

In March, in a statement by Chang Lien-hua (Secretary-General of the All-China Athletic Federation), China announced that it had decided not to take part in the 3rd Asian Games to be held in Tokyo in May, 1958. He noted: "We would unquestionably compete in these games if Taiwan athletes were entered as a part of the Chinese team."[55]

A more striking development occurred on August 19, 1958. In a long statement by Chang Lien-hua, the Chinese Olympic Committee (ACAF) announced that it had decided to withdraw its affiliation with the International Olympic Committee, in protest over the "unlawfully extended recognition to the [sports organ] of the Chiang Kai-shek clique in Taiwan."[56] It further announced that, for the same reason, it was withdrawing from the following international sports organizations:

    International Amateur Swimming Federation
    International Amateur Basketball Federation
    International Amateur Athletic Federation (track and
        field)
    International Weightlifting Federation
    International Shooting Union

International Amateur Wrestling Federation
International Cyclist's Union
Asian Table Tennis Federation[57]

Earlier that year (June 9), Communist China had withdrawn from the International Federation of Football Associations.[58]

It should be pointed out that, although the International Olympic Committee is the chief administrative body of the Olympic Games, for a country to participate in any particular event, it must belong to the corresponding international sports organization. Thus, for Communist China to again participate in the Olympics, after this mass resignation, she would have had to be accepted for membership by the IOC all over again; and would also have had to be accepted for membership once again by each of the international sports organizations which had jurisdiction over any event in which she might have wished to compete.

The All-China Athletic Federation statement, at the time of the withdrawal of Communist China from the IOC, offers no explanation that is new or different and was not used before in its criticism of the Olympic organization. Of course, in any discussion of this period, one must bear in mind the spirit of the "Great Leap Forward." The withdrawal of the Chinese from the IOC coincides with the general hardening of the political line which was characteristic of the "Great Leap." The Chinese justified their resignation with the usual arguments: the admission of the Chiang clique as a violation of Olympic rules; the use of international sports by the United States to further imperialist policies (with IOC President Brundage as the principal U.S. lackey); etc.[59] However, as the following outlines of correspondence between Brundage and Tung Shou-yi (of the ACAF) indicate, tensions between the IOC and Communist China had been building up to a fever pitch since the beginning of 1958. The general contents of the correspondence are as follows:[60]

Brundage to Tung, January 8, 1958

Brundage mentions that "there is a separate government in Taiwan," recognized internationally and by the United Nations, which "was last a part of Japan and not China." He further cites the Olympic Code, which separates sports from politics.[61]

Tung to Brundage, April 23, 1958

Tung acknowledges the rectification of the error of misnaming the People's Republic of China: " 'The Democratic People's Republic of China,' in the minutes of the 53rd session of the IOC."

Tung goes on to say that the statement about Taiwan "last" being "part of Japan" was false since it was restored to China after the Second World War in accordance with the Cairo and Potsdam agreements. He disagrees with Brundage's statement that "the natives [of Taiwan] are neither Chinese nor Japanese," saying that they are 90% Han Chinese. His letter concludes by saying that the fact that "there is a separate government in Taiwan" was wholly brought about by U.S. intervention, and that it is Brundage, not he, who is introducing politics into sports.[62]

Brundage to Tung, June 1, 1958

Brundage says that the International Olympic Committee has nothing to do with politics, and neither recognizes nor deals with governments. He further accuses Tung of violating his obligations as a member of the IOC by constantly introducing political questions which violate the spirit and letter of the Olympic Code.[63]

Tung to Brundage, August 19, 1958

He calls Brundage's actions a truthful indication that "you are a faithful menial of the U.S. imperialists bent on serving their plot of creating 'two Chinas.' " He concludes by saying: "A man like you . . . has no qualifications whatsoever to be IOC President. . . . I will no longer cooperate with you or have any connection with the IOC while it is under your domination."[64]

On September 5, 1958, at a meeting in Lausanne, Switzerland, the IOC issued a statement notifying sports organizations throughout the world that the IOC had received the August 19 resignation of IOC member, Professor Tung Shou-yi; had removed Communist China from its records and lists; and would thus bar her from the 1960 Olympic Games.[65] They later stated that there was no prospect of the Mainland Committee being readmitted in time to participate in the 1960 Games.[66]

With Communist China having relinquished any claim to compete in the Olympics, it would seem that the IOC would have been willing and eager to leave things pretty much as they were. Nevertheless, on May 22, 1959, the IOC saw fit to make it clear that the Nationalist Chinese Olympic Committee was not a body representing all of China. In the future, it said, Nationalist China would be referred to as Taiwan.[67] Theoretically, this made room for Communist China's readmission. Further, on May 28, in its 55th session at Munich, Germany, the IOC removed Nationalist China from its rolls as a body representing all of China (by a 48-7 vote) telling her that she could reapply later as a representative of Taiwan, since she "no longer represents sports in the entire country of China." Avery Brundage, in a significant statement, said that if Communist China reapplied for IOC membership at this time, she would be readmitted as "the representative of China."[68]

AFTERMATH TO THE CHANGE OF STATUS OF TAIWAN

The IOC action was misconstrued[69] as having "expelled" Formosa and, brought immediate censure from the U.S. State Department, which called the decision "totally inconsistent with its non-political traditions."[70] Another U.S. government statement called the IOC move "a clear act of political discrimination." In the House of Representatives, Francis D. E. Dorn of New York introduced a resolution favoring reversal of the IOC decision and calling for the barring of future readmission of Communist China. He said that he thought that, should the Nationalists not be permitted to compete, the U.S. should not compete either.[71] On June 3, the House of Representatives voted to prohibit the use of any army personnel or equipment at the 1960 Winter Games at Squaw Valley, California, if any "free nation" was banned.[72] The American Legion also threatened to withdraw its aid to the 1960 Winter Games.[73] Even President Eisenhower commented that asking the Nationalists to discard the name of the Republic of China seemed to belong to the realm of politics rather than sports.[74] The implication being that the IOC had no right to take the action that it had taken. Perhaps a statement by the U.S. representative at the United Nations, Henry Cabot Lodge, aptly summarized U.S. public opinion at this time. He called on the IOC to reverse its decision to expel Taiwan, and said that if this was not done, "many Americans are surely going to doubt the value of U.S. participation in the Olympic Games."[75]

Because of this barrage of unfavorable U.S. sentiment, the IOC was forced to clarify its stand somewhat.[76] One of the motivating factors in this clarification was, no doubt, the U.S. government's threat not to contribute $400,000 that it had pledged to the Squaw Valley Games. Thus, on June 6, IOC Chancellor Otto Mayer announced reassuringly that Nationalist China would immediately be accepted back into the IOC if it would only change its name.[77] A few days later he elaborated on this statement and said that Taiwan had to drop the word "China" from the name of its Olympic committee.[78]

On June 11, Avery Brundage said that the IOC would find a solution to assure the participation of Nationalist China in the Squaw Valley Games. However, he also said that unless they dropped all reference to China in the title of their Olympic committee, they could no longer belong to the IOC. Nevertheless, he said that they could be allowed to compete at Squaw Valley on the grounds that they had received an invitation before they were expelled.[79] (Conceivably, this would give the IOC more time to re-examine, and possibly rectify, their position before the 1960 Summer Games without having to capitulate, and thus lose face.)

Avery Brundage obviously was under a great deal of pressure at this time to further clarify the IOC stand. He indicated this when, on July 19, in Philadelphia, he said that he personally would support the Nationalist Chinese in their application for readmission to the IOC, because they now applied under the name of their country: The Olympic Committee of the Republic of China.[80] They had been calling themselves the Chinese Nationalist Olympic Committee (not a very significant change at first glance). Apparently, the word "nationalist" signifying the *entire* China was the key term here. This was quite a shift in position from his original statement that the word "China" would have to be dropped.

The entire problem turned out to be merely academic because neither China participated in the Squaw Valley Games, although the Nationalists did send a token delegation of officials.[81]

THE 1960 SUMMER GAMES AT ROME

After the 1958 events, Communist China made no attempt nor expressed any further desire to compete in the 1960 Games at Rome. The Nationalists did compete, although they were forced (though under protest) to make their entry seem as though it was being received from the island of Taiwan. During the inaugural parade of athletes, on the first day of the Rome Games, one Taiwan athlete was seen carrying a sign reading: "Under Protest."[82] The Nationalists also competed at the Tokyo Olympiad in 1964 and in 1968 at Mexico City.

EVENTS PRECEDING THE GAMES OF THE NEW EMERGING FORCES

In 1963, a new sports organization was started. It was initiated at a meeting held in Djakarta, Indonesia, during April, 1963, mainly with the blessings of Communist China and Indonesia. This organization became known as the Games of the New Emerging Forces. Its purpose was to give nations which, for political and other reasons, could not or did not wish to participate in the Olympic Games, an opportunity to compete in sporting events of high calibre.[83]

The establishment of the Games of the New Emerging Forces (GANEFO) can be directly linked to Indonesia's refusal to issue visas to athletes from Taiwan and Israel at the time of the Fourth Asian Games, held in Djakarta, in the summer of 1962.[84] The Chinese Communists apparently took advantage of this incident to serve their own purposes.

The Chinese have always considered international sports to be an important political tool for them. They evidently felt that by not competing in the Olympic Games, their international stature was being hurt considerably. Thus, immediately after the Asian Games, before the IOC could serve any sanctions on Indonesia for her treatment of Taiwan and Israel (although one could feel that a rebuke was forthcoming), and before Indonesia herself had expressed any desire to hold a sports competition outside of the jurisdiction of the recognized international sports bodies, the Chinese Communists began to plant seeds in the minds of the Indonesians.

On October 4, 1962, *T'i Yü Pao,* the influential Communist Chinese bi-weekly sports newspaper, declared in an editorial that ". . . Indonesian public opinion has favored the proposed holding of Afro-Asian Games and the founding of an Afro-Asian Sports Organization." The editorial further indicated that the Chinese sportsmen heartily endorsed such a proposal. The editorial then indicated how these games would serve the best interests of the people of Asia and Africa:

1) By conforming to the spirit of the Bandung Conference of 1955, they will help promote unity among the peoples of Asia and Africa, because:

    a) these nations are engaged in a similar struggle, against imperialism and colonialism, for independence;

    b) they have a similar need to develop their national culture and economy stifled by imperialism and colonialism;

    c) sports is a good means of promoting mutual understanding and friendship among the people of various countries.

2) The proposed organization and games (GANEFO) would help develop sports and raise the level of performance in Asia and Africa. Although sports is flourishing in Asia and Africa, there is still much room for improvement.

3) Sports in Asian and African countries has long been discriminated against by the forces of imperialism and sports organizations manipulated by imperialist countries.[85]

THE RESIGNATION AND EXPULSION OF INDONESIA FROM THE IOC AND THE BEGINNING OF THE GAMES OF THE NEW EMERGING FORCES

At a meeting held in Lucerne, Switzerland, on Feb. 8, 1963, the IOC passed a resolution designed to bar from the Olympics any nation which was guilty of discrimination against foreign athletes on political, racial, or religious grounds.[86] Sukarno apparently saw the handwriting on the wall (the inevitability of Indonesia's expulsion), and, one week later, announced his withdrawal from the Olympic movement. (Indonesia was subsequently expelled.) He immediately ordered his Minister of Sports to organize rival games.[87]

The Preparatory Conference of GANEFO was held in Djakarta, April 27-29, 1963. Taking part actively in this conference were: Cambodia, Communist China, Guinea, Indonesia, Iraq, Mali, Pakistan, North Vietnam, the U.A.R., and the Soviet Union; while Ceylon and Yugoslavia sent along observers. This Preparatory Conference established the following ground rules and guiding principles:

1) GANEFO was to be based on the spirit of the 1955 Bandung Conference and the Olympic ideals, and was to promote the development of sports in new emerging nations so as to cement friendly relations among them.
2) The first GANEFO meet would be held in November, 1963, in Djakarta, Indonesia.
3) GANEFO was to be held every four years (like the Olympic Games).
4) Invitations to compete were to be sent to the following: countries who participated in the 1955 Bandung Conference and who were faithful to its precepts; countries present at the April 27-29 Preparatory Conference; countries who promise to support GANEFO; socialist countries; other countries of the new emerging forces in Asia, Africa, Latin America and Europe who apply and indicate that they wish to participate.
5) The following sports would be included in the competition providing that at least three countries wished to participate in them: track and field, swimming and diving, soccer, volleyball, basketball, weightlifting, shooting, fencing, wrestling, boxing, cycling (road racing only), table tennis, tennis, badminton, water polo, hockey (field hockey), archery, yachting, judo, and gymnastics. With the exception of table tennis (which is the forte of the Chinese), tennis, and badminton, all of these sports were Olympic events at the time.
6) The Games would not exceed twelve days in length.

One of the more interesting developments of this Preparatory Conference was a statement made by President Sukarno. After denouncing the IOC for professing not to mix sports and politics, but, in fact, doing so, he said: "Let us declare frankly that sport has something to do with politics. And Indonesia now proposes to mix sports with politics."[88]

The Chinese decided immediately to compete and, on June

26, held a preparatory meeting in Peking. The events in which they planned to participate were: track and field, cycling, swimming and diving, archery, gymnastics, weightlifting, soccer, basketball, volleyball, table tennis, tennis, badminton, and shooting.[89] It should be noted that the Chinese (who, as it will be seen, were one of the few nations to really take these Games seriously) only competed in those events (13 out of 20) in which they had a reasonable chance of doing well.

National trials for the Chinese team were scheduled for Peking in September, 1963, and Vice-Premier Ho Lung (long time sports luminary as well as political figure) was elected chairman of the Preparatory Committee for the Games.[90]

The selective trials for the Chinese GANEFO team took place in Peking from September 15-22. The Chinese made every attempt to glamourize the event as much as possible, and the trials were therefore inaugurated on September 14, with a grand parade. Over 1,000 athletes competed for spots on the Chinese squad in the first large scale sports meeting held in China since the national sports meeting of 1959. An examination of the quality of the Chinese athletes at the selective trials possibly indicates why the Chinese were anxious to compete in easier company, and did not continue to press for admission to the Olympic Games.[91]

A statistical comparison between the performances of the Chinese athletes at the GANEFO selective trials, and the winning performances of the champions at the 1960 Olympic Games at Rome, in men's and women's track and field, men's and women's swimming, and weightlifting (men only) shows that only in the weightlifting events, where the Communists had several world class performers, might the Chinese have been able to capture a 1960 Olympic medal.[92] The Chinese women in general would have fared better than the men, and had an outside chance of capturing several medals in track and field. In short, the Chinese, for a nation of their size, would have been humiliated had they participated in world class competition in 1963, and this may have played a part in their decision not to attempt to participate in future Olympic Games for the time being—aside from any political influences which may have been brought to bear.

At the close of the trials held in Peking, a team of approximately 238 Chinese athletes was selected to participate in the first GANEFO. The delegation was to be headed by Jung Kao-t'ang (Vice-Chairman of the Physical Culture and Sports Commission). Huang Chung, Li Meng-hua, and Chao Cheng-hung were deputy leaders of the delegation. The team was to compete in the 13 events (or 14, if swimming and diving are considered as two) mentioned above.[93] One may be sure that the Chinese sent the very best team possible to compete in Djakarta.

THE GANEFO MEETING (NOVEMBER 10-22, 1963)

The opening ceremonies, before a capacity crowd of 100,000 enthusiastic fans in flag-bedecked Bung Karno Stadium, were a carbon copy of Olympic pageantry, and consisted of the usual parade of athletes, the torch relayed by athletes (this one from Java instead of Mt. Olympus in Greece), and the athlete's pledge.[94] They created a GANEFO motto: "Onward, No Retreat!"[95] There was even a "Song of GANEFO":

Whose is the GANEFO, whose is the GANEFO?
It is the GANEFO of the people throughout the world,
the GANEFO of the people throughout the world.[96]

Another direct parallel with Olympic custom was President Sukarno's pronouncement which brought to a close the Games of the New Emerging Forces: "I call upon all the young men, all the young women, all the countries of the new emerging forces to participate in the next GANEFO."[97]

In China, Chairman Liu Shao-Ch'i and Premier Chou En-lai sent telegrams of congratulations to President Sukarno, and in the press the Games were hailed. *Jen Min Jih Pao* called the Games "a brilliant epoch-making event in the history of international sports." *Ta Kung Pao* said that GANEFO would surely become a permanent institution.[98]

From 47-55 nations, and from 2,000 to 3,000 athletes (the exact figures were cause for much controversy among GANEFO officials themselves), competed in the Games. Indonesia had the largest delegation with approximately 341 athletes (including 112 women), and China was next with 238[99] (here, too, figures are conflicting and cannot be completely trusted). Thus two nations supplied approximately 20% of the athletes. Among the other nations which were listed as having competed were: Bolivia, Somali, Dominican Republic, Japan, Philippines, Algeria, Mali, Guinea, Argentina, Cambodia, the U.A.R., Albania, North Korea, Iraq, Lebanon, North Vietnam, Morocco, Chile, Finland, Poland, France, Soviet Union, Brazil, Uraguay, Saudi Arabia, Bulgaria, Czechoslovakia, the German Democratic Republic and Yugoslavia.[100]

Athletically, things went very well for the Chinese. Among their successes were 20 gold medals in track and field, 12 of 18 in swimming and diving, several weightlifting victories, and victories in badminton, table tennis, and basketball.[101] By the time the competition was over, the Chinese had garnered 65 gold medals, 56 silver, and 47 bronze, which was double the number of any other participant. The Soviet Union, with a contingent of less than 100 athletes, was second with 31 gold medals and a total of 59 (gold, silver, and bronze). Though several world records were set, they were not recognized internationally, and the quality of performance generally was acknowledged to be well below top level standards.[102]

Although the Chinese, quite literally, swept everything in sight, the Chinese press reports of these Games lead one to believe that the athletic competition was of secondary importance, and that the primary purpose of participation in the Games was to establish strong friendships and to project a favorable national image.

Reports by the Chinese tried to portray the Games of the New Emerging Forces as being morally superior to the Olympic Games: ". . . in contrast to the imperialist-controlled Olympic Games, GANEFO has no discriminatory rules or regulations. . . . To enable late-comers to take part, new regulations were instituted as regards the deadline for entries. Thus, in track and field, entries could be made two hours before an event began."[103]

As they came to an end, the Chinese hailed the Games as a tremendous success for the people of the "whole world against imperialism and old and new colonialism, . . . a triumph of historical significance . . . in foiling the imperialist manipulation of international sports. . . ."[104] The importance of holding GANEFO every four years was stressed. When the Chinese athletes returned from Indonesia, a tremendous rally was held for them in Canton. In addition, the Korean and Vietnamese delegations were honored in China on their way home.[105] If one were to base all his conclusions about GANEFO solely on Communist reports, he would justifiably conclude that it was every bit as successful as the Olympic Games.

A DIFFERENT PERSPECTIVE ON GANEFO

In reality, the Games of the New Emerging Forces could hardly be compared to the Olympic Games. True, the approximately 50 nations that competed compared favorably with the number that competed in any of the first ten meetings of the Olympic Games.[106] However, most of the athletes at GANEFO did not really represent their nations. For the most part, they were unofficial representatives from student and other associations. Further, many delegations were only made up of five or six participants. This was generally brought about by a fear that any nation entering an official team in the GANEFO would be barred from the Olympic Games. As an example, although approximately 62 athletes were present from Japan, the Japan Amateur Athletic Federation had refused to send an official team, and very few of the athletes from Japan were of Olympic calibre. The same was true of the Soviet Union. If the comment by a Philippine sports columnist, that his country was sending "not even second-rate" athletes, is generalized (as appears fair), the domination of China becomes more readily understandable.[107]

An air of uneasiness apparently hung over the Djakarta meeting. Of special significance is the fact that precise instructions were given that no one was allowed in the special area occupied by the Chinese delegation.[108] Further, amid reports that anti-government rebels were trying to sabotage the running of the Games, a tight security guard was clamped around the sports complex.[109]

WERE THE INDONESIANS THE REAL FORCE BEHIND THE FIRST GANEFO?

When one reads about the Games of the New Emerging Forces as described in Communist inspired literature, he is left with a feeling that the Chinese Communists were more than just participants. One gets the impression that they were the moving force behind these Games. Small bits of evidence which seeped into the Japanese press lend substance to this feeling. One report said that ". . . the transport costs for all delegations are reliably reported to have been paid by the Chinese."[110] Another rumor reported that the Chinese had secretly given the Indonesians an eighteen million dollar gift so that they might hold the Games. This gift was to remain secret.[111]

In the original agreement between the Indonesians and the Chinese, China was to give Indonesia $18,000,000 in exchange for 18 billion Indonesian rupiahs. The Chinese were then expected to destroy the rupiahs, and the $18,000,000 would in fact be a gift. Unpleasantness apparently developed when the Chinese arrived in Indonesia with an unusually large number of rupiahs in their pockets.[112]*

From all this it appears that perhaps the first GANEFO was not the great success portrayed by the Chinese. To encourage participation, the Chinese appear to have absorbed the expense of transporting many of the delegations to Indonesia. But, even with the inducement of free passage, very few nations were willing to run the risk of expulsion from the Olympic Games by sending an *official* national team.

Yet, perhaps GANEFO did serve a positive function for the Chinese. It certainly served as an ego-builder for their government. To the Chinese people it had now been "proved" that the imperialists could be surpassed in the sports area as well. As far as the Chinese *people* were aware, the first GANEFO was every bit as exciting and successful as any Olympic Games ever held.

EVENTS SINCE THE FIRST GANEFO

According to its charter, GANEFO is scheduled to be held every four years. For a long while, it appeared that this plan would be carried out. At a meeting held during the first GANEFO in November, 1963, it was decided to hold the next GANEFO in Cairo, in October, 1967. Should the U.A.R. be unable to provide suitable facilities, Peking would then be the alternate site.[113]

The Chinese apparently felt that the GANEFO could do them a great deal of good, and they did not intend to let it die. In August, 1964, the Chinese elected a national GANEFO

---

* Though this financial participation on the part of China is noted in only one source, confirmation of Chinese financial assistance to Cambodia at the time of the Asian GANEFO in 1966 lends credence to the report.

committee of 23 members (with Ho Lung as Honorary Chairman; Jung Kao-t'ang, Chairman; Huang Chung, Vice-Chairman; and Chang Lien-hua, Secretary-General).[114] A week later, a five man group, (headed by Huang and Chang) left for Djakarta to attend the Congress of the Executive Board of the GANEFO.[115] At this meeting (August 19-21), a report was given on the progress of the Cairo preparations for 1967, and it was decided to add three sports to the GANEFO program, as well as to form a permanent secretariat.[116]

In honor of the first anniversary of GANEFO, the Chinese staged a two week celebration in Peking in November, 1964. At this time, Vice-Premier Ho Lung sent a telegram of congratulations to President Sukarno. The festivities were highlighted by a rally of 15,000 people at which diplomats from GANEFO countries, as well as Premier Chou En-lai and Vice-Premiers Ho Lung and Ch'en Yi, were present. A color documentary of the first GANEFO was shown in nine Peking movie houses and on Peking television.[117] The Chinese clearly had no intention of letting the concept of GANEFO die.

In September, 1965, the second session of the Council of the Federation of GANEFO was held in Peking. Thirty-nine delegations were present at this meeting. The following attended as regular members: Albania, Arab Palestine, Bulgaria, Cambodia, Ceylon, China, Cuba, Czechoslovakia, the Dominican Republic, Finland, the German Democratic Republic, Guinea, Hungary, Indonesia, Iraq, Italy, the Democratic People's Republic of Korea, Laos, Mongolia, Pakistan, Poland, Syria, Somali, the U.S.S.R., the U.A.R., the Democratic Republic of Vietnam, Yemen, Lebanon, and the South African Non-Racial Olympic Committee. Attending as observers were delegates from: Afghanistan, Algeria, the Central African Republic, the Congo (Brazzaville), France, Mali, Mauritania, Nepal, Rumania, the Sudan, Tanzania, Uganda, and Morocco.[118] If the first GANEFO may be taken as an indication, most of these delegations probably did not represent the official sports bodies in their countries. This, however, did not disturb the organizers of the first GANEFO, and it is doubtful that it had any effect on the planning or execution of the second GANEFO.

The scope of GANEFO was expanded in September, 1965, with the formation of the Asian Committee of the Games of the New Emerging Forces. The Executive Committee consisted of Arab Palestine, Cambodia, Ceylon, China, Indonesia, Iraq, the Democratic People's Republic of Korea, Pakistan, and North Vietnam.[119] It was decided to hold the first Asian GANEFO meet November 25-December 6, 1966, at Phnom Penh, Cambodia. The Preparatory Committee for the People's Republic of China was formally established in July, 1966, with Jung Kao-t'ang as Chairman. The Chinese at that time announced their plans to compete in soccer, basketball, volleyball, table tennis, badminton, track and field, swimming and diving, shooting, archery, gymnastics, weightlifting, and cycling —the same sports which they competed in at the earlier GANEFO.[120]

The timing of the first Asian GANEFO reveals its primary purpose. Just as the GANEFO of 1963 was intended to show underdeveloped nations that an alternative did exist to the western-oriented Olympic Games, so the first Asian GANEFO wished to provide such an alternative for Asian sports. The Fifth Asian Games were scheduled to open December 9, 1966, in Bangkok, Thailand. Holding a rival GANEFO at this time would provide a place to compete for those nations not willing, or ineligible, to participate in the International Olympic Committee-supported Asian Games, as well as force the acknowledged international sports authorities to censure those nations competing in the outlawed GANEFO, and thus, indirectly, publicize them.

The first Asian GANEFO was held as planned and appears to have been successful. Some 2,000 athletes from 17 countries and areas competed. In addition to those belonging to the Executive Committee, delegations were sent from Lebanon, Nepal, Mongolia, Japan, Laos, Syria, Yemen, and Singapore.[121] As was the case in the prior GANEFO, it can be assumed that many of these delegations were unofficial. Also following the pattern of 1963 was the underwriting of a large part of the expenses by the Chinese. At the opening ceremonies Prince Sihanouk of Cambodia took care to state that: ". . . I still want to stress the important part played by our Chinese friends whose material aid and recommendations are extremely valuable."[122]

Athletically, too, the meet was a repeat of the GANEFO of 1963. The Chinese delegation swept 113 gold medals, far outdistancing North Korea's 30.[123] Included were two world records by Chinese weightlifters: a lift of 118.5 kgs. by bantam-

Chinese world-class high jumper Ni Chih-chin.

weight Chen Man-lin, and a lift of 157.5 kgs. by featherweight Hsiao Ming-hsiang. All in all 59 GANEFO records were broken including a leap of 2.27 meters by Chinese high jumper Ni Chih-chin that came within one centimeter of tying the world record. Despite their decided superiority, the Chinese followed their previous precedent of not competing in events in which they weren't strong. Of the 20 events on the program (which were identical to those of 1963 with the exception of rowing which replaced field hockey), they did not compete in eight.[124]

During the course of the first Asian GANEFO, it was decided to hold the second GANEFO in Peking in September, 1967, as had been stipulated earlier, in the event that Cairo was not prepared to do so.[126] Without any formal explanation, this meet was never held; undoubtedly because of the Cultural Revolution.

STANDINGS OF THE FIRST ASIAN GANEFO[125]

COUNTRY	NO. OF ATHLETES	GOLD	SILVER	BRONZE	TOTAL
Ceylon	35	—	1	4	5
China	208	113	58	37	208
Indonesia	51	7	9	5	21
Iraq	47	2	9	7	18
Japan	49	10	13	8	31
N. Korea	201	30	40	34	104
Laos	16	—	—	—	—
Lebanon	27	3	3	7	13
Mongolia	10	—	1	—	1
Nepal	20	—	—	—	—
Palestine	59	1	3	3	7
Pakistan	27	—	—	—	—
Singapore	27	2	3	—	5
Syria	27	2	3	—	5
N. Vietnam	106	4	11	14	29
Yemen	28	—	—	—	—
Cambodia	332	13	34	57	104
TOTAL	1,270	185	186	181	552

The future fate of GANEFO remains very much up in the air. Had this manuscript been completed several months earlier, it would have carried the conclusion that the Games of the New Emerging Forces would very likely be reinstituted as soon as China emerged from the last throws of the Cultural Revolution. The logical conclusion today has to be quite different. After more than 20 years of self-imposed isolation, the Chinese have at last begun to cast their lot with that of the larger world. GANEFO was an expression of isolationist China. Now that China seems to be shedding her isolationist garb, we can expect her to once more seek a rapproachment with the Olympic Games—if not in time for Munich in 1972, then certainly for Canada in 1976. This rapproachment, when it does come about, will be the strongest indication through sports that China can give that she is headed in a new direction.

When the research for this chapter was first completed, before the Cultural Revolution, it was my conclusion that we would be wise to keep sports in mind as a possible first link in the establishment of contacts with Communist China. The intervening few years have seen the realization of this prediction. What has been related in this chapter has shown that international sports competition did not suddenly become a soft spot in the harsh exterior that China presented to the world for over 20 years. As far back as 1952, the Communists were sorely disenchanted with the Olympic Games, yet they waited six years until 1958 until finally divorcing themselves from them completely. In 1956, it even appeared that they were ready to compete in the Olympics regardless of whether or not Taiwan was to be a participant. Athletic contact with the U.S.S.R. continued for several years despite the Sino-Soviet split. More than once American and Mainland athletes have met on the same field in the darkest years of U.S.-Chinese relations.

Despite the distinct recent improvement in Sino-American relations, complete mutual understanding in some of the touchier areas will not come quickly. More likely than not, sports will continue to provide a primary avenue of cultural communication between the two nations. This contact through sports could help buy the vital time that will doubtlessly be needed to iron out the more vital outstanding issues between the two nations.

Summary

OUR ATTEMPT in these pages has been to highlight the major themes in the history of modern sports and physical culture in China. As part of this effort, we have first discussed the introduction of modern athletics—a process which, like others, involving modernization in China, was initiated by people from the West. Over-riding all other western influences was that of the YMCA.

The role of the YMCA in Chinese physical culture was so great until the mid-1920's that the Y was practically synonymous with physical education in China. In the widest sense, their greatest contribution was orientational. They played the major role in introducing and developing those aspects of physical culture which predominated during the Republican period and were later adopted by the Communist regime.

The YMCA's first influence was on the local level. Through the Physical Departments in the various branches of the YMCA, thousands were introduced to sports for the first time. The introduction of competitive meets as early as 1902 encouraged a constantly ascending level of performance. The YMCA was able to continue expanding this program through the initiation of two major series of meets during this period.

In 1910, they introduced the first National Athletic Meet. As we have seen, this was the first of a series that had a strong influence on the future organization of sports in China. It was responsible for the division of China into five athletic sections and, doubtlessly, encouraged the formation of the many regional athletic associations which sprang up between 1910 and 1924. The formation of the China Amateur Athletic Union in 1919 and the China National Amateur Athletic Federation in 1924 were plainly natural extensions of the influence which the YMCA brought to bear. This, in turn, led to the first government involvement in physical culture on a national scale in the 1930's.

The Far Eastern Championship Games series, initiated by the YMCA, is another example of YMCA influence in this area. The FECG did several things for Chinese athletics:

1. It alerted government to the importance of sports, and thus contributed to its later involvement in it.

2. It sensitized people to western sports and physical education who had never known about them before.

3. It developed a positive attitude toward sports on the part of women because of the female competition incorporated in the meets.

4. Because it became involved in competition with other nations, it helped to present the concept of a nation to the Chinese people, and thus served as a unifying factor.

In the area of physical culture within the school system, the YMCA was less successful. As has been pointed out, school physical education was a weak point in Republican China. In the case of the YMCA, they were unable to train sufficient personnel capable of developing the necessary programs required to permit physical education to continue to expand. This inadequacy was actually but an echo of the overall national condition. Yet, in spite of the generally deficient condition in which school physical education found itself during the early part of the Republican period, the Nationalist government, which was established in 1928, saw sufficient promise in it to make it a focal point for further development in the ensuing years.

Two themes stand out in the post-YMCA period (1928-49). The first is government control; the second, the reintroduction of a military-flavored physical education. Both foretold developments in physical culture during the Communist regime.

The military flavor in modern Chinese physical education, as we have seen, is as old as western physical education in China. The first physical education instructors were German or Japanese; those who were Chinese had studied in Japan. The tradition which they brought with them placed its stress on spartan-like military gymnastics. Games or organized sports had no place in their system. Between 1910 and 1920 this influence declined as the Far Eastern Championship Games, the National Athletic Meets, and other types of competition began to arouse an increasing interest in competitive sports among the Chinese. German and Japanese influence was all but absent in the 1920's as American educational theories and practices began to replace those of Japan.

With the establishment of the Nationalist government in 1928, the German tradition of military-flavored physical education once more began to be influential. German instructors were brought in to head physical education departments, and Chinese students began to study in Germany. Sports competition *per se,* however, continued to retain its place in the physical education program. This tendency toward militarism in sports was first inspired by the spirit of the Three People's Principles which became the watchword of the Nationalist regime. The Three People's Principles Physical Education Program distinctly advocated military physical education. The war conditions of the 1930's and 1940's made this a necessary course.

The mere fact that the Nationalist government took control of sports is not especially noteworthy. Indeed, they made an effort to control many aspects of Chinese life. What is of particular significance is that they concentrated on physical culture as deeply as they did. Their efforts in this respect took three avenues: the convening of physical education conferences, the passing of legislation, and the provision within the structure of government for the administration of physical culture. All were firsts for China.

Government control of sports, school physical education programs, physical education with an eye toward national defense, and international athletics—introduced into physical education during the Republican period—all underwent further development during the Communist period.

Summary

When the Communists came to power in 1949, they were in a more advanced position with respect to physical culture than the Nationalists had been when they came to power. Over 20 years of experience in the South and the Northwest had taught them the direction that they wanted physical culture to take. They were able to pursue immediately the further development of those themes introduced during the Republican period.

In the area of organization, the Communists have worked out an elaborate system of sports organization, extending through several levels of government, which guarantees maximum state jurisdiction over the sports and physical culture system. The refinement of this control evolved slowly, though apparently with precise planning. The All-China Athletic Federation (formed October, 1949) was the sole administrative body over athletics until the formation of the Physical Culture and Sports Commission in November, 1952. Though a "mass" or "people's" organization (and, thus, strictly speaking, non-governmental), the ACAF performed most of the functions of the government commission as is seen by the similarity in structure between the ACAF in its early years and the PCSC. The apparent reason for the lag between the formation of the ACAF and the PCSC was the desire to staff the government commission with politically reliable personnel who also had some sports experience. Though experienced sports personnel were available immediately after the formation of the regime, they apparently did not satisfy political requirements.

Our examination into the sports system below the national level has cast some doubt on the oft held hypothesis that, at every level, the Party oversees government operations. In the case of Shanghai, we have seen that there has been an overlap in membership between the Municipal Physical Culture and Sports Committee and the local level Party department which controls physical culture. The introduction of Political Departments in government organs which took place just before the Cultural Revolution suggests an increased assertion of Party control from *within* the government organization.

In the area of school physical education, the haphazard provisions made during the Nationalist period have been replaced by a sophisticated system geared to all levels of education. Contrary to Republican experiences, the policy decided upon in this area seems to have been implemented. Generally, it calls for physical education at all levels of schooling. The physical culture institutes, and various normal schools, provide training for prospective physical culture instructors and other personnel. Nevertheless, a shortage of trained personnel continues to plague the People's Republic much as it did its predecessor.

Two characteristics of Chinese Communist school physical education stand out because of their contrast to the type of physical education familiar to us. For one thing, the Communists make use of the school as a breeding ground for future athletes. The process originates in the spare-time athletic school where boys and girls, as young as eight years old, who have stood out in the regular school physical education program, are sent for special training. Though the spare-time school is not strictly a part of the formal educational system, its awareness of the students' scholastic progress coupled with its reliance on the school as a source of talent, link it very closely with the regular school program.

A student who shows promise in the spare-time school (or elsewhere) can eventually hope to gain admission to one of the physical culture institutes. These institutes produce physical education instructors for middle schools and universities, coaches, and researchers. They are unique, however, in that they enable an athlete to devote a substantial amount of time to perfecting his particular specialty under the guidance of expert coaches. This is accomplished through enrollment in a Sports Department which makes minimum demands on pedagogical or theoretical studies.

The other unique feature of school physical education on Mainland China, mirrored by the degree of militarism inherent in it, is merely the reflection of a theme applied to physical culture as a whole. "National defense physical culture" is a theme which can be traced to the origins of the "labor-defense system" in the early 1950's. Its exact nature has varied within the course of the last 20 years. What has remained constant throughout this span is the influence which the Chinese Communist experiences, before they came to power, have had upon their program. Forced marches, military camping, swimming, fording rivers, and handling weapons, all stem from the Communist experience in Chingkanshang, during the Long March and during the civil war in the 1940's. Their continuing stress on this type of activity reflects their enduring commitment to the guerilla mode of warfare.

Perhaps the richest legacy which the Nationalist period has bequeathed to the Communists in physical culture is in international athletics. The Far Eastern Championship Games was the strongest institution in Republican sports. It encouraged further international competition on a dual meet basis, and also helped prepare China for participation in the Olympic Games. The Communists have made full use of this legacy, and have engaged prominently in international competition. The length of time which they waited before withdrawing entirely from the Olympic movement, and the great effort which they expended as the moving force behind the Games of the New Emerging Forces (including underwriting the expenses of other nations) point to their positive commitment in this area.

Communist motives in international athletics are propagandist as well as ideological. They recognize that through sports they are able to enhance China's image abroad; hence, their heavy concentration on hosting other delegations at receptions during meets abroad. At the same time, they proclaim that traditionally, sports has been monopolized by "imperialist" countries. By promoting movements such as the GANEFO, which cater specifically to underdeveloped nations, they hope to provide an alternative to sports which has been dominated by "exploiting" societies, and thus present China as a true champion of oppressed people.

The one area where the Republican and the Communist experiences are least alike is in the ideological realm. The CCP physical culture program since 1949 has benefited from an ideological basis, many years in the making. Thus, from the very inauguration of the Communist regime, China has had a definite idea what her commitment to physical culture is.

The road that the Communists see as proper for physical culture is that which they see for all aspects of education and culture—a physical culture which is national, scientific, and mass oriented. Many interpretations have been given these three terms and we have given our analysis of them in these pages. What is important to note here is that none of these terms is mutually exclusive. Physical culture in its broadest sense must be geared to the good of the nation. As such, it must be based on scientific principles; it must be organized strongly on a national basis; and it must embrace people from diverse backgrounds. These three elements taken together, form a strong ideological bond from which physical culture on the Mainland draws its strength. It is this ideological framework woven into the very essence of the state which guarantees sports and physical culture an enduring future in the People's Republic of China.

Notes

PROLOGUE

1. Shih Chi-wen, *Sports Go Forward in China* (Peking, Foreign Languages Press, 1963), p. 1.
2. *Ibid.*; Tseng Wei-chi, "An Ancient Form of Physical Culture," *China Reconstructs*, 1955, Vol. 4, No. 8, pp. 27-28; and G. G. Tan, "A Review of the Development of Athletics in Chinese History," *China Today*, Vol. 2, No. 8 (August, 1959), pp. 82-91.
3. G. G. Tan, *ibid.*, and Tseng Wei-chi, *op. cit.*
4. G. G. Tan, *op. cit.*
5. Tseng Wei-chi; and Julius Eigner, "The Ancient Art of Chinese Boxing," *The China Journal*, Vol. 28, No. 1 (Jan. 1938), pp. 11-12.
6. Robert W. Smith, ed., *Secrets of Shaolin Temple Boxing* (Rutland, Vt., Charles E. Tuttle, 1964).
7. Eigner, *op. cit.*
8. Smith, *op. cit.*
9. "Chuan Shu," *China's Sports*, 1957, No. 1; G. G. Tan, *op. cit.*; Tseng Wei-chi, *op. cit.*; and "Traditional Sports in China," *People's China*, 1954, No. 1, pp. 17-23.
10. Boxing, nevertheless, did continue during the Ch'ing dynasty. For an example of a place where boxing existed during the Ch'ing, see Frederick Wakeman Jr., *Strangers at the Gate—Social Disorder in South China—1839-1861* (Berkeley, Univ. of California, 1966), p. 40.
11. Herbert A. Giles, "Football and Polo in China," *The Nineteenth Century and After*, Vol. 5 (March, 1906), pp. 508-513; G. G. Tan, *op. cit.*; and G. G. Tan, "Chinese Origins of Diverse Types of Ball Games," *China Today*, Vol. 2, No. 10 (October, 1959), pp. 71-75. The precise citations for these quotations are not given.

12. Giles, *op. cit.*
13. Edward H. Schafer, "Falconry in T'ang Times," *T'oung Pao*, 1958, Vol. 46, No. 3-5, pp. 293-338.
14. Shih Chi-wen, *Sports Go Forward in China, op. cit.*
15. G. G. Tan, "A Review of the Development of Athletics in Chinese History," *op. cit.*
16. Liu Hou-sheng, "Chinese Acrobats," *China Reconstructs*, 1954, Vol. 3, No. 1, pp. 23-27.

CHAPTER 1

1. Lo Jung-pang, ed., *K'ang Yu-wei—A Biography and a Symposium* (Tucson, University of Arizona, 1967), pp. 2-3.
2. Stuart R. Schram, *Une Étude de l'Éducation Physique* (Paris, Mouton, 1962), p. 27.
3. Benjamin I. Schwartz, *In Search of Wealth and Power—Yen Fu and the West* (Cambridge, Mass., Harvard, 1968), p. 86.
4. Wu Wen-chung, *T'i Yü Shih* (Taipei, Ku Li Pien Yi Kuan, 1962), pp. 321-325.
5. Wu Chih-kang, "The Influence of the Y.M.C.A. in the Development of Physical Education in China" (U. of Michigan, unpublished Ph.D. thesis, 1956), p. 55. Wu Yün-jui, "San Shih Wu Nien Lai Chung Kuo chih T'i Yü," in Chang Yüan-chi, ed., *Tsui Chin San Shih Wu Nien chih Chung Kuo Chiao Yü* (Shanghai, Commercial Press, 1931), pp. 225-241. Wu Wen-chung, *ibid.*
6. Wu Chih-kang, *op. cit.*, and Wu Wen-chung, *op. cit.*, pp. 321-325.
7. Kuo P'ing-wen, *The Chinese System of Public Education* (New York, Teachers College, 1914), p. 108.
8. *The China Yearbook*, 1916 (Tientsin, North China Daily News, 1916).
9. *Ibid.*, 1925-26.
10. Wu Chih-kang, *op cit.*
11. Wu Yün-jui, *op. cit.*
12. Martin Yang, *A Chinese Village* (New York, Columbia Univ., 1945), p. 24. A similar portrayal is presented in Lin Yüeh-hwa, *The Golden Wing—A Family Chronicle* (New York, Institute of Pacific Relations, 1944), p. 44.
13. Wu Yün-jui, *op. cit.*; Wu Wen-chung, *op. cit.*; and Hoh Gunsun, "T'i Yü," in Wu Chün-cheng, ed., *Chung Hua Min Kuo Chiao Yü Chih* (Taipei, Chung Hua Wen Hua Ch'u Pan Shih Yeh Wei Yüan Hui, 1955).
14. Wu Wen-chung, p. 351.
15. Wu Yün-jui, *op cit.*
16. Wu Wen-chung, pp. 321-325, 351-352.
17. *Ibid.*, pp. 330-337.
18. *China Mission Yearbook*, 1912 (Shanghai, Christian Literature Society), pp. 356-62.
19. Wu Yün-jui, *op. cit.*
20. Wu Chih-kang, p. 110.
21. *Ibid.*, p. 76.
22. *Ibid.*, pp. 89-91.
23. J. H. Gray, "The Present Status of Physical Education in China," *American Physical Education Review*, Vol. 31 (Dec., 1926), pp. 1169-74.
24. Wu Chih-kang, pp. 96-97.
25. C. H. Robertson, Report for the Year Ending Sept. 30, 1909.
26. Wu Chih-kang, p. 112.

27. *Ibid.*, pp. 115-116.
28. *Ibid.*
29. Max J. Exner, YMCA National Physical Director, Report for the Year Ending Sept. 30, 1910.
30. Max J. Exner, "Physical Training in China," *Physical Training*, Vol. VIII, No. 6 (April, 1911), p. 19.
31. *Ibid.*
32. *Ibid.*
33. Wu Wen-chung, p. 380.
34. Gunsun Hoh, *Physical Education in China* (Shanghai, Commercial Press, 1926), p. 96 and Max J. Exner, "Physical Training in China," *op cit.*
35. *North China Herald*, Oct. 28, 1910, pp. 221-2.
36. Wu Chih-kang, pp. 123-127.
37. *China Mission Yearbook*, 1912, p. 359.
38. *North China Herald*, May 16, 1914 and May 23, 1914, and Hoh, *op. cit.*, pp. 94-95.
39. Wu Wen-chung, p. 380.
40. Hoh, *op. cit.*, pp. 162-201, Wu Chih-kang, p. 122, and Wu Wen-chung, pp. 321-325.
41. Wu Chih-kang, *ibid.*
42. Hoh, pp. 162-201.
43. Hoh, *ibid.*, and *Chung Kuo T'i Yü Shih Ts'an K'ao Tzu Liao*, Vol. III (Peking, Jen Min T'i Yü Ch'u Pan She, 1958), pp. 98-108.
44. Hoh, *ibid.*
45. Kwei Chung-shu, ed., *The Chinese Yearbook*, 1935-36 (Shanghai, Commercial Press), pp. 550-551, and William Z. L. Sung, "The Development of Modern Athletics in China," *China Weekly Review* (Oct. 10, 1928 supplement), pp. 47-50.
46. Hoh, pp. 162-201.
47. *The Chinese Yearbook*, 1935-36, *op. cit.*
48. Hoh, pp. 162-201.
49. *Ibid.*
50. Hoh, pp. 201-207 and Wu Chih-kang, p. 160.
51. Wu Wen-chung, p. 410.
52. Hoh, p. 93.
53. *Ti Wu Chieh Ch'uan Yün Chuan Chi* (Shanghai, Hua Mei Shu T'u Shu Kung Szu, 1933).
54. Hoh, pp. 201-207, and Hoh Gunsun, "T'i Yü," in Wu Chün-sheng, ed., *Chung Hua Min Kuo Chiao Yü Chih* (Taipei, Chung Hua Wen Hua Ch'u Pan Shih Yeh Wei Yüan Hui, 1955).
55. Wu Chih-kang, p. 22.
56. Hoh, *Physical Education in China*, pp. 208-220.
57. George E. Goss, "Survey of Physical Education in YMCA's Around the World" (1923), p. 27. In the YMCA Historical Library.
58. A. H. Swan, Annual Report for the Year Ending Sept. 30, 1915.
59. A. H. Swan, Physical Director Shanghai YMCA, Annual Report for the Year Ending Sept. 30, 1913.
60. A. H. Swan, "Physical Education in a City Association," *China's Young Men*, Vol. XI, No. 10 (June 15, 1916), pp. 537-546.
61. Appendix III, Report of Statistics, Sept. 1, 1916-Aug. 31, 1917, Shanghai YMCA.
62. Hoh, *Physical Education in China*, pp. 208-220.
63. Goss, *op cit.*

64. J. H. Crocker, National YMCA Physical Director, Report for the Year Ending Sept. 30, 1915.
65. "Annual National Hexathlon Championships of the YMCA of China for 1923," mimeographed sheets in the YMCA Historical Library.
66. Wu Chih-kang, p. 150.
67. *Ibid.*, p. 156.
68. *Ibid.*, p. 118.
69. C. A. Siler, Physical Director Tientsin YMCA, Report for the Year Ending Sept. 30, 1915.
70. J. H. Crocker, National YMCA Physical Director, Report for the Year Ending Sept. 30, 1917.
71. C. H. McCloy, National YMCA Physical Director, Report for the Year Ending Sept. 30, 1914.
72. J. H. Gray, National YMCA Physical Director, Quarterly Report, April-June, 1923.
73. Wu Chih-kang, p. 144.
74. J. H. Crocker, Extract of a Report of January 10, 1917.
75. Letter from J. H. Crocker to John R. Mott, Feb. 5, 1917.
76. J. H. Crocker, National YMCA Physical Director, Report for the Year Ending Sept. 30, 1916.
77. "Circular of Information—School of Physical Education of the Association College of China," Autumn, 1918.
78. Wu Chih-kang, pp. 145-148.
79. Archives, YMCA Historical Library, box 24, folder b.
80. J. H. Gray, "History of the Physical Department in China," report of April 9, 1921.
81. Wu Chih-kang, p. 148.
82. Alfred H. Swan, "The Contribution of the Physical Department of the Young Men's Christian Association to the Christian Movement in China," in *China Mission Yearbook*, 1918, *op. cit.*, pp. 284-290.
83. Wu Chih-kang, pp. 96-97.
84. *Tientsin Young Men*, Vol. 2, No. 40 (Nov. 21, 1903), p. 4.
85. Swan, "The Contribution of the Physical Department . . . ," *op. cit.*
86. C. H. McCloy, National YMCA Physical Director, Report for the Year Ending Sept. 30, 1914.
87. A. N. Hoagland, Physical Director Peking YMCA, Report for the Year Ending Sept. 30, 1914.
88. Wu Chih-kang, pp. 141-144.
89. J. H. Crocker, National YMCA Physical Director, Report for the Year Ending Sept. 30, 1915, and Wu Chih-kang, p. 119.
90. Hoh, *Physical Education in China*, pp. 208-220, and J. H. Crocker, Report of Jan. 15, 1916.
91. J. H. Gray, National YMCA Physical Director, Quarterly Report, April-June, 1923.
92. J. H. Gray, Report of Oct. 30, 1923.
93. Wu Chih-kang, p. 178.
94. Letter from J. H. Crocker to E. C. Jenkins, Jan. 24, 1917. YMCA Historical Library.
95. J. H. Crocker, Report of Jan. 15, 1916.
96. *Chung Kuo T'i Yü Shih Ts'an K'ao Tzu Liao*, Vol. IV, *op. cit.*, pp. 61-62.

CHAPTER 2

1. Hoh, "T'i Yü," *op. cit.*
2. Wu Yün-jui, *op. cit.*
3. *China Mission Yearbook, op. cit.,* Chapter I, 1925, pp. 292-293.
4. Cyrus H. Peake, *Nationalism and Education in Modern China* (New York, Columbia U., 1932), pp. 83-84.
5. Hoh, "T'i Yü," pp. 5-6.
6. Wu Yün-jui, *op cit.*
7. Wu Wen-chung, pp. 344-349.
8. *Ibid.,* and *The Chinese Yearbook,* 1935-36, *op. cit.,* Chapter I, pp. 543-44.
9. H. G. W. Woodhead, ed., *The China Yearbook,* 1929-30 (Tientsin, North China Daily News), p. 521.
10. Wu Wen-chung, pp. 325-330.
11. Wang Hsüeh-cheng, *T'i Yüu Kai Lun* (Taipei, Taiwan Shang Wu Yin Shu Kuan, 1967), pp. 104-111.
12. *Ibid.,* pp. 95-99, and Wu Yün-jui, *op. cit.*
13. Wang Hsüeh-cheng, *op. cit.,* pp. 100-101.
14. Wu Wen-chung, pp. 325-330.
15. *Ibid.,* pp. 325-337.
16. *The China Yearbook,* 1933, p. 526.
17. *Ibid.; The Chinese Yearbook,* 1935-36, p. 542; and Chang Huei-lan, "A Collegation of Facts and Principles Basic to Sound Curriculum Construction for Physical Education in China" (U. of Iowa, unpublished doctoral dissertation, 1944), p. 14.
18. *The Chinese Yearbook,* 1935-36, pp. 541-553.
19. *Ibid.,* pp. 544-545.
20. Wu Wen-chung, pp. 330-337.
21. Wu Chih-kang, p. 175.
22. Wu Wen-chung, pp. 325-330.
23. *Ibid.,* pp. 330-337.
24. Wu Chih-kang, pp. 178-179.
25. *The Chinese Yearbook,* 1935-36, pp. 544-45.
26. Wu Wen-chung, pp. 325-330.
27. Wu Chih-kang, p. 182.
28. *North China Herald,* April 8, 1930, p. 45.
29. T'ang Leang-li, *Reconstruction in China* (Shanghai, China United Press, 1935), p. 104.
30. Wu Chih-kang, pp. 183-185, and *North China Herald,* Oct. 11, 1933, p. 67, Oct. 18, 1933, p. 106.
31. Wu Wen-chung, p. 419.
32. Wu Chih-kang, p. 185.
33. *North China Herald,* Oct. 9, 1935, p. 45.
34. Wu Chih-kang, p. 186.
35. Wu Wen-chung, pp. 424-25.
36. *Ibid.,* pp. 340-345, and Wu Chih-kang, pp. 189-190.
37. Hoh Gunsun, "T'i Yü," *op cit.,* pp. 38-39, and Wu Wen-chung, pp. 325-330.
38. Hoh, *ibid.*
39. Wu Wen-chung, pp. 337-340.
40. *Ibid.,* pp. 330-337.
41. Hoh, "T'i Yü," pp. 39-40.
42. Arthur N. Young, *China's Wartime Finance and Inflation, 1937-1945* (Cambridge, Mass., Harvard, 1965), p. 358.
43. Hoh, "T'i Yü," pp. 41-42.

CHAPTER 3

1. *Preliminary Announcement—Far Eastern Championship Games* (Shanghai, 1914), p. 5.
2. "The Story of the Far Eastern Athletic Association—A Record of Seven Years 1913-1920." Report in the archives of the YMCA Historical Library, box 38, folder K.
3. *Preliminary Announcement*, p. 5. Although the participation of Siam and the Malay States was approved very soon after the First Games, World War I made their participation impractical. Until Indian athletes participated in 1930, only athletes from China, Japan, and the Philippines were involved in the games.
4. William Tutherly, "The World at Play—A Program of Practical Athletics for the Millions." Report, YMCA Historical Library.
5. Gunsun Hoh, *Physical Education in China* (Shanghai, Commercial Press, 1926), p. 206.
6. *Preliminary Announcement*, p. 6.
7. Hoh, *op. cit.*, pp. 100-101.
8. The Far Eastern Championship Games were known originally as the Far Eastern Olympic Games. The word "Olympic" was subsequently changed to "Championship" before the 1915 Games at the request of the International Olympic Committee. Nevertheless, the term "Far Eastern Olympic Games" was popularly used throughout the history of the games and may be considered synonymous with it. Wu Wen-chung, *T'i Yü Shih* (Taipei, Ku Li Pien Yi Kuan, 1962), p. 400.
9. Hoh, p. 108.
10. Elwood S. Brown, "Far Eastern Olympic Games," *Physical Training*, Vol. 10 (April, 1913), pp. 173-174.
11. *Ibid.*, and Hoh, p. 108.
12. "Far Eastern Olympic Games," *North China Herald*, Vol. 106 (Jan. 25, 1913), p. 255.
13. "Far Eastern Olympic Games," *North China Herald*, Vol. 106 (Feb. 22, 1913), p. 540.
14. The Second Far Eastern Championship Games were originally to be held in the fall of 1914. The outbreak of World War I forced their postponement until May, 1915. From a July, 1914 report letter of J. H. Crocker in the YMCA archives.
15. *Ibid.*
16. Alfred H. Swan, Physical Director Shanghai YMCA, Annual Report for the Year Ending September 30, 1915, and Elwood S. Brown, "A Few Highlights of the Second Far Eastern Championship Games," report in the YMCA Historical Library.
17. J. H. Crocker, report letter of July, 1914, *op. cit.*
18. J. H. Crocker, YMCA National Physical Director, Annual Report for the Year Ending Sept. 30, 1915, and *ibid.*
19. J. H. Crocker, Annual Report for the Year Ending Sept. 30, 1915, and J. Wang-Quincy, "The Far Eastern Championship Games." *China's Young Men*, Vol. 10, No. 110 (June 15, 1915), pp. 423-432.
20. *Official Report of the Ninth Far Eastern Championship Games* (Tokyo, Japan Contest Committee FEAA, 1930), p. 70.
21. "The Far Eastern Olympiad," *North China Herald*, Vol. 115 (April 3, 1915), p. 44, and "The Far Eastern Olympic Games," *North China Herald*, Vol. 115 (May 22, 1915), pp. 530-534.

22. Elwood S. Brown, "A Few Highlights of the Second Far Eastern Championship Games," *op. cit.*
23. Swan, Report of Sept. 30, 1915, *op. cit.*
24. Franklin H. Brown, "The Third Far Eastern Championship Games," *Physical Training*, Vol. 14, No. 9 (Sept., 1917), pp. 386-393.
25. "The Story of the Far Eastern Athletic Association . . . ," *op. cit.*
26. Hoh, p. 114. Several sources mention the difficulty which the Filipino team had in adapting to the colder climate of Japan and cite this as a reason for the lack of a better showing by the Philippines.
27. "The Story of the Far Eastern Athletic Association . . . ," *op. cit.*
28. Brown, "The Third Far Eastern Championship Games," *op. cit.*
29. Hoh, pp. 115-116.
30. "The Story of Far Eastern Athletic Association . . . ," *op. cit.*
31. J. H. Gray, "Fifth Far Eastern Championship Games, Shanghai, 1921," report by the National Physical Director of the YMCA in China. YMCA Historical Library.
32. E. H. Lockwood, "Far Eastern Games at Shanghai," report of June, 1921. YMCA Historical Library.
33. Hoh, p. 120.
34. "The Far Eastern Games," *North China Herald*, Vol. 139 (June 11, 1921), p. 754.
35. Hoh, pp. 116-117.
36. Gray, "Fifth Far Eastern Championship Games," *op. cit.*
37. Wu Chih-kang, "The Influence of the Y.M.C.A. on the Development of Physical Education in China," *op. cit.* (see chapter 1). Gray, in his report, says that the profit was from $5,000 to $10,000.
38. "Chinese Girls to Be in Far Eastern Games," *Millard's Review of the Far East*, Vol. 16, No. 13 (May 28, 1921), p. 695.
39. Hoh, pp. 121-124 and Franklin H. Brown, "The Sixth Far Eastern Championship Games," *Physical Training*, Vol. 20, No. 10 (October, 1923), pp. 375-377.
40. Wu Wen-chung, *op. cit.*, p. 400.
41. Hoh, pp. 124-134.
42. Letter from E. Stanton Turner of the YMCA to C. A. Herschleb of the YMCA National Council, dated June 23, 1925. In YMCA Historical Library.
43. "The Far Eastern Olympiad," *North China Herald*, Vol. 155 (May 23, 1925), p. 333, and May 30, 1925, p. 387.
44. Wu Wen-chung, *op. cit.*, p. 404.
45. *Ibid.*
46. Private conversation with Mr. Charles Lo.
47. *Official Report of the Ninth Far Eastern Championship Games, op. cit.*, pp. 15-23.
48. "Far Eastern Games in Manila," *North China Herald*, Vol. 191 (May 23, 1934), pp. 277-278.
49. Japan had brought up the participation of Manchukuo a month before the holding of the games, but had been unable to get it approved. For a time she considered not competing in the Tenth Games at all, but finally decided to do so. "Far Eastern Olympiad Quarrels," *North China Herald*, Vol. 191 (April 18, 1934), p. 81.
50. "Result of Manila Games Quarrels," *North China Herald*, Vol. 191 (May 30, 1934), p. 318, and Wu Wen-chung, p. 402.
51. Statistics are from the following sources: Hoh, p. 131, John Kiernan and Arthur Daley, *The Story of the Olympic Games* (Philadelphia, J. B. Lip-

pincott Co., 1961), and *Story of the Ninth Far Eastern Championship Games, op. cit.*
52. Elwood S. Brown, "Report of the Relationship Established Between the Y.M.C.A. and the International Olympic Committee at Antwerp," Sept., 1920. In YMCA Historical Library.
53. Charles A. Siler, "Physical Education in China," *The Chinese Students' Christian Journal,* Vol. 6, No. 1 (Oct., 1919), pp. 28-30.
54. Wu Wen-chung, pp. 403-404, and Hoh, pp. 109-114.

CHAPTER 4

1. Edgar Snow, *Red Star Over China* (New York, Random House, 1938), p. 141.
2. Stuart R. Schram, *Une Étude de l'Éducation Physique* (Paris, Mouton, 1962), p. 27. This publication contains the original Chinese text.
3. *Ibid.,* p. 30; citing, *Hsin Ch'ing Nien,* Vol. 1, No. 2 (1915), p. 6.
4. *Chung Kuo T'i Yü Shih Ts'an K'ao Tzu Liao,* Vol. V (Peking, Jen Min T'i Yü Ch'u Pan She, 1958), pp. 1-11.
5. Schram, pp. 37-44. Original Chinese provided in text.
6. *Ibid.,* p. 44.
7. *Ibid.*
8. *Ibid.,* pp. 44-46.
9. *Ibid.,* pp. 47-50.
10. *Ibid.,* pp. 50-52.
11. *Ibid.,* pp. 52-56.
12. Snow, *op. cit.,* pp. 308-311.
13. "Ke Chung Ch'ih Se T'i Yü Kuei Tse" (Red Area Sports Rules), 1933. From archives of Ch'en Ch'eng collection, reel no. 5.
14. "Chinese Communists in Wartime, 1931-1949," *China's Sports,* 1959, No. 5, pp. 24-25.
15. Tse Chi, "Sports Activities in Yenan During the Anti-Japanese War," *China's Sports,* 1966, No. 6.
16. Wu Chiang-p'ing, "Yi Yen An" (Recalling Yenan), *Hsin T'i Yü,* 1957, No. 2, pp. 4-5.
17. Tse Chi, *op. cit.*
18. Wu Chiang-p'ing, *op. cit.*
19. "The First Revolutionary Physical Culture Department in Yenan," *China's Sports,* 1966, No. 6.
20. Tse Chi, *op. cit.*
21. *Hsin Min Chu Chu Yi te Kuo Min T'i Yü* (n.p., Chung Hua Ch'uan Kuo T'i Yü Tsung Hui Ch'in Pei Wei Yüan Hui Mi Shu Ch'u, 1949).
22. *Sheng Hsüeh Chih Tao, Kao Teng Hsüeh Hsiao Chao Sheng* (Chinese People's Republic Ministry of Higher Education, 1958), pp. 183-185. This text does not cite the source in Marx.
23. Henry W. Morton, *Soviet Sport* (New York, Collier Books, 1963), pp. 111-112, citing, I. M. Koriakoviskii, ed., *Teoriia Fizicheskogo Vospitaniia* (Moscow, Fizkultura i Sport, 1953), p. 26.
24. *Sheng Hsüeh Chih Tao, op. cit.,* pp. 183-185.
25. Morton, *op. cit.,* citing, E. A. Babaeva, *Fizicheskaia Kultura i Povyshenie Proizvoditelnosti Truda* (Moscow, Goskultprovetizdat, 1952), p. 7.
26. Li Ch'ao, *Hsüeh Hsiao Chung te T'i Yü* (Hupei, Jen Min Ch'u Pan She, 1956), pp. 1-6.
27. *Chiao Yü Hsüeh* (Nanking, Kiangsu Jen Min Ch'u Pan She, 1959), pp. 295-300. These quotations are presented here without citation. They are commonly seen on placards at mass sports meets.

Notes

28. Su Shih-yi, "Hsüeh Hsi T'i Yü Yen Chiu te Tien Ti T'i Hui" (A Little Understanding Through the Study of Physical Education Research), *Hsin T'i Yü*, 1960, No. 4.
29. *Sheng Hsüeh Chih Tao, op. cit.*, pp. 183-185. These quotations are provided without citation.
30. *Selections from China Mainland Magazines* (SCMM), No. 388, Sept., 1963, p. 16 and *Chiao Yü Hsüeh, op. cit.*, pp. 295-300.
31. C. T. Hu, ed., *Chinese Education Under Communism* (New York, Teachers College, Columbia University, 1962), p. 30.
32. *Hsin Min Chu Chu Yi te Kuo Min T'i Yü, op. cit.*, p. 3.
33. *Ibid.*, and *T'i Yü Kung Tso Che Hsüeh Hsi Ts'an K'ao Tzu Liao*, Vol. 1 (Hua Nan Ch'u Pan Pien Ch'u, 1950), pp. 29-32.
34. *SCMM*, No. 452, Dec., 1964, p. 22.
35. *T'i Yü Kung Tso Che Hsüeh Hsi Ts'an K'ao Tzu Liao, op. cit.*
36. *SCMM*, No. 217, June 1, 1960, p. 13.
37. *Ibid.*
38. Mao Tse-tung, *Selected Works*, Vol. II, Chinese version, p. 468.
39. *SCMM*, No. 477, June 14, 1965, pp. 14-29.
40. Li Chung-ch'uan, "Shen T'i Hao yü Kung Tso Hao te Pien Cheng Kuan Hsi" (The Dialectical Relationship Between Good Health and Good Work), *Hsin T'i Yü*, 1964, No. 7, p. 9.
41. *Survey of the China Mainland Press* (SCMP), No. 3505, July 4, 1965, p. 9.
42. *SCMM*, No. 477, *op. cit.*
43. *SCMP*, No. 3393, Dec. 23, 1964, p. 17.
44. *Hsin Min Chu Chu Yi te Kuo Min T'i Yü, op. cit.*
45. *SCMP*, No. 2922, January 30, 1963, pp. 5-6.
46. "T'i Yü Lao Tung Neng Tai T'i Yü Tuan Lien Ma?" (Can Physical Labor Take the Place of Physical Training?), *Wen Hui Pao*, April 2, 1958.
47. *SCMM*, No. 217, June 1, 1960, p. 13.
48. Jung Kao-t'ang, "Wei Kuo Min T'i Yü Yün Tung te P'u Chi ho Ching Ch'ang erh Fen Tou" (Let Us Struggle for the Popularization and Regularization of the People's Sports and Physical Culture), *Jen Min Shou Ts'e*, 1953 (Peking, Ta Kung Pao), pp. 373-375.
49. *T'i Yü Kung Tso Che . . . , op. cit.*
50. Jung, *op. cit.*
51. *Current Background*, No. 759, January 19, 1965, p. 10.
52. *A Glossary of Chinese Communist Terms and Phrases*, Joint Publication Research Service, 1966.
53. *SCMM*, No. 452, Dec., 1954, p. 22.

CHAPTER 5

1. *Jen Min Shou Ts'e* (People's Handbook), 1953 (Peking, Ta Kung Pao), pp. 377-378.
2. *T'i Yü Kung Tso Che Hsüeh Hsi Ts'an K'ao Tzu Liao, op. cit.*, see chapter 4.
3. *Fa Chan T'i Yü Yün Tung, Tseng Ch'iang Jen Min T'i Chih* (Peking, Ch'ing Nien Ch'u Pan She, 1952), p. 64.
4. *T'i Yü Kung Tso She Hsüeh Hsi Ts'an K'ao Tzu Liao, op. cit.*, pp. 90-91.
5. *Jen Min Shou Ts'e, op. cit.*, 1949, p. 15.
6. *Jen Min Shou Ts'e*, 1953, pp. 375-377.
7. *Intelligence Research Aid, Directory of Chinese Communist Officials*, March 1966, U.S. Department of State, and *Chuka Jinmin Kyōwakoku Soshiki Betsu Jinmei Hyō*, 1966 (Tokyo, Japanese Cabinet, 1966).

8. A. Doak Barnett, *Cadres, Bureaucracy, and Political Power in Communist China* (New York, Columbia Univ., 1967), pp. 48-70.
9. *Jen Min Shou Ts'e*, 1953, pp. 373-375 and *China's Sports.*
10. *Chuka Jinmei Kyōwakoku* . . . , *op. cit.*, 1959 and 1961.
11. *Jen Min Shou Ts'e*, 1965, pp. 140-141.
12. *Ibid.*, 1950; *Jen Min Shou Ts'e*, 1952, p. 257; and *Jen Min T'i Yü Yün Tung te Fang Chen yü Jen Wu* (Peking, Ch'ing Nien Ch'u Pan She, 1951).
13. Most of the information presented here has been gathered from the following sources: *Who's Who in Communist China* (Hong Kong, Union Research Service, 1966); American Consulate General Biographical and Organizational Files on microfilm; *Intelligence Research Aid*, 1966, *op. cit.; Directory of Party and Government Officials of Communist China*, 1960, U.S. Department of State; *Chuka Jinmei Kyowakoku* . . . , *op. cit.; Genzai Chugoku Jinmei Jiten* (Tokyo, Zaidan Hōjin Kasumisankai, 1966).
14. *Ibid.*
15. *T'i Yü Kung Tso Che Hsüeh Hsi Ts'an K'ao Tzu Liao, op. cit.*
16. *Intelligence Research Aid,* March, 1966, *op. cit.*
17. American Consulate General Organizational File, microfilm.
18. Barnett, *op. cit.*, pp. 274-275.
19. *Intelligence Research Aid*, March, 1966, and *Chuka Jinmei Kyōwakoku* . . . , *op. cit.*
20. *Jen Min Jih Pao,* November 18, 1954, in John W. Lewis, *Leadership in Communist China* (Ithaca, N. Y., Cornell U., 1963), p. 143.
21. Wang Chang-ling, "Kung Fei Chao K'ai T'i Yü Kung Tso Hui Yi" (Communists Convene a Physical Culture Work Conference), *Fei Ch'ing Yüeh Pao*, Vol. 8, No. 3 (April 30, 1965), pp. 29-34.
22. Interview that I conducted in April, 1969.

CHAPTER 6

1. *Jen Min T'i Yü Yün Tung te Fang Chen yü Jen Wu* (Peking, Ch'ing Nien Ch'u Pan She, 1951).
2. C. T. Hu, ed., *Chinese Education Under Communism* (New York, Teachers College, Columbia Univ., 1962), p. 26.
3. Chang Chih-hsüeh, "Tsen Yang Tsai T'i Yü Hsüeh Chung Yün Yung Su Lien te Chiao Yü Fang Fa" (How to Apply the Soviet Union's Educational Methods in the Study of Physical Education), *Jen Min Chiao Yü* (JMCY), 1953, No. 4, pp. 56-57.
4. Su Ch'ing-ts'un, "Hsüeh Hsi Su Lien Hsüeh Hsiao T'i Yü te Hsien Chin Ching Yen, Ming Ch'üeh Chung Hsiao Hsüeh T'i Yü Kai Ke" (Study the Progressive Experience of the Soviet Union's School Physical Education, Understand More Clearly the Reform of Primary and Middle School Physical Education), *JMCY*, 1954, No. 7, pp. 68-69.
5. "T'i Yü Shih Kung Ch'an Chu I Chiao Yü Pu K'e Fen Ke te Pu Fen" (Physical Education Is an Inseparable Aspect of Communist Education), *Hsin T'i Yü* (HTY), 1957, No. 2, pp. 9-10.
6. Su Ch'ing-ts'un, *op. cit.*
7. Chang Chih-hsüeh, *op. cit.*
8. *Hsiao Hsüeh Chiao Shih*, 1955, No. 5, p. 31, and *Chiao Yü Hsüeh* (Nanking, Kiangsu Jen Min Ch'u Pan She, 1959), pp. 143-144.
9. Li Ch'ao, *Hsüeh Hsiao Chung te T'i Yü* (Hupei, Jen Min Ch'u Pan She, 1956), pp. 1-6.
10. *SCMM*, No. 434, July 6, 1964, p. 34.

11. *Chiao Yü Hsüeh, op. cit.,* pp. 306-309.
12. *Ibid.,* pp. 300-306.
13. Interview of Refugees, Dec., 1963. By permission of author Ezra Vogel.
14. *Chiao Yü Hsüeh,* pp. 300-306.
15. Interviews of Refugees, Ezra Vogel, Jan., 1963, Dec., 1963.
16. *SCMP,* No. 837, June 26, 1954, p. 54.
17. "Hsiao Hsüeh Wei Shemma Pu T'ui Hsing 'Lao Wei Chih'" (Why Don't Primary Grades Push the "Labor-Defense System"), *HTY,* 1957, No. 6, p. 26.
18. New China News Agency (NCNA), November 14, 1958.
19. "Women Tsen Yang Chih Ting Chiao Yü Chi Hua" (How We Formulate Education Plans), *HTY,* 1957, No. 2, pp. 26-27.
20. *Fei Ch'ing Yüeh Pao—Yearbook on Chinese Communism* (in Chinese), 1967 (Taipei, Institute for the Study of Chinese Communist Problems), pp. 1336-37.
21. Sun Ming-yi, "T'i Yü K'e Tsen Yang Chin Hsing Ssu Hsiang Chiao Yü" (How Physical Education Courses Can Advance Thought Education), *HTY,* 1960, No. 2, p. 25, and "Tsen Yang Tsai T'i Yü K'e Li Chin Hsing Ssu Hsiang Chiao Yü" (How to Advance Thought Education in Physical Education Courses), *HTY,* 1958, No. 18.
22. "Tsen Yang Tsai T'i Yü K'e Chung Kuan Ch'e Cheng Chih Ssu Hsiang Chiao Yü" (How to Inject Political Thought Education into Physical Education Courses), *JMCY,* 1953, No. 4, pp. 55-56.
23. *Chiao Yü Hsüeh,* pp. 300-306.
24. Refugee interviews by Ezra Vogel, Dec., 1963.
25. *SCMP,* No. 2978, April 18, 1963, pp. 12-13.
26. *Chiao Yü Hsüeh,* pp. 300-306.
27. *SCMM,* No. 440, July 6, 1964, pp. 22-28.
28. "Tsen Yang Tsu Chih K'e Wai Huo Tung" (How to Organize Extracurricular Activities), *HTY,* 1959, No. 7, p. 30, and Chang Hsi-liang, "Tsu Chih K'e Wai T'i Yü Huo Tung te Pan Fa" (Methods of Organizing Extracurricular Physical Education Activities), *HTY,* 1959, No. 8, p. 30.
29. "Tui Hsüeh Hsiao K'e Wai T'i Yü Huo Tung te Chi Tien I Chien" (Several Opinions on Extracurricular School Physical Education Activities), *HTY,* 1957, No. 3, p. 13.
30. *SCMM,* No. 440, July 6, 1964, pp. 22-28. *op. cit.*
31. "Simplified Regulations Governing the Organization of the Physical Culture and Sports Commission," Joint Publication Research Service (JPRS) No. 14,673, pp. 51-53.
32. *Chung Hua Jen Min Kung Ho Kuo T'i Yü Yün Tung Wen Chien Hui Pien* (Peking, Jen Min T'i Yü Ch'u Pan She, 1957), pp. 143-145; and "Chiao Yü Pu, Kuan Yü 1957 Nien Hsueh Hsiao T'i Yü Kung Tso te Chi Tien I Chien te T'ung Chih" (Several Notes from the Ministry of Education on Opinions Regarding 1957 School Physical Education Work), *Kuo Wu Yüan Pao,* 1957, No. 12, pp. 230-235.
33. *Compendium of Laws and Regulations of the People's Republic of China,* Vol. 3 (Peking, 1956), in JPRS No. 14,673, pp. 731-743.
34. Ch'eng Tzu-li, "San ke Pai Fen chih Pai Shih Tsen Yang Te Lai te" (How Can You Get 300%), *HTY,* 1958, No. 19, pp. 14-19.
35. Chang Yi, "Ch'ing Hua T'i Yü Shih Nien" (Ten Years of Physical Education at Tsinghua), *HTY,* 1959, No. 18, pp. 17-20.
36. Feng Wen-pin, *Pa Hsin Chung Kuo te T'i Yü Yün Tung Ch'eng Wei Ching Ch'ang te Kuang Fa te Yün Tung* (Peking, Ch'ing Nien Ch'u Pan She, 1951), p. 75.

37. *Sheng Hsüeh Chih Tao, 1954 Nien Shu Ch'i Kao Teng Hsüeh Hsiao Chao Sheng* (Peking, Commercial Press, 1954), p. 165.
38. *Su E chi Ch'i Fu Yung Chi T'uan T'i Yü Shih Kuang Fa Chan Shih K'uang chih Yen Hsi* (Taiwan, Ssu Fa Hsing Cheng Pu Tiao Ch'a Chu, 1958), p. 100.
39. "Chiao T'i Yü Yu Mei Yu Ch'ien T'u" (Is There Any Future in Teaching Physical Education?), *HTY*, 1958, No. 2, pp. 11-12.
40. *Sheng Hsüeh Chih Tao, Kao Teng Hsüeh Hsiao Chao Sheng* (Chinese People's Republic, Ministry of Higher Education, 1958), pp. 118-119.
41. *Ibid.*, p. 185.
42. *Fei Ch'ing Yüeh Pao—Yearbook on Chinese Communism*, 1967, *op. cit.*, pp. 1335-1337.
43. "Pao K'ao T'i Yü Yüan Hsiao te Chi ke Wen T'i" (Problems in Taking Entrance Examinations for Physical Culture Institutes and Schools), *HTY*, 1957, No. 10, p. 29.
44. Refugee interviews by Ezra Vogel, April, 1964.
45. *T'ou K'ao Ta Hsüeh Chih Tao* (Hong Kong Student Book Co., 1954), p. 64.
46. *Sheng Hsüeh Chih Tao*, 1958, *op. cit.*, p. 185.
47. "Pao K'ao T'i Yü Yüan Hsiao te Chi ke Wen T'i," *op. cit.*
48. *Sheng Hsüeh Chih Tao*, 1958, *op. cit.*, p. 185, and *Fei Ch'ing Yüeh Pao*, *op. cit.*
49. *Jen Min Shou Ts'e*, 1963, pp. 418-420, and *SCMP*, No. 3350, Dec. 1, 1964, p. 16.
50. *SCMP*, No. 1311, June 13, 1956, p. 17.
51. *SCMP*, No. 2010, April 19, 1959, p. 4.
52. *Pei Ching T'i Yü Hsüeh Yüan* (Peking, Jen Min T'i Yü Ch'u Pan She, 1956), and *Jen Min Shou Ts'e*, 1963, pp. 418-420.
53. *SCMP*, No. 922, Nov. 3, 1954, p. 29, and No. 3095, Nov., 1963, p. 23.
54. Shih Chi-wen, *Sports Go Forward in China* (Peking, Foreign Languages Press, 1963), p. 10.
55. *SCMP*, No. 2417, Jan. 10, 1961, p. 15.
56. *Sheng Hsüeh Chih Tao*, 1958, pp. 118-119.
57. *Ibid.*, and *SCMP*, No. 3539, Sept., 1965, p. 20.
58. *Kung Fei Chung Teng Chiao Yü chih Yen Chiu*, p. 31.
59. "Pao K'ao T'i Yü Yüan Hsiao te Chi ke Wen T'i," *op. cit.*
60. *Kung Fei Chung Teng Chiao Yü chih Yen Chiu*, p. 207.
61. Tung Nien-li, "Pa Ch'ing Shao Nien Yeh Yü T'i Yü Pan te Keng Hao" (Do Better Work With Youth Spare-time Physical Education), *HTY*, 1964, No. 1, pp. 17-19.
62. "Kuan Yü Yeh Yü T'i Yu Hsueh Hsiao te Wen Chien" (Documents Relating to Spare-time Physical Education Schools), in *Chung Hua Jen Min Kung Ho Kuo T'i Yü Yün Tung Wen Chien Hui Pien*, 1957, *op. cit.*, pp. 151-158; and "Shemma Shih Ch'ing Nien ho Shao Nien Yeh Yü T'i Yü Hsüeh Hsiao" (What Are Teenage and Youth Spare-time Physical Education Schools?), *HTY*, 1957, No. 4, p. 32.
63. *HTY*, *ibid.*
64. *SCMP*, No. 1880, October 18, 1958, p. 33.
65. *SCMP*, No. 1670, December, 1957, p. 3.
66. NCNA, October 22, 1958.
67. *SCMP*, No. 2026, May, 1959, p. 4.
68. "Young Athletes Get a Start," *China's Sports*, 1960, No. 1.
69. Tung Nien-li, *op. cit.*

70. Wang Tseng-hua, "Shihchahai Junior Spare-time Athletic School," *China's Sports,* 1959, No. 4, pp. 11-12.
71. "Chiao T'i Yü Yu Mei Yu Ch'ien T'u," *op. cit.,* and "Notification of the Committee for Physical Culture Concerning In-Service Training of Physical Culture Instructors in 1956," JPRS No. 14,763, pp. 746-51.

CHAPTER 7

1. "Chinese Communists in Wartime 1931-1949," *China's Sports* (CS), 1959, No. 5, pp. 24-25.
2. *Jen Min Shou Ts'e,* 1959, p. 267.
3. "T'i Yü Yün Tung Chih Shih, Shemma Shih Lao Wei Chih" (Physical Culture and Sports Information, What Is the Labor-Defense System?), *Kuang Chou Jih Pao,* June 22, 1956.
4. *Jen Min Shou Ts'e,* 1952, pp. 456-460.
5. *SCMP,* No. 748, Feb. 9, 1954, p. 14.
6. See note 3, and *Ibid.*
7. "Joint Directive for Launching the Mass Sports Movement in Institutes of Learning Above the Middle School Standard," *Huang Ming Jih Pao,* May 4, 1956, in "Compulsory Sports and Physical Training," Union Research Service, Vol. 4, No. 17 (August 28, 1956), pp. 245-262.
8. "Shemma Shih Lao Wei Chih" (What Is the Labor Defense System?), *T'ieh Tao Chien She* (Railroad Construction), June 12, 1956. Translation my own.
9. "Kuan yü Lao Wei Chih Cheng Chang, Cheng Shu Chi ke Wen T'i te Ta Fu" (Response to Several Questions Regarding the Labor-Defense System Badges and Certificates), *Kuang Ming Jih Pao,* May 4, 1955.
10. "We Must Not Ask Too Much and Expect Quick Results from the Preparation for Labor and National Defense System," *Huang Ming Jih Pao,* July 3, 1956, in "Compulsory Sports and Physical Training," *op. cit.*
11. "How Did Li Yüan-hua Die?" and "Let the Labor-Defense System Be Implemented Objectively and Practically Through a Gradual Course," *Chung Kuo Ch'ing Nien Pao,* June 16, 1956 and July 16, 1956 respectively, in "Compulsory Sports and Physical Training," *op. cit.*
12. Su Ch'ing-ts'un, "Ju Ho Yi Lao Wei Chih Wei Chung Hsin Kai Chin Chung Teng Hsüeh Hsiao T'i Yü K'e ho K'e Wai T'i Yü Huo Tung (How Come We Should Concentrate on the Labor-Defense System to Advance Middle School Physical Education Courses and Extracurricular Sports Activity), *Jen Min Chiao Yü,* September, 1955.
13. "It Is Necessary to Push Ahead the Labor-Defense System," *HTY,* 1956, No. 14 (July 21, 1956), in "Compulsory Sports and Physical Training," *op. cit.*
14. *SCMP,* No. 1881, October 20, 1958, p. 18.
15. "Regulations Governing the System of Physical Culture for Labor and National Defense," *SCMP,* No. 1899, Oct. 20, 1958, p. 9.
16. *SCMP,* No. 1899, Oct. 20, 1958, p. 11.
17. "Chung Hua Jen Min Kung Ho Kuo Lao Tung Wei Kuo T'i Yü Chih Tu Shao Nien Chi Hsiang Mu Piao Chun" (Standards for the Youth Stage of the Labor-Defense System of the Chinese People's Republic), *Chung Kuo Ch'ing Nien Pao,* October 27, 1958.
18. *Ibid.,* and "Chung Hua Jen Min Kung Ho Kuo Lao Tung Wei Kuo T'i Yü Chih Tu Ehr Chi Hsiang Mu Piao Chun" (Standards for the Second Stage of the Labor-Defense System of the Chinese People's Republic), *Chung Kuo Ch'ing Nien Pao,* Oct. 27, 1958.

19. *SCMP*, No. 1899, Oct. 20, 1958, p. 11.
20. *SCMP*, No. 1899, Oct. 26, 1958, p. 14.
21. *SCMP*, No. 1963, Feb. 21, 1959, p. 32.
22. The term "mass sports" does not seem to be well defined as to the exact nature of its contents. It is clear that this term has a broader scope than "national defense physical culture." I might be reading a little bit too much into it, but it seems to me that there is a definite implication of "usefulness for national defense" in the Chinese usage of "mass sports" (ch'ün chung hsing t'i yü).
23. Jung Kao-t'ang, "Let Physical Culture Better Serve Socialist Construction," *Hung Ch'i*, in SCMM, No. 217, June 1, 1960, p. 13.
24. Tsai Shu-fang, "The Springtime of Physical Culture and Sports in China," *China's Sports* (CS), 1958, No. 5, pp. 2-3.
25. "Sports in a Factory," *CS*, 1958, No. 2, pp. 8-9.
26. Lin Chung-yu, "Sports in the Countryside," *CS*, 1959, No. 5, pp. 28-31.
27. "Kuang Fan K'ai Chan Nung Ts'un Jen Min Kung She te T'i Yü Huo Tung" (Extensively Develop the Sports Activities of the Rural People's Communes), *HTY*, No. 171 (March 21, 1960), pp. 1-3.
28. "Sports Activities Widespread in Rural Areas," *SCMP*, No. 1847, Sept. 1, 1958, p. 17.
29. "China's 1958 Sports Year in Retrospect," *SCMP*, No. 1927, Dec. 26, 1958, p. 31.
30. "A Sporting People's Commune," *CS*, 1959, No. 2, p. 12.
31. *SCMP*, No. 2978, April 18, 1963, pp. 12-13.
32. *Jen Min Shou Ts'e*, 1965.
33. "Develop the Mass Movement for Defense Training," *Jen Min Jih Pao*, in *SCMP*, No. 1257, March 7, 1956, p. 5.
34. *Jen Min Shou Ts'e*, 1965.
35. *SCMP*, No. 1490, Feb. 26, 1957, p. 6.
36. Franz Schurmann, *Ideology and Organization in Communist China* (Berkeley, University of California Press, 1966), pp. 480-1.
37. "Summer Military Camps for Students and Workers," Union Research Service, Vol. 36, No. 12 (August 11, 1964), pp. 174-188.
38. "Everyone a Soldier Movement," Union Research Service, Vol. 13, No. 2 (October 7, 1958), p. 16.
39. "Field Camping in Communist China," Union Research Service, Vol. 22, No. 21 (March 14, 1961), pp. 323-340.
40. "Summer Military Camps for Students and Workers," *op. cit.*
41. "Field Camping in Communist China," *op. cit.*
42. "Sports for National Defense," *CS*, 1958, No. 5, pp. 12 and 17.
43. *SCMP*, No. 3434, March 19, 1965, p. 20 and *SCMP*, No. 3612, Dec. 22, 1965, pp. 2-4.
44. *SCMP*, No. 3454, April 17, 1965, pp. 2-4.
45. Jung Kao-t'ang, *op. cit.* (note 23).
46. Chao Cheng-hung, "Do a Still Better Job of Physical Culture for National Defense," *HTY*, in *SCMM*, No. 362, March 6, 1963, p. 37.
47. "Improve the Physique of the People and Turn Out Intellectually and Physically Capable Personnel," *Jen Min Jih Pao*, in *SCMP*, No. 3279, July 25, 1964, p. 11.
48. *SCMP*, No. 2054, July 7, 1959, p. 29.
49. "Improve the Physique of the People and Turn Out Intellectually and Physically Capable Personnel," *op. cit.*
50. *SCMP*, No. 3454, April 17, 1965.
51. Fang Ch'en, "Fly High in the Sky—A General Picture of the Booming

Growth of Gliding Activity in Our Country," *T'i Yü Pao*, in *SCMP*, No. 3424, March 10, 1965, p. 14.
52. "Sports for National Defense," *CS, op. cit.*
53. "Actively Develop Amateur Gliding and Foster Militia Airmen," *T'i Yü Pao*, in *SCMP*, No. 3368, Dec. 4, 1964, pp. 6-7; and "Spare-time Gliding for Young People Must Be Run Properly," *T'i Yü Pao*, in *SCMP*, No. 3538, August 27, 1965, p. 21.
54. Fang Ch'en, *op. cit.*
55. "Modern Air Sports in Ancient Chinese Capital (Sian)," *SCMP*, No. 2778, July 11, 1962, p. 16.
56. "Sports for National Defense," *op. cit.*
57. "China's Largest Aviation Club in Peking," *SCMP*, No. 2710, March 27, 1962, p. 16.
58. Edgar Snow, *Red Star Over China* (New York, Random House, 1938).
59. Wang Ming-li, "Swimming Is a Kind of Ability to Win a War," *SCMP*, No. 3542, Sept. 1, 1965, p. 13.
60. "Mass Swimming," Union Research Service, Vol. 43, No. 20 (June 7, 1966), pp. 294-309.
61. "Mao Tse-tung Swims Across the Yangtse," Union Research Service, Vol. 44, No. 13 (August 12, 1966), pp. 183-199; and Yang Yung, "Swimming in the Ming Tombs Reservoir with Chairman Mao and Chairman Liu," *Hsin T'i Yü*, 1965, No. 6, in *SCMM*, No. 489, June 6, 1965, p. 27.
62. "Sports Activities Widespread in Rural Areas," *op. cit.*
63. "Mass Swimming," *op. cit.*
64. *SCMP*, No. 1838, August 15, 1958, p. 28.
65. The same point is made by Wang Chang-ling, "Kung Fei Chao K'ai T'i Yü Kung Tso Hui Yi" (Communists Convene a Physical Culture Work Conference), *Fei Ch'ing Yüeh Pao*, Vol. 8, No. 3 (April 30, 1965), pp. 29-34.
66. "Tang te Tsung Lu Hsien Tsai T'i Yü Chan Hsien Shang te Hui Huang Sheng Li" (The Party's General Line in the Glorious Victory of the Physical Culture Front), *HTY*, No. 160 (Oct. 6, 1959), pp. 1-2.
67. "Spare-time Sports Schools for Chinese Children," *SCMP*, No. 2510, May 30, 1961, p. 27.
68,. Jung, *op. cit.* (note 23), and "Launch Physical Training for the People's Militia and National Defense Movement on a Large Scale," *SCMP*, No. 2267, February 21, 1960, pp. 4-6.
69. *SCMP*, No. 2978, April 18, 1963, pp. 12-13.
70. *Who's Who in Communist China* (Hong Kong, Union Research Service, 1966), pp. 48-49.
71. Chao Cheng-hung, *op. cit.*
72. Hu K'e-shih, "Let the Whole League Do Physical Culture Work," *Chung Kuo Ch'ing Nien Pao*, in *SCMP*, No. 3234, May 12, 1964, p. 14.
73. "Improve the Physique of the People and Turn Out Intellectually and Physically Capable Personnel," *op. cit.*
74. "Promote Revolutionization of Youth by Vigorously Developing Military Sports," *Chung Kuo Ch'ing Nien Pao*, in *SCMP*, No. 3435, March 25, 1965, p. 7; and *SCMP*, No. 3393, Dec. 25, 1964, pp. 15-16.
75. "Summer Military Camps for Students and Workers," *op. cit.*
76. *SCMP*, No. 3435, March 25, 1965, pp. 9-11.
77. "One Should Join in Military Physical Education Activity with Enemy Activity in Mind," *Chung Kuo Ch'ing Nien Pao*, in *SCMP*, No. 3454, p. 1.
78. *SCMP*, No. 3462, May 17, 1965, p. 17.
79. *SCMP*, No. 3495, June 18, 1965, p. 10.
80. Hung Chou, "An Account of Military Sports Activities Conducted at

Tsinghua University," *HTY,* 1965, No. 5, in *SCMM,* No. 479, May 6, 1965, p. 8.
81. *SCMP,* No. 3469, May 13, 1965, p. 2.
82. *SCMP,* No. 3585, Nov. 21, 1965, p. 13.
83. "China Calls for Nationwide Promotion of Swimming Activities," *SCMP,* No. 3467, May 23, 1965, p. 18.
84. "Mass Swimming," *Peking Review,* Vol. 8, No. 23 (June 4, 1965), p. 4.
85. Yang Yung, *op. cit.*
86. *SCMP,* No. 3467, May 23, 1965, p. 18.
87. "Mass Swimming," *Peking Review, op. cit.*
88. "Mass Swimming Along China's Coasts and Rivers," *SCMP,* No. 3469, May 27, 1965, p. 3.
89. *SCMP,* No. 3474, June 5, 1965, p. 13.
90. "Height of Swimming Season in Peking," *SCMP,* No. 3478, June 12, 1965, p. 15.
91. *SCMP,* No. 3479, May 23, 1965, pp. 12-13.
92. "Mass Swimming," Union Research Service, *op. cit.* (note 60).
93. "On the Lane Charted by Chairman Mao," *HTY,* 1966, No. 7-8, in *SCMM,* No. 552, August 24, 1966, p. 14, and *SCMP,* No. 3752, July 28, 1966, p. 20.
94. *The New York Times Official Sports Record Book* (New York, Bantam, 1967), p. 267.
95. "Mass Swimming," Union Research Service, *op. cit.*
96. See note 27.
97. Detailed information is not available on Lin and Chao Chün-yi.
98. *Who's Who in Communist China, op. cit.,* and U.S. Consulate General microfilm biographical file.
99. See note 66.
100. *SCMP,* No. 3561. October 4, 1965, p. 21.
101. "Fan Tang Ts'uan Chün Fan Ke Ming Hsiu Cheng Chu I Fen tzu Ho Lung te Tsui Hsing" (The Crime of the Anti-Party, Anti-Military, Anti-Revolutionary, Revisionist Ho Lung), *T'i Yü Chan Hsien,* No. 8-9 (joint issue), Feb. 9, 1967. Translated by Hsü Wen-hsiung.

CHAPTER 8

1. *Chung Kuo T'i Yü Shih Ts'an K'ao Tzu Liao,* Vol. I (Peking, Jen Min T'i Yü Ch'u Pan She, 1957).
2. Chi Ying, "Ts'ung Kuo Chi Ching Sai K'an Chung Kuo T'i Yü te Yüeh Chin" (Looking at China's Leap Forward in Sports from the Point of View of International Competition), *Chung Kuo Hsin Wen T'ung Hsün Kao),* January 20, 1959.
3. *Chung Kuo Ch'ing Nien Pao,* May 27, 1956.
4. *SCMP* (Survey of the China Mainland Press), No. 389, August 2, 1952.
5. *SCMP,* No. 863, Aug. 5, 1954, pp. 5-6, Aug. 6-8, 1954, p. 23.
6. *SCMP,* No. 3917, April 9, 1967, p. 41.
7. Of the 25 members of the Chinese Olympic Committee before 1949, 19 fled to Taiwan in 1949. From minutes of the IOC meeting in Helsinki, Finland, July, 1952—received through correspondence with the IOC.
8. *The New York Times,* Feb. 14, 1952, p. 33.
9. After receiving this initial correspondence from Communist China, the IOC immediately contacted all of the international sports organizations to see if Communist China was affiliated with them. (To compete in an Olympic event, a nation must belong to the international organization which governs that event.) It was found that Communist China was only

affiliated with the basketball and swimming federations. From IOC documents.
10. *The New York Times*, Feb. 18, 1952, p. 22.
11. From documents received from the IOC and *The New York Times*, June 18, 1952, p. 37.
12. *The New York Times*, June 25, 1952, p. 36.
13. *Ibid.*, July 3, 1952, p. 21, and July 11, 1952, p. 21.
14. Ho Gun-sun, representing Taiwan, and Sheng Chih-pai, representing the Mainland, both appeared at this meeting, and each asked that the other's country be excluded from the Olympics.

    The vote to accept athletes from both countries was deemed "provisional" by the IOC Executive Committee pending "a precise determination of the international status of both countries." From IOC minutes of the July, 1952 meeting.
15. *The New York Times*, July 19, 1952, p. 9.
16. *Ibid.*, July 21, 1952, p. 23.
17. *SCMP*, No. 375, July 15, 1952.
18. *The New York Times*, July 24, 1952, p. 22; July 26, 1952, p. 17; and July 30, 1952, p. 26.
19. *Ibid.*, July 22, 1952, p. 30.
20. *SCMP*, No. 388, July 30, 1952 and No. 389, August 2, 1952.
21. *The New York Times*, August 1, 1952, p. 10.
22. *Ibid.*, July 29, 1952, p. 24.
23. *SCMP*, No. 390, August 6, 1952.
24. *The New York Times*, August 21, 1953, p. 36.
25. *Ibid.*, May 15, 1954, p. 1.

    On April 9, 1954, Jung Kao-t'ang sent a letter to Avery Brundage of the IOC asking to have the IOC "settle the question of uninterrupted recognition of our status on the International Olympic Committee" at the May 14, 1954, meeting of the IOC. A Constitution of the Chinese Olympic Committee was also sent to the IOC at this time. Strangely enough, the Chinese asked the Olympic ommittee of the Soviet Union to forward these documents to the IOC rather than doing so themselves.
26. *The New York Times*, May 15, 1954, p. 1.
27. *Ibid.*, Nov. 2, 1954, p. 35; and Dec. 22, 1954, p. 31.
28. *SCMP*, No. 992, Feb. 19, 1955, p. 28.
29. *SCMP*, No. 1067, June 10, 1955, p. 17 and June 12, 1955, p. 17.
30. *Ibid.*
31. *SCMP*, No. 1069, June 14, 1955, p. 21.
32. *SCMP*, No. 1180, Nov. 29, 1955, p. 47.
33. *The New York Times*, Nov. 22, 1955, p. 43.
34. *SCMP*, No. 1223, February 1, 1956, p. 24.
35. *SCMP*, No. 1252, March 18, 1956, p. 40.
36. *SCMP*, No. 1278, April 25, 1956, p. 35.
37. *SCMP*, No. 1323, July 2, 1956, p. 42.
38. *SCMP*, No. 1364, Sept. 1, 1956, p. 10.
39. *The New York Times*, October 19, 1956, p. 30.
40. *SCMP*, No. 1367, Sept. 2, 1956, p. 10.
41. *SCMP*, No. 1387, October 6, 1956, p. 5 and No. 1395, October 20, 1956, p. 4.
42. *SCMP*, No. 1398, Oct. 23, 1956, p. 31, and No. 1395, Oct. 20, 1956, pp. 4-5.
43. *SCMP*, No. 1397, Oct. 22, 1956, p. 30.
44. *SCMP*, No. 1398, Oct. 23, 1956, p. 29.
45. *SCMP*, No. 1407, Nov. 4, 1956, p. 41.

46. *SCMP,* No. 1408, Nov. 6, 1956, p. 25.
47. *The New York Times,* Oct. 30, 1956, p. 49.
48. *SCMP,* No. 1408, Nov. 6, 1956, p. 26.
49. New China News Agency (NCNA), Nov. 3, 1956.
50. NCNA, Nov. 18, 1956.
51. *SCMP,* No. 1453, Jan. 15, 1957, p. 34.
52. *SCMP,* No. 1615, Sept. 18, 1957, p. 52. At this meeting, Tung Shou-yi of the All-China Athletic Federation requested that the misnaming of his country (it had been called the "Democratic People's Republic of China") be rectified in the IOC minutes. (From minutes of the September, 1957 Sofia meeting of the IOC.)
53. *The New York Times,* September 11, 1957, p. 10.
54. *Ibid.,* Sept. 18, 1957, p. 1.
55. *SCMP,* No. 1734, March 15, 1958, p. 38.
56. Made available by the International Olympic Committee, Lausanne, Switzerland.
57. *SCMP,* No. 1839, August 20, 1958, p. 55.
58. *China's Sports,* 1958, No. 3, p. 2, and *SCMP,* No. 1790, June 9, 1958, p. 46.
59. Made available by the IOC.
60. *SCMP,* No. 1839, August 20, 1958, p. 57.
61. Made available by the IOC.
62. *Ibid.*
63. *Ibid.*
64. *Ibid.*
65. *Ibid.*
66. *The New York Times,* Sept. 9, 1958, p. 46.
67. *Ibid.,* May 23, 1959, p. 20.
68. *Ibid.,* May 29, 1959, p. 1.
69. Because the IOC felt that the developments at their May 28th meeting had been misconstrued, Avery Brundage issued a statement on June 3, 1959, to make it clear that the action taken with respect to Taiwan was merely intended to clarify exactly which athletes the Olympic Committee from Taiwan represented. He reiterated that there was no "pressure" from anyone to bring about this action, and that the vote had been virtually unanimous.
70. *The New York Times,* May 29, 1959, p. 1.
71. *Ibid.,* June 3, 1959, p. 9.
72. *Ibid.,* June 4, 1959, p. 15.
73. *Ibid.,* June 19, 1959, p. 11.
74. *Ibid.,* June 18, 1959, p. 14.
75. *Ibid.,* August 4, 1959, p. 30.
76. Made available by the IOC.
77. *The New York Times,* June 6, 1959, p. 3.
78. *Ibid.,* June 9, 1959, p. 3.
79. *Ibid.,* June 11, 1959, p. 3.
80. *Ibid.,* June 20, 1959, p. 18.
81. *Ibid.,* Feb. 18, 1960, p. 4.
82. *Ibid.,* Aug. 26, 1960, p. 16.
83. "Birth of the GANEFO Organization Announced," *China's Sports* (CS), 1963, No. 3, p. 1.
84. *The New York Times,* Feb. 9, 1963, p. 14.
85. *SCMP,* No. 2835, Oct. 4, 1962, p. 20.
86. *The New York Times,* Feb. 9, 1963, p. 14.
87. *Ibid.,* Feb. 15, 1963, p. 3.

88. "Birth of the GANEFO Organization Announced," *op. cit.*
89. "China to Participate in GANEFO," *CS*, 1963, No. 4, p. 1.
90. "Chinese Sports Delegation for GANEFO," *CS*, 1963, No. 5-6, p. 13 and *ibid.*
91. *CS*, 1963, No. 5-6.
92. *Ibid.*, and promotional booklet published by the U.S. Olympic Committee (exact title not available).
93. *SCMP*, No. 3075, Oct. 3, 1963, p. 22.
94. *Peking Review*, Vol. VI, No. 46 (Nov. 15, 1963), pp. 21-22.
95. "First GANEFO Comes Through With Flying Colors," *Peking Review*, Vol. VI, No. 48 (Nov. 29, 1963), pp. 18-20.
96. NCNA, Nov. 13, 1963.
97. *Japan Times*, November 24, 1963.
98. NCNA, Nov. 10, 1963 and *SCMP*, No. 3101, Nov. 10, 1963, pp. 29 and 31.
99. *Japan Times*, Nov. 6, 1963, p. 6, Nov. 10, 1963; and "Hail the First Games of the New Emerging Forces," *Peking Review*, Vol. VI, No. 46 (Nov. 15, 1963), pp. 21-22.
100. List of participants gathered from *SCMP*, *Japan Times*, and *China's Sports*.
101. "GANEFO: New Wave in Sports and Friendship," *Peking Review*, Vol. VI, No. 47 (Nov. 22, 1963), pp. 16-18; *China's Sports*, 1964, No. 1; and *Japan Times* (many issues throughout duration of games).
102. *Japan Times*, Nov. 24, 1963.
103. "First GANEFO Comes Through With Flying Colors," *op. cit.*
104. *SCMP*, No. 3114, Nov. 22, 1963, p. 21.
105. *SCMP*, No. 3121, Dec. 12, 1963, p. 23.
106. *SCMP*, No. 3101, Nov. 10, 1963, p. 31.
107. *Japan Times*, Nov. 6, 1963, p. 6 and Nov. 24, 1963.
108. *Ibid.*, Nov. 10, 1963.
109. *Ibid.*, Nov. 11, 1963.
110. *Ibid.*, Nov. 24, 1963.
111. *Ibid.*, Nov. 22, 1963.
112. *Ibid.*
113. "GANEFO's Splendid Achievements," *China's Sports*, 1964, No. 1, p. 1.
114. *SCMP*, No. 3275, August 4, 1964, p. 25.
115. *SCMP*, No. 3279, August 11, 1964, p. 19.
116. *China's Sports*, 1964, No. 6, p. 8.
117. *SCMP*, No. 3346, Nov. 24, 1964, pp. 22-23.
118. *SCMP*, No. 3544, Sept. 21, 1965, p. 28.
119. *SCMP*, No. 3547, Sept. 25, 1965, p. 28.
120. *SCMP*, No. 3749, July 25, 1966, p. 22.
121. NCNA, Nov. 26, 1966.
122. NCNA, Nov. 28, 1966.
123. "Successful Closing of First Asian Games," *Peking Review*, Vol. 9, No. 5 (Dec. 9, 1966), pp. 21-22.
124. NCNA, Nov. 26, 27, 29, Dec. 1, 3, 1966.
125. "The First Asian Games of the New Emerging Forces," *Kambuja*, 1966, No. 21 (Dec. 15, 1966), pp. 39-67.
126. NCNA, Nov. 29, 1966.

Bibliography

WESTERN LANGUAGE BOOKS, PAMPHLETS, AND DISSERTATIONS

Barnett, A. Doak, *Cadres, Bureaucracy, and Political Power in Communist China.* New York, Columbia University, 1967.

Chang Hwei-lan, "A Collegation of Facts and Principles Basic to Sound Curriculum Construction for Physical Education in China." Unpublished doctoral dissertation, State University of Iowa, 1944.

China Mission Yearbook, 1910-1925 (published as *China Christian Yearbook* 1926-1939). Shanghai, Christian Literature Society.

"Circular of Information—School of Physical Education of the Association College of China." Shanghai, Autumn, 1918.

A Compendium of Laws and Regulations of the People's Republic of China, Vol. 3. Peking, 1950, in Joint Publication Research Service No. 14,673.

A Glossary of Chinese Communist Terms and Phrases. Joint Publication Research Service, 1966.

Goss, George E., "Survey of Physical Education in YMCA's Around the World." Report in YMCA Historical Library, 1923.

Hoh, Gunsun, *Physical Education in China.* Shanghai, Commercial Press, 1926.

Hu, C. T., ed., *Chinese Education Under Communism.* New York, Bureau of Publications, Teachers College, Columbia U., 1962.

Intelligence Research Aid, Directory of Chinese Communist Officials. U.S. Department of State, March, 1966.

Japan Contest Committee, Far Eastern Athletic Association, *Official Report of the Ninth Far Eastern Championship Games.* Tokyo, 1930.

Kiernan, John and Daley, Arthur, *The Story of the Olympic Games.* Philadelphia, J. B. Lippincott Co., 1961.

Kuo P'ing-wen, *The Chinese System of Public Education.* New York, Teachers College, 1914.

Kwei Chung-shu, ed., *The Chinese Yearbook,* 1935/36-1944/45. Shanghai, Commercial Press.

Lewis, John W., *Leadership in Communist China.* Ithaca, N. Y., Cornell Univ., 1963.

Lin Yüeh-hwa, *The Golden Wing—A Family Chronicle.* New York, Institute of Pacific Relations, 1944.

Liu, Snowpine, "The Needs of China in Physical Education." M.S. thesis, Springfield College, 1931.

Lo Jung-pang, ed., *K'ang Yu-wei—A Biography and a Symposium.* Tucson, Arizona, University of Arizona, 1967.

Morton, Henry W., *Soviet Sport.* New York, Collier Books, 1963.

The New York Times Official Sports Record Book. New York, Bantam Books, 1967.

Peake, Cyrus H., *Nationalism and Education in Modern China.* New York, Columbia University Press, 1932.

Preliminary Announcement, Far Eastern Championship Games. Shanghai, 1914.

Schram, Stuart, *Une Étude de l'Éducation Physique.* Paris, Mouton, 1962.

Schurmann, Franz, *Ideology and Organization in Communist China.* Berkeley, University of California Press, 1966.

Schwartz, Benjamin I., *In Search of Wealth and Power—Yen Fu and the West.* Cambridge, Mass., Harvard, 1968.

Shih Chi-wen, *Sports Go Forward in China.* Peking, Foreign Languages Press, 1963.

Smith, Robert W., ed., *Secrets of Shao Lin Temple Boxing.* Rutland, Vt., Charles E. Tuttle, 1964.

Snow, Edgar, *Red Star Over China.* New York, Random House, 1938.

T'ang Leang-li, *Reconstruction in China.* Shanghai, China United Press, 1935.

Wakeman, Frederick Jr., *Strangers at the Gate—Social Disorder in South China—1839-1861.* Berkeley, Univ. of California, 1966.

Wee, Kok Ann, *Physical Education in Protestant Christian Colleges and Universities in China.* New York, Columbia University publication of Ph.D. thesis, 1937.

Who's Who in Communist China. Hong Kong, Union Research Service, 1966.
Woodhead, H. G. W., ed., *The China Yearbook,* 1912-1940. Tientsin, North China Daily News.
Wu Chih-kang, "The Influence of the Y.M.C.A. on the Development of Physical Education in China." Ann Arbor, Univ. of Michigan unpublished Ph.D. thesis, 1956.
Yang, Martin, *A Chinese Village.* New York, Columbia Univ. 1945.

CHINESE AND JAPANESE LANGUAGE BOOKS

Chūka Jinmin Kyōwakoku Soshiki Betsu Jinmei Hyō (Organizational Personnel of the Chinese People's Republic). Tokyo, Japanese Cabinet, 1957, 1959, 1962, 1964, 1966.
Chung Hua Jen Min Kung Ho Kuo T'i Yü Yün Tung Wen Chien Hui Pien (A Compendium of Documents Relating to Sports and Physical Culture in the People's Republic of China), 2 vols. Peking, Jen Min T'i Yü Ch'u Pan She, 1955 (Vol. 1) and 1957 (Vol. 2).
Chung Kuo T'i Yü Shih Ts'an K'ao Tzu Liao (Source Material Relating to the History of Chinese Physical Culture), 5 vols. Peking, Jen Min T'i Yü Ch'u Pan She, 1957 (Vols. I and II) and 1958 (Vols. III, IV, V).
Fa Chan T'i Yü Yün Tung, Tseng Chiang Jen Min T'i Chih (Develop Sports and Physical Culture, Strengthen the People's Physique). Peking, Ch'ing Nien Ch'u Pan She, 1952.
Fei Ch'ing Yüeh Pao—Yearbook on Chinese Communism. Taipei, Institute for the Study of Chinese Communist Problems, 1967.
Feng Wen-pin, *Pa Hsin Chung Kuo te T'i Yü Yün Tung Ch'eng Wei Ching Ch'ang te Kuang Fan te Yün Tung* (To Make a Commonplace Widespread Physical Culture of China's Sports and Physical Culture). Peking, Ch'ing Nien Ch'u Pan She, 1951.
Genzai Chūgoku Jinmei Jiten (Dictionary of Present-day Chinese Personnel). Tokyo, Zaidan Hōjin Kasumisankai, 1966.
Hoh, Gunsun, "T'i Yü" (Physical Education), in Wu Chün-sheng, ed., *Chung Hua Min Kuo Chiao Yü Chih* (Record of Education of the Republic of China). Taipei, Chung Hua Wen Hua Ch'u Pan Shih Yeh Wei Yüan Hui, 1955.
Hsin Min Chu Chu I te Kuo Min T'i Yü (The People's Physical Culture of the New Democracy). Peking, All-China Athletic Federation Preparatory Committee, 1949.
Jen Min Shou Ts'e (People's Handbook). Peking, Ta Kung Pao, 1949-present (excluding 1954).
Jen Min T'i Yü Yün Tung te Fang Chen yü Jen Wu (Directions

and Responsibilities of the People's Sports and Physical Culture). Peking, Ch'ing Nien Ch'u Pan She, 1951.
Kung Fei Chung Teng Chiao Yü chih Yen Chiu (Research in Chinese Communist Middle School Education). No other information given.
Li Ch'ao, *Hsüeh Hsiao Chung te T'i Yü* (School Physical Education). Hupei, Jen Min Ch'u Pan She, 1956.
Mao Tse-tung, *Selected Works,* Vol. II. Peking, People's Publishing House, 1960.
Nanching Shih Fan Hsüeh Yüan Chiao Yü Hsi, *Chiao Yü Hsüeh* (Education). Nanking, Kiangsu Jen Min Ch'u Pan She, 1959.
Pei Ching T'i Yü Hsüeh Yüan 1955-56 Hsüeh Nien K'e Hsüeh T'ao Lun Hui Pao Kao Chi (Excerpts from the Report of the 1955-56 Peking Physical Culture Institute Scientific Conference). Peking, Jen Min T'i Yü Ch'u Pan She, 1956.
Sheng Hsüeh Chih Tao, Kao Teng Hsüeh Hsiao Chao Sheng (Guide to Admission, Promotion in Schools of Higher Learning). People's Republic of China, Ministry of Higher Education, 1958.
Sheng Hsueh Chih Tao—1954 Nien Shu Ch'i Kao Teng Hsüeh Hsiao Chao Sheng (Guide to Admission, 1954 Summer Higher Education Recruitment). Peking, Commercial Press, 1954.
Su E chi Ch'i Fu Yung Chi T'uan T'i Yü Fa Chan Shih K'uang chih Yen Hsi (Detailed Research into the Developmental Affairs of Physical Culture in Soviet Russia and Her Satellites). Taiwan, Ssu Fa Hsing Cheng Pu Tiao Ch'a Chu, 1958.
Ti Wu Chieh Ch'uan Yün Chuan Chi (Complete Record of the Fifth Meet). Shanghai, Hua Mei Shu T'u Shu Kung Szu, 1933.
T'i Yü Kung Tso Che Hsüeh Hsi Ts'an K'ao Tzu Liao (Study Source Material for Physical Culture Workers). Hua Nan Ch'u Pan Pien Hao, 1950.
T'ou K'ao Ta Hsüeh Chih Tao (Guide to Entrance Examinations for Universities). Hong Kong, Hong Kong Student Book Co., 1954.
Wang Hsüeh-cheng, *T'i Yü Kai Lun* (A Summary of Physical Education). Taipei, Taiwan Shang Wu Yin Shu Kuan, 1967.
Wu Wen-chung, *Chung Kuo Chin Pai Nien T'i Yü Shih* (A History of China's Last Hundred Years of Physical Culture). Taiwan, Taiwan Shang Wu Yin Shu Kuan, 1967.
―――, *T'i Yü Shih* (A History of Physical Culture). Taipei, Kuo Li Pien Yi Kuan, 1962.
Wu Yün-jui, "San Shih Wu Nien Lai Chung Kuo chih T'i Yü" (The Last 35 Years of Chinese Physical Education), in Chang Yüan-chi, ed., *Tsui Chin San Shih Wu Nien chih Chung Kuo*

Chiao Yü (The Last 35 Years of Chinese Education). Shanghai, Commercial Press, 1931.

Yün Tung Yüan Szu Hsiang Hsiu Yang Chiang Hua (Lectures on Thought Cultivation for Athletes). Peking, Jen Min T'i Yü Ch'u Pan She, 1964.

PERIODICALS CITED

THE TRADITIONAL AND PRE-COMMUNIST PERIODS

American Physical Education Review (APER)
The China Journal (CJ)
China's Young Men (CYM)
China Today (CT)
China Weekly Review (CWR)
Chinese Students' Christian Journal (CSCJ)
Millard's Review of the Far East (MR)
The Nineteenth Century and After (NCA)
North China Herald (NCH)
People's China (PC)
Physical Training (PT)
Tientsin Young Men (TYM)
T'oung Pao (TP)

THE COMMUNIST PERIOD

China Reconstructs (CR)
China's Sports (CS)
Chung Kuo Ch'ing Nien Pao (CKCNP)
Chung Kuo Hsin Wen (CKHW)
Current Background (CB)
Fei Ch'ing Yüeh Pao (FCYP)
Hsiao Hsüeh Chiao Shih (HHCS)
Hsin T'i Yü (HTY)
Japan Times (JT)
Jen Min Chiao Yü (JMCY)
Jen Min Jih Pao (JMJP) —People's Daily
Jen Min Shou Ts'e (JMST)
Joint Publication Research Service (JPRS)
Kambuja
Kuang Chou Jih Pao (KCJP)
Kuang Ming Jih Pao (KMJP)
Kuo Wu Yüan Pao (KWYP)
The New York Times
Peking Review (PR)

Selections from China Mainland Magazines (SCMM)
Survey of the China Mainland Press (SCMP)
T'ieh Tao Chien She (TTCS)
T'i Yü Chan Hsien (Red Guard publication)
T'i Yü Pao (TYP)
Union Research Service (URS)
Wen Hui Pao

PERIODICAL ARTICLES IN ENGLISH

"Actively Develop Amateur Gliding and Foster Militia Airman." *TYP,* in *SCMP,* No. 3368, Dec. 4, 1964, pp. 6-7.
"Birth of the 'GANEFO' Organization." *CS,* 1963, No. 3, p. 1.
Brown, Elwood S., Far Eastern Olympic Games." *PT,* Vol. 10 (April, 1913), pp. 173-174.
Brown, Franklin H., "The Third Far Eastern Championship Games." *PT,* Vol. 14, No. 9 (Sept., 1917), pp. 386-393.
———, "The Sixth Far Eastern Championship Games." *PT,* Vol. 20, No. 10 (Oct., 1923), pp. 375-377.
Chao Cheng-hung, "Do a Still Better Job of Physical Culture for National Defense." *HTY,* in *SCMM,* No. 362, March 6, 1963, p. 6.
"China Calls for Nationwide Promotion of Swimming Activities." *SCMP,* No. 3467, May 23, 1965, p. 18.
"China's Largest Aviation Club in Peking." *SCMP,* No. 2710, March 27, 1962, p. 21.
"China's 1958 Sports Year in Retrospect." *SCMP,* No. 1927, Dec. 26, 1958, p. 31.
"China to Participate in GANEFO." *CS,* 1963, No. 4, p. 1.
"Chinese Communists in Wartime, 1931-1949." *CS,* 1959, No. 5, pp. 24-25.
"Chinese Girls to Be in Far Eastern Games." *MR,* Vol. 16, No. 13 (May 28, 1921), p. 695.
"Chinese Sports Delegation for GANEFO." *CS,* 1963, No. 4, p. 1.
"Chuan Shu." *CS,* 1957, No. 1.
"Compulsory Sports and Physical Training." *URS,* Vol. 4, No. 17 (August 28, 1956), pp. 245-262.
"Develop the Mass Movement for Defense Training." *JMJP,* in *SCMP,* No. 1257, March 7, 1956, p. 5.
Eigner, Julius, "The Ancient Art of Chinese Boxing." *CJ,* Vol. 28, No. 1 (January, 1938), pp. 11-12.
"Everyone a Soldier Movement." *URS,* Vol. 13, No. 2 (Oct. 7, 1958), p. 16.
Exner, Max J., "Physical Training in China." *PT,* Vol. VIII, No. 6 (April, 1911), p. 19.

Fang Ch'en, "Fly High in the Sky—A General Picture of the Booming Growth of Gliding Activity in Our Country." *TYP,* in *SCMP,* No. 3424, March 10, 1965, p. 14.

"Field Camping in Communist China." *URS,* Vol. 22, No. 21 (March 14, 1961), pp. 323-340.

"The First Asian Games of the New Emerging Forces." *Kambuja,* 1966, No. 21 (Dec. 15, 1966), pp. 39-67.

"First GANEFO Comes Through With Flying Colors." *PR,* Vol. VI, No. 48 (Nov. 29, 1963), pp. 18-20.

"GANEFO: New Wave in Sports and Friendship." *PR,* Vol. VI, No. 47 (Nov. 22, 1963), pp. 16-18.

"GANEFO's Splendid Achievements." *CS,* 1964, No. 1, p. 1.

Giles, Herbert A., "Football and Polo in China." *NCA,* Vol. 5 (March, 1906), pp. 508-573.

Gray, J. H., "The Present Status of Physical Education in China." *APER,* Vol. 31 (Dec., 1926), pp. 1169-74.

"Hail the First Games of the New Emerging Forces." *PR,* Vol. VI, No. 46 (Nov. 15, 1963), pp. 21-22.

Ho Chen-liang, "GANEFO—New Spirit in Sports." *China Reconstructs,* Vol. XIII, No. 2 (Feb., 1964).

Hu K'e-shih, "Let the Whole League Do Physical Culture Work." *CKCNP,* in *SCMP,* No. 3234, May 12, 1964, p. 14.

Hung Chou, "An Account of Military Sports Activities Conducted at Tsinghua University." *HTY,* 1965, No. 5, in *SCMM,* No. 479, May 6, 1965, p. 8.

"Improve the Physique of the People and Turn Out Intellectually and Physically Capable Personnel." *JMJP,* in *SCMP,* No. 3279, July 25, 1964, p. 11.

Jung Kao-t'ang, "Let Physical Culture Better Serve Socialist Construction." *Hung Ch'i,* in SCMM, No. 217, June 1, 1960, p. 13.

"Launch in a Practical Way Sports Activities Among the Workers." *SCMP,* No. 2922, Jan. 30, 1963, pp. 5-6.

"Launch Physical Training for the People's Militia and National Defense Movement on a Large Scale." *SCMP,* No. 2267, Feb. 21, 1960, pp. 4-6.

Lin Chung-yi, "Sports in the Countryside." *CS,* 1959, No. 5, pp. 28-31.

Liu Hou-sheng. "Chinese Acrobats." *CR,* Vol. 3, No. 1 (1954), pp. 23-27.

"Mao Tse-tung Swims Across the Yangtse." *URS,* Vol. 44, No. 13 (August 12, 1966), pp. 183-199.

"Mass Swimming." *PR,* Vol. VIII, No. 23 (June 4, 1965), p. 4.

"Mass Swimming." *URS,* Vol. 43, No. 20 (June 7, 1966), pp. 294-309.

"Mass Swimming Along China's Coasts and Rivers." *SCMP*, No. 3469, May 27, 1965, p. 3.
"Modern Air Sports in Ancient Chinese Capital (Sian)." *SCMP*, No. 2778, July 11, 1962, p. 16.
"Notification of the Committee for Physical Culture Concerning In-Service Training of Physical Culture Instructors in 1956." *JPRS*, No. 14, 673, pp. 746-51.
"One Should Join in Military Physical Education Activity with Enemy Activity in Mind." *CKCNP*, in *SCMP*, No. 3454, p. 1.
"On the Lane Charted by Chairman Mao." *HTY*, 1966, No. 7-8, in *SCMM*, No. 552, August 24, 1966, p. 14.
"Politics Must Play Its Part a Hundred Percent of the Time." *Chieh Fang Chün Pao* (PLA News), in *SCMP*, No. 3452, April 9, 1965, p. 2.
"Promote Revolutionization of Youth by Vigorously Developing Mass Sports." *CKCNP*, in *SCMP*, No. 3435, March 25, 1965, p. 7.
"Regulations Governing the System of Physical Culture for Labor and National Defense." *SCMP*, No. 1899, Oct. 20, 1958, p. 9.
Schafer, Edward H., "Falconry in T'ang Times." *TP*, Vol. 46, No. 3-5 (1958), pp. 293-338.
Siler, Charles A., "Physical Education in China." *CSCJ*, Vol. 6, No. 1 (Oct., 1919), pp. 28-30.
"Simplified Regulations Governing the Organization of the Physical Culture and Sports Commission." *JPRS*, No. 14, 673, pp. 51-53.
"Spare-time Physical Education to Be Popularized." *SCMP*, No. 1880, Oct. 18, 1958, p. 33.
"Spare-time Sports School for Chinese Children." *SCMP*, No. 2510, May 30, 1961, p. 27.
"A Sporting People's Commune." *CS*, 1959, No. 2, p. 12.
"Sports Activities Widespread in Rural Areas." *SCMP*, No. 1847, Sept. 1, 1958, p. 17.
"Sports for National Defense." *CS*, 1958, No. 5, pp. 12 and 17.
"Sports in a Factory." *CS*, 1958, No. 2, pp. 8-9.
Sung, William Z. L., "The Development of Modern Athletics in China." *CWR*, October 10, 1928 supplement, pp. 47-50.
Swan, A. H., "Physical Education in a City Association." *CYM*, Vol. XI, No. 10 (June 15, 1916), pp. 537-546.
———, "The Contribution of the Physical Department of the Young Men's Christian Association to the Christian Movement in China." *China Mission Yearbook*, 1918, pp. 284-290.
Tan, G. G., "A Review of the Development of Athletics in Chinese History." *CT*, Vol. 2, No. 8 (August, 1959), pp. 82-91.

———, "Chinese Origins of Diverse Types of Ball Games." *CT*, Vol. 2, No. 10 (October, 1959), pp. 71-75.
"Traditional Sports in China." *PC*, 1954, No. 1, pp. 17-23.
Tse Chi, "Sports Activities in Yenan During the Anti-Japanese War." *CS*, 1966, No. 6.
Tseng Wei-chi, "An Ancient Form of Physical Culture." *CR*, Vol. 4, No. 8 (1955), pp. 27-28.
Wang Ming-li, "Swimming Is a Kind of Ability to Win a War." *SCMP*, No. 3542, Sept. 1, 1965.
Wang-Quincy, J., "The Far Eastern Championship Games." *CYM*, Vol. 10, No. 110 (June 15, 1915), pp. 423-432.
Wang Tseng-hua, "Shihchahai Junior Spare-time Athletic School." *CS*, 1959, No. 4, pp. 11-12.
"When Friends Meet at International Village." *CS*, 1964, No. 1.
Yang Yung, "Swimming in the Ming Tombs Reservoir with Chairman Mao and Chairman Liu." *HTY*, 1965, No. 6, in *SCMM*, No. 489, June 6, 1965, p. 27.
"Young Athletes Get a Start." *CS*, 1960, No. 1.

PERIODICAL ARTICLES IN CHINESE

Chang Chih-hsüeh, "Tsen Yang Tsai T'i Yü Hsüeh Chung Yün Yung Su Lien te Chiao Yü Fang Fa" (How to Apply the Soviet Union's Educational Methods in the Study of Physical Education). *JMCY* (People's Education), 1953, No. 4, pp. 56-57.
Chang Hsi-liang, "Tsu Chih K'e Wai T'i Yü Huo Tung te Pan Fa" (Methods of Organizing Extracurricular Physical Education Activities). *HTY* (New Physical Culture), 1959, No. 8, p. 30.
Chang Yi, "Ch'ing Hua T'i Yü Shih Nien" (Ten Years of Physical Education at Tsinghua). *HTY*, 1959, No. 18, pp. 17-20.
Ch'eng Tzu-li, "San ke Pai Fen chih Pai Shih Tsen Yang Te Lai te?" (How Can You Get 300%?). *HTY*, 1958, No. 19, pp. 14-19.
"Chiao T'i Yü Yu Mei Yu Ch'ien T'u?" (Is There Any Future in Teaching Physical Education?). *HTY*, 1958, No. 2, pp. 11-12.
"Chiao Yü Pu Kuan yü 1957 Nien Hsüeh Hsiao T'i Yü Kung Tso te Chi Tien I Chien te T'ung Chih" (Several Notes from the Ministry of Education on Opinions Regarding 1957 School Physical Education Work). *KWYP*, 1957, No. 12, pp. 230-35.
Chi Ying, "Ts'ung Kuo Chi Ching Sai K'an Chung Kuo T'i Yü te Yüeh Chin" (Looking at China's Leap Forward in Sports from the Point of View of International Competition). *CKHW*, Jan. 20, 1959.
"Chung Hua Jen Min Kung Ho Kuo Lao Tung Wei Kuo T'i Yü

Chih Tu Shao Nien Chi Hsiang Mu Piao Chun" (Standards for the Youth Stage of the Labor-Defense System of the Chinese People's Republic). *CKCNP*, Oct. 27, 1958.

"Fan Tang Ts'uan Chün Fan Ke Ming Hsiu Cheng Chu I Fen tzu Ho Lung te Tsui Hsing" (The Crime of the Anti-Party, Anti-Military, Anti-Revolutionary, Revisionist Ho Lung). *T'i Yü Chan Hsien* (Sports Battlefront), No. 8-9, Feb. 9, 1967.

"Hsiao Hsüeh Wei Shemma Pu T'ui Hsing 'Lao Wei Chih' " (Why Primary Grades Don't Push the "Labor-Defense System"). *HTY*, 1957, No. 6, p. 26.

Jung Kao-t'ang, "Wei Kuo Min T'i Yü Yün Tung te P'u Chi ho Ching Ch'ang erh Fen Tou" (Let Us Struggle for the Popularization and Regularization of the People's Sports and Physical Culture). *JMST*, 1953, pp. 373-375.

"Kuang Fan K'ai Chan Nung Ts'un Jen Min Kung She te T'i Yü Huo Tung" (Extensively Develop the Sports Activities of the Rural People's Communes). *HTY*, No. 171, March 21, 1960, pp. 1-3.

"Kuan yü Lao Wei Chih Cheng Chang, Cheng Shu Chi ke Wen T'i te Ta Fu" (A Response to Several Questions Regarding the Labor-Defense System Badges and Certificates). *KMJP*, May 4, 1955.

Li Chung-ch'uan, "Shen T'i Hao yü Kung Tso Hao te Pien Cheng Kuan Hsi" (The Dialectic Relationship Between Good Health and Good Work). *HTY*, 1964, No. 7, p. 9.

"Pao K'ao T'i Yü Yüan Hsiao te Chi ke Wen T'i" (Problems in Taking Entrance Examinations for Physical Culture Institutes and Schools). *HTY*, 1957, No. 10, p. 29.

"Shemma Shih Ch'ing Nien ho Shao Nien Yeh Yü T'i Yü Hsüeh Hsiao?" (What Are Teenage and Youth Spare-time Physical Education Schools?). *HTY*, 1957, No. 4, p. 32.

"Shemma Shih Lao Wei Chih" (What Is the Labor-Defense System?). *T'ieh Tao Chien She* (Railroad Construction), June 12, 1956.

Su Ch'ing-ts'un, "Hsüeh Hsi Su Lien Hsueh Hsiao T'i Yü te Hsien Chin Ching Yen Ming Ch'üeh Chung Hsiao Hsüeh T'i Yü Kai Ke" (Study the Progressive Experience of the Soviet Union's School Physical Education, Understand More Clearly the Reform of Primary and Middle School Physical Education). *JMCY*, 1954, No. 7, pp. 68-69.

―――, "Ju Ho Yi Lao Wei Chih Wei Chung Hsin Kai Chin Chung Teng Hsüeh Hsiao T'i Yü K'e ho K'e Wai T'i Yü Huo Tung" (How Come We Should Concentrate on the Labor-Defense System to Advance Middle School Physical Education Courses and Extracurricular Sports Activities?). *JMCY*, Sept. 9, 1955.

Su Shih-yi, "Hsüeh Hsi T'i Yü Yen Chiu te Tien Ti T'i Hui" (A Little Understanding Through the Study of Physical Education Research). *HTY*, 1960, No. 4.

Sun Ming-yi, "T'i Yü K'e Tsen Yang Chin Hsing Ssu Hsiang Chiao Yü" (How to Advance Thought Education in Physical Education Courses). *HTY*, 1958, No. 18.

"Tang te Tsung Lu Hsien Tsai T'i Yü Chan Hsien Shang te Hui Huang Sheng Li" (The Party's General Line in the Glorious Victory of the Physical Culture Front). *HTY*, No. 160, Oct. 6, 1959, pp. 1-2.

"T'i Yü Lao Tung Neng Tai T'i T'i Yü Tuan Lien Ma?" (Can Physical Labor Take the Place of Physical Training?). *Wen Hui Pao*, April 2, 1958.

"T'i Yü Shih Kung Ch'an Chu I Chiao Yü Pu K'e Fen Ke te Pu Fen" (Physical Education Is an Inseparable Aspect of Communist Education). *HTY*, 1957, No. 2, pp. 9-10.

"T'i Yü Yün Tung Chih Shih, Shemma Shih Lao Wei Chih" (Physical Culture and Sports Information, What Is the Labor-Defense System?). *KCJP*, June 22, 1956.

"Tsen Yang Tsai T'i Yü K'e Chung Kuan Ch'e Cheng Chih Ssu Hsiang Chiao Yü" (How to Inject Political Thought Education into Physical Education Courses). *JMCY*, 1953, No. 4, pp. 55-56.

"Tsen Yang Tsu Chih K'e Wai Huo Tung" (How to Organize Extracurricular Activities). *HTY*, 1959, No. 7, p. 30.

"Tui Hsüeh Hsiao K'e Wai T'i Yü Huo Tung te Chi Tien I Chien" (Several Opinions on Extracurricular School Physical Education Activities). *HTY*, 1957, No. 3, p. 13.

Tung Nien-li, "Pao Ch'ing Shao Nien Yeh Yü T'i Yü Pan te Keng Hao" (Do Better Work with Youth Spare-time Physical Education). *HTY*, 1964, No. 1, pp. 17-19.

Wang Chang-ling, "Kung Fei Chao K'ai T'i Yü Kung Tso Hui Yi" (Communists Convene a Physical Culture Work Conference). *Fei Ch'ing Yüeh Pao*, Vol. 8, No. 3 (April 30, 1965), pp. 29-34.

"Women Tsen Yang Chih Ting Chiao Yü Chi Hua" (How We Formulate Education Plans). *HTY*, 1957, No. 2, pp. 26-27.

Wu Chiang-p'ing, "Yi Yen An" (Recalling Yenan). *HTY*, 1957, No. 2, pp. 4-5.

ARCHIVES CONSULTED

In the course of this study, extensive use was made of the archival material at the YMCA Historical Library in New York City. Much of the information in chapters 1-3 was obtained there.

OTHER SOURCES OF INFORMATION

American Consulate General Biographical and Organizational Files of Chinese Communist Leaders. Available on microfilm.

Ch'en Ch'eng collection dealing with pre-1949 Chinese Communist affairs, especially reel No. 5 (microfilm).

Documents supplied by the International Olympic Committee in Laussane, Switzerland. This included correspondence between Communist China and the IOC as well as minutes of IOC meeting involving the question of Communist China.

Interviews of refugees from Mainland China performed by Ezra Vogel of Harvard University.

New China News Agency releases.

Union Research Institute (Hong Kong) Chinese language clipping file available on microfilm.

Index

ACAF (see All-China Athletic Federation)
Acrobatics, xix
Administration of physical education and physical culture, 38
  In schools, 119
Adrianov, Constantin, 174
Afghanistan, 197
Africa, 169, 183, 190, 191
Afro-Asian Games, 190
Akabe, 62
Albania, 194, 197
Algeria, 193-194, 197
All-China Athletic Federation (ACAF), 86, 88, 98, 100-109, 172, 174, 179, 183, 184, 185, 205
  Preparatory Conference (1949), 93
  Preparatory Committee, 98
  Branch organizations: provincial, county, municipal, 99
  As of June, 1952, 100
  After formation of PCSC, 100
  Fourth Congress, 104
  Interlocking leadership with PCSC, 104-105
All-China Federation of Democratic Women, 98, 103
All-China Federation of Democratic Youth, 103
All-China Federation of Labor, 103
All-China Federation of Trade Unions, 98, 106, 107, 108, 147
  Dept. of Physical Culture, 107
All-China Students' Federation, 98, 103, 137
Amateur Athletic Federation of the Orient, 66
American Indemnity College (Tsinghua), 15
American influence, 32, 35
Amoy YMCA, 17, 25

Amsterdam, 45
Anhwei, 16
Anking, 16
Annual Athletic Meet, 9
Anti-U.S. propaganda, 148
Antwerp, Belgium, 68
"Apparatus Work," 30
Arab Palestine, 197, 198
Archery, xv, xvi, 191, 192, 198
Army (Chinese), 103, 136
Asahi Shimbun, 63
Asia, 190, 191
Asian Committee of the GANEFO, 197
Asian Games, 68
  Third, 183
  Fourth, 189
  Fifth, 198
Asian Table Tennis Federation, 185
Athens, Greece, 174
"Athletic days," 26
August 1st, 83, 114
Australia, 28, 168
Austria, 173
Aviation activities, 148, 152-154
  Gliding, 152
  Model airplanes, 152-153
  Parachuting, 152-153
Aviation Club of Peking, 153-154
Aviation Dept. (PCSC), 100, 102

"Backward Areas," 66, 68
Badminton, 106, 129, 183, 191, 192, 194, 198
Balkan States, 68
Ball games, xvii, 75, 83, 124, 127
Ball Games Dept. (PCSC), 100, 102
Bandung Conference, 190, 191
Bangkok, Thailand, 198
Barnett, A. Doak, 106, 107
Baseball, 8, 13, 15, 54, 55, 59

Basketball, 8, 18, 19, 45, 46, 59, 64, 83, 84, 89, 114, 124, 125, 128, 129, 130, 144, 169, 172, 179, 191, 192, 194, 198
Basketball Championships of Friendly Countries 169
Bayonet-charge, 152, 158
Berlin (Olympics), 45, 66
Board of Education (*Hsüeh Pu*), 5, 7
Bodhidharma (Ta Mo), xvi
Bodily development, 80
Bolivia, 193
Book of Rites, xv
Boxing, xvi, 45, 124, 183, 191
Boy Scouts (*t'ung tzu chün*), 46, 57
Branch organizations (ACAF)—provincial, municipal, county, 99
Brazil, 183, 194
Broadcast exercises, 76, 95, 102, 118, 145-146, 156
Brockman, Fletcher S., 8
Brown, Elwood S., 52, 53, 55, 57, 68
Brown, Franklin H., 58, 61, 63
Brundage, Avery, 173, 174, 177, 181, 182, 188
   Correspondence with Tung Shou-yi, 185-186
Bucharest, Rumania, 170
Buddhism, xvi
Budget (see Financing of physical education)
Bulgaria, 194, 197
Bung Karno Stadium, 193
Burma, 45, 169
"The Bushido of China," 3, 78

Cadres, Bureaucracy and Political Power in Communist China, 106
Cadres Dept. (PCSC), 100, 101
Cadres Education Dept., 101
Cairo, 196
Cairo Agreement, 186
Calisthenics, 40, 83, 138
Cambodia, 169, 191, 197, 198
"Camping on a nearby ground," 149
Canada, 173
Canoeing, 144
Canton, 3, 17, 42, 57, 125, 161
Canton Athletic League, 17
Canton government, 60
Canton Tennis and Volleyball League for Girls, 17
Canton YMCA, 17, 20, 25
Capitalism, 87
Caribbean Games, 68
Central African Republic, 197

Central China, 12, 16, 17, 18, 20
Central China Athletic Federation, 17
Central China Athletic Meet, 16, 17
Central government physical education appropriations, 48
Central National Defense Physical Culture Club (*Chung Yang Kuo-fang T'i Yü Chü-le-pu*), 147
Central Physical Culture Institute, 125
Ceylon, 169, 173, 191, 197, 198
Chang Chih-tung, 4
Chang Ch'ing-chi, 107
Chang Lien-hua, 177, 178, 184, 197
Chang Po-ling, 18, 19, 39, 44, 55, 68
Chang, T. B., 16
Changchou, Szechuan, 161
Changsha, 16, 77, 158
Changsha YMCA, 25
Chao Cheng-hung, 156, 163, 193
Chao Chün-yi, 163
Charioteering, xv
Chekiang, 6, 16, 42
Chen Ching-kia, 183
Chen, H. C., 16
Chen Man-lin, 199
Ch'en Tu-hsiu, 78
Chen Yi, 197
Cheng k'e (regular physical education), 40
Chengtu Physical Culture Institute, 123
Ch'i (state of), xvi, xvii
Chialingkiang River, 161
Chiang Kai-shek, 33, 44, 52, 158, 180, 184, 185
Chiang K'un-ti, 78-79
Chile, 194
Ch'in Fen Book Company, 42
China Amateur Athletic Union (*Chung Hua Yeh Yü Yün Tung Lien Ho Hui*), 18, 19, 29, 53, 203
China Archery Sports Association (ACAF), 102
China Aviation Sports Association (ACAF), 102
China Badminton Association (ACAF), 102
China Basketball Association (ACAF), 102
China Cycling Association (ACAF), 102
China Gymnastics Association (ACAF), 102
China Maritime Sports Association (ACAF), 102

Index

China Mountainclimbing Association (ACAF), 102
China National Amateur Athletic Federation (*Chung Hua Ch'uan Kuo T'i Yü Hsieh Chin Hui*), 18, 19, 25, 29, 42, 45, 48, 53, 203
China Shooting Sports Association (ACAF), 102
China Soccer Association (ACAF), 102
China Table Tennis Association (ACAF), 102
China Tennis Association (ACAF), 102
China Track and Field Association (ACAF), 102
China Volleyball Association (ACAF), 102
China Watersports Association (ACAF), 102
China Weightlifting Association (ACAF), 102
China Wireless Sports Association (ACAF), 102
China Wrestling Association (ACAF), 102
China Wu Shu Association (ACAF), 103
Chinan, 15
Chinese boxing, xvi, 20, 45
Chinese Communist Party (CCP), 52, 92, 93, 95, 104, 107, 108, 109, 163
Chinese Communist policy of physical culture, 88-96
Chinese National Physical Education Research Association (*Chung Hua Ch'uan Kuo T'i Yü Yen Chin Hui*), 32-33
Chinese Nationalist Amateur Athletic Federation, 172-177
Chinese Olympic Committee (Communist), 177, 182
Chinese Olympic team, 183
Chinese People's National Defense Physical Culture Association, 108, 147, 156
Chinese People's Political Consultative Conference, 99
 Culture and Education Committee, 99
Chinese Physical Training School (*Chung Kuo T'i Ts'ao Hsüeh Hsiao*), 6, 7, 32
Chinese Progressive Education Association, 32, 33
Chinese Public School, 16

Ch'ing Dynasty (1644-1911), xvii, xviii, xix, 6, 37
Chingkanshan, 82, 207
Chinsha River, 154
Chou Dynasty (1122-255 B.C.), xv, xvi
Chou En-lai, 87, 193, 197
Christianity, 22, 26
Christian schools, 7, 12
Chu En-te, 62
Chu Pao-san, 55
Chu Teh, 83, 84, 87, 136
Ch'üan neng chin piao, 64
Chuang Tse-tung, 125
Chungking (Szechwan), 46, 47
Chung Kuo Ch'ing Nien Pao, 158
Chung Mun-yew, 55
Chungshan, Kwangtung, 128
Ch'üan shu (pugilistic skills), xv, xvi
Chüeh Yüan, xvii
Civil service system, 4
Class nature (class origin), 87, 96
Cock fighting, xviii
Collective spirit, 94
Commercial Press, 42, 45
Common Program, 86, 88
Communes, 142, 143, 145, 163
Communications, 150-152, 157
Communist Bloc, 169
Communist period, part II
Communist physical culture in pre-1949 China, 82-85
Comparison of Chinese and American records, 13
Competitive athletics (see Sports competition)
"Construction of By-laws of Athletic Governing Bodies," 30
Contradictions, 87
Corbillon Cup, 170
Cortina D'Ampezzio, Italy, 177, 178
Crocker, J. H., 16, 19, 24, 26, 27, 28, 29, 30, 53, 54, 55, 56, 69
Crone, Frank L., 52
Cuba, 197
Cultural Revolution, 90, 99, 144, 149, 160, 163, 164, 166, 169, 170, 200
Culture and education, 88, 110
Culture, Education and Health Dept. (of commune or equivalent), 106
Curricula, 39
Cycling, 45, 46, 129, 144, 191, 192, 198
Czechoslovakia, 167, 173, 194, 197

Dance, 84
  As a part of Communist physical education program, 114
Davis Cup, 61
Decathlon, 54-55, 59, 62, 64
de Coubertin, Baron Pierre, 68
Denmark, 169
Department of Physical Education (*T'i Yü Tsu*), 46
Dialectical relationships, 91, 92
Dice, xviii
"Director of Physical Education," 24
Diving (also see Swimming), 129
Djakarta, Indonesia, 189, 191
Doctrine, 77
Dominican Republic, 193, 198
Dorn, Francis D. E., 187
Draft Committee (ACAF), 98, 99
Du, L. K., 60
Dual meet competition, 169
"Dual track school physical education system" (*shuang kuei chih hsüeh hsiao t'i yü*), 32
Dulles, John Foster, 183

Early morning exercises (*tsao ts'ao*), 40, 118
East Asia, 167
East China, 12, 15, 16, 17, 18
East China Athletic Federation, 16
East China Intercollegiate Athletic Association, 16
East China Physical Culture Institute (see Shanghai P. C. Institute)
Eastern European countries, 167
Economics, 75
Edstrom, Sigfried, 171
Egypt (U.A.R.), 183, 191, 197
English system, 62
Eighth Party Congress (1956), 87
  Eleventh Plenary Session, 163
Eisenhower, Dwight D., 184, 187
Elliot, T. M., 17
Emperor Huang, xvii
Emperor's Cup, 62
Employed Officers' Conference, 23
Equipment, 41, 115, 116, 139, 145, 150
  Improvisation, 84
Eton, 34
Europe, 191
Evaluation, 47
Evening men's gymnasium class, 10
"Every man a soldier" (Everyone a soldier), 115, 147

Exercise (as a part of Communist school physical education program), 114
Exner, Dr. Max J., 9, 10, 11, 19, 23, 29
Extra-curricular (*k'e wai*) sports, 40, 41, 118, 119

Facilities (YMCA), 20
Factories, 136, 143, 144
  Factory workers, 149
Falconry, xviii, xix
Far East, 68
Far Eastern Athletic Association (FEAA), 16, 53, 59, 66, 68
  Constitution, 65
Far Eastern Athletic Committee for China, 53
Far Eastern Championship Games (FECG), 18, 26, 28, chapter 3, 203, 204, 207
  First FECG, 54-55
  Second FECG, 13, 55, 58
  Third FECG, 58
  Fourth FECG, 17, 18, 58-59, 62
  Fifth FECG, 59-60, 62
  Sixth FECG, 60-61
  Seventh FECG, 61-63
  Eighth FECG, 63-64
  Ninth FECG, 64-65
  Tenth FECG, 65-66
  Team performance (charts), 71-72
  Inception of FECG, 52
  Events, 53-54
  Competition for women, 61, 65, 68
  Level of performance, 66-67
  Indirect influences, 66
  Federation Affairs (*Hui Wu T'ung Hsün*), 98
Fencing, xv, 191
Feng Wen-pin, 88, 104
Field hockey, 191
Financing of physical education, 36, 47-49
Finland, 172, 173, 194, 197
Fire lighting, 57
First Asian GANEFO, 198-200
  Standings, 200
First Degree Sportsman, 89, 121
First National Education Conference, 34
First National Middle School Education Conference (1950), 86
First National Physical Education Conference (1932), 38-42
First Normal School (Hunan), 78

First Physical Culture Scientific Conference (1956), 126
First Physical Directors' Conference, 23
First Private Middle School, 8
"Five Arts," xv
"Five good" soldier, 91-92, 157
"Five know hows," 157
Five Year Plan, 87
Foochow YMCA, 20, 25
Food, 80
Football, xvii, xviii
Forced march, 149, 206
Fording rivers, 84
Formosa (see Taiwan)
"Formosa China," 180, 181
"Four firsts," 91-92
"Four-fold Program," 22, 40
"Four good" company," 91-92, 157
Fourth Conference of the National Federation of Educational Assemblies, 32
France, 169, 194, 197
Friendly competition, 169
Fukien, 17
Full marathon, 54
Full pack (running with), 83, 84

Gailey, Robert R., 8
Games (as aspect of Communist physical education program), 114
Games of the New Emerging Forces (GANEFO), 170, 189-201, 207
  Beginning of GANEFO, 190-193
  Trials for Chinese team (1963), 192-193
  1963 GANEFO, 193-195
  A different perspective, 195
  The real force behind GANEFO, 195-196
  Financing of, 195-196
GANEFO motto, 193
General Office (PCSC), 100. 101
Geographic sections (see Regional athletic sections)
German Democratic Republic (East Germany), 169, 173, 194, 197
German influence, 5-6, 31, 35, 204
Germany, 45-46
Ginling College (Nanking), 32
Gliding, 152
Government Administrative Council, 99, 100
Government control (era of), chapter 2, 85, 203

Control of National Athletic Meets, 39
Government schools, 8, 12, 27, 32, 42
Gray, J. H., 18, 19, 23, 25, 28, 29, 60, 61, 69
Great Britain, 34, 168, 173, 183
"Great Leap Forward" (1958), 117, 128, 129, 140, 142, 147, 156, 162, 167, 170, 185
Great Proletarian Cultural Revolution, 170
Grenade throwing, 82, 83, 115, 138
Group consciousness, 34
Group traits, 37
Guerilla warfare, 155
Guinea, 191, 194, 197
Gymnasium classes, 22
Gymnasiums, 116, 125
Gymnastics, 18, 19, 84, 85, 106, 124, 127, 128, 129, 138, 144, 179, 191, 192, 198
Gymnastic bridge building, 57

Haichün (Woosung), 6
Han Dynasty (206 B.C.-220 A.D.), xvi, xviii, xix
Hangchow, 23, 32, 42
Hankow, 16
Harbin, 123, 141, 161
Harbin Physical Culture Institute, 123
Hawking, xviii
Health, 75, 112, 113
Helsinki, Finland, 167, 171, 173, 174
"Hexathlon Championships," 22, 28
Historical view of sports (CCP), 87
Hoagland, A. N., 13, 15
Hochi, 63
Hofei Mining Institute (Anhwei), 121
Ho Lung, 84, 164, 165, 192, 197
Hoh, C. G., 10, 18, 28
Hoh Gunsun, 25, 44, 172, 174
Honkew Recreation Park, 56, 59, 60
Hong Kong, 15, 17, 52, 62, 179
Hong Kong YMCA, 25
Honolulu (Chinese baseball team), 55, 56
Horseback riding, xviii
House of Representatives (U.S.), 187
Hsi Tsung, xviii
Hsiang (expanded village), 142
Hsiang River, 78
Hsiao Ming-hsiang, 199
Hsin T'i Yü (New Physical Culture), 99, 101
Hsü Fu-lin, 6, 7
  His wife, 7

Hsü Ping-san, 18
Hsü Te-li, 134
Hsü Yi-ping, 6
Hsüan Tsung, xviii
Hua T'o, xvi
Huang Chung, 193, 197
Huang Yen-pei, 27
Hui Min-fei, 25
Hunan, 16, 82
Hunan Provincial Library (Changsha), 77
Hungary, 167, 168, 169, 197
Hupei, 4, 16, 122
Hupei Recreational Grounds, 16
Hygiene education, 46

Ice hockey, 129, 183
Ice skating, 83, 84, 106, 114, 129, 141, 183
Ice sports, xix
Ideological training, 92
Ideology, chapter 4
Imperialism, 87, 88, 158, 185, 207
India, xvi, 64, 168, 178
Indonesia, 45, 168, 183, 190, 191, 194, 195, 196, 197, 198
Inner Mongolia, 143, 150
"Inner" School, xvii
In-service training of physical education teachers, 27, 39, 130, 131
Institutes of physical culture:
  Nationalist period, 29
  Communist period, 90, 122-126, 206
"Instructor of Physical Training," 24
International Amateur Athletic Federation, 64, 173, 184
International Amateur Basketball Federation, 172, 184
International Amateur Swimming Federation, 172, 184
International Amateur Wrestling Federation, 185
International athletic relations, 52, 89, chapter 8, 207
International Cyclist's Union, 185
International Federation of Football Associations, 185
International Friendly Shooting Competition, 169
International Liaison Dept. (PCSC), 100, 101
International Olympic Committee, 19, 45, 53, 66, 87, 166, 170, 171, 174, 177, 181, 182, 184, 185
International Shooting Union, 184

International Weightlifting Federation, 184
International Working Women's Day, 83
Iraq, 191, 194, 197, 198
Ireland, 168
Israel, 189
Italy, 197

Japan, 43, 44, 45, chapter 3, 170, 183, 193, 195, 198
Japanese Amateur Athletic Association, 63
Japanese influence, 5, 6, 31, 32, 204
Japanese war, 7, 46-48, 154
Java, 45, 193
Jen Min Jih Pao (see *People's Daily*)
Johnson, Chalmers, 107
Johnson, Lyndon, 158
"Joint Directive Concerning Strengthening Physical Education in Institutions of Higher Education," 120
"Joint Directive for Launching the Mass Sports Movement in Institutions of Learning above the Middle School Standard," 137
Judo, 191
Jung Kao-t'ang, 90-94, 172, 174, 177, 179, 181, 193
  Biography, 90
  Reproduction of letter, 174

Kaifeng, 15
K'ang Yu-wei, 3
Kano, Dr. Jigoro, 58
Kaot'ang, Shantung, 143
Karate, xvii
Khoo Hui-yi, 64
Kiangnan Civic Center, 44
Kiangnan Intercollegiate Athletic Federation, 16
Kiangsi, 16, 82
Kiangsi Soviet (1931-34), 82
Kiangsu, 16, 27
Kiangsu Educational Association, 27
Kiangsu Higher Normal School (Soochow), 6
"Kill the enemy," 148, 157
Knowledge (the seat of virtue), 78, 79
Kuan-tzu, xvi
Kulangsoo, 17
Kuomintang (Nationalist Party), 34, 37, 50, 52
Kwangchow, 123

Kwangchow Physical Culture Institute, 123
Kwangsi, 17
Kwangtung, 15, 17, 27, 128
Kwangtung Physical Education College, 25
Kweichow, 150

Laos, 197, 198
"Labor-defense System," 76, 85, 102, 113, 115, 118, 120, 121, 130, 133, 146, 147
  1951-1958, 135-140
  Events, 138, 141-142
  Criticism, 139-140
  In 1958, 140-144
  Badges and certificates, 141
Land activities, 148, 149-152
  Markmanship, 149-150
  Mountaineering, 150
  Communications, 150-152
Land Sports Dept. (PCSC), 100, 102
Language problems, 29, 30
Large gymnasium class, 20
Latin America, 169-191
Lau, F. K., 60
"Leader's Class," 10
"Learn from the PLA," 148, 157
Lebanon, 194, 197, 198
Legislative Yüan, 35
Lenin, 85-86
Lenin Club, 82-83
Lewis, R. E., 8
Li Fu-ch'un, 83
Li Hung-chang, 4
Li Meng-hua, 193
Li Ta, 163
Li Yüan-Hua, 139
Li Yüan-hung, 56
Liang Ch'i-ch'ao, 3, 78
Lianghsiang Airport (Peking), 154
Liaotung military district, 163
Liberation Daily (*Chieh Fang Jih Pao*), 83
Lin K'ai, 163
Liu Ai-feng, 112
Liu Ch'ang-ch'un, 45
Liu Ch'eng-lieh, 6
Liu Chia-hsiu, 34
Liu Hsüeh-sung (Snowpine Liu), 25
Liu Shao-ch'i, 87, 90, 160, 168, 193
Lo, Charles, 69
Local government, 36, 39
Lodge, Henry Cabot, 188
London, 46

Long March, 79, 154, 206
Los Angeles, 45
Lu Han, 105
Lucerne, Switzerland, 190
Lum, Gordon, 64

Ma Hsü-lun, 104
Ma Yüeh-han (John Ma), 104, 179
Macao, 179
Malaya, 45, 64
Mali, 191, 194, 197
Manchukuo, 45, 65, 66
Manchuria, 18, 38, 43, 44, 45, 65
Manila, 18, 45, 52, 54, 61
Manila Carnival, 52, 53
Manpower, 28, 30, 41, 122, 150, 206
Mao Tse-tung, 77-82, 86, 96, 154, 164-165
  Swimming, 154, 160, 162, 170
"Maoism," 77
Marco Polo Bridge Incident, 44
Marksmanship, 82, 129, 149, 157, 158, 164, 179, 191, 198
Marquis Okuma, 58
Marx, 85-86
Marxism-Leninism, 124
Mass calisthenics, 84
Mass demonstrations, 57, 60, 68
  For girls, 60, 61
"Mass education," 150
Mass line, 90
"Mass organization," 98, 103, 205
Mass (*ta chung te*) physical culture, 88, 94, 96, 110, 207
Mass Physical Culture Department (PCSC), 100, 102
Mass Sports, 34, 38, 121, 133, 143, 146, 147, 156
Mass Sports and the Concept of National Defense Physical Culture, chapter 7
  Labor-defense system—1951-1958, 135-140
  Labor-defense system in 1958, 140-144
  Sports in factories, 144
  Sports in communes, 145
  Equipment, 145
  Broadcast exercises, 145-146
  Sports for national defense, 146-148
  Military camping, 148-149
  Land activities, 148-152
  Navigation activities, 154-155
  The period after 1958, 155-164

Master of Sport (*Chien Chiang*), 89, 121, 149
Mauritania, 197
May 4th, 83, 114
May 4th Movement (1919), 52, 60
May 30, 1925 Incident, 16, 29
Mayer, Otto, 171, 174, 188
McCloy, Charles H., 23, 24, 25, 26, 27, 28, 29, 33, 42
Melbourne, Australia, 174, 178, 181, 182
   Melbourne Games, 176-178
Metric system, 61
Mexico City, 174
Middle school, 40, 76, 157
   Communist program, 110-120
Military (sports in), 108-109
Military camping, 148-149, 206
Military exercise, military drill, military flavored physical education, 34, 35, 85, 204, 206
Military spirit, 35
"Military sports" (*chün-shih t'i yü*), 164
Military sports events, 84, 158, 159
Military training, 4, 33, 38, 40, 147, 157, 163
Ming Dynasty (1368-1644), xvii, xviii, xix
Ming Tombs, 44, 160
Ministry of Education, 7, 32, 34, 36, 38, 39, 40, 42, 43, 46, 47, 103, 108, 120, 131, 137, 147
"Ministry of Education Middle School Teaching Plan," 113
Ministry of Higher Education, 131, 137
Ministry of Public Health, 103, 112, 113, 137
Ministry of the Interior, 36
Mirror of History, xviii
Missionaries, 16
Model airplanes, 57, 152-153, 164
Model naval vessels, 155, 164
Modern school physical education in military tradition, 5-8
   German, 6
   Swedish, 6
Modernization, 202
Mokanshan, 23
Mongolia, 169, 197
Morocco, 194, 197
Mount Muztagh Ata (Pamir Range, Tibet), 150
Mount Olympus, 193
Mountaineering, 150, 157

Mountaineering Dept. (PCSC), 100, 102
Mukden Incident, 38, 43, 52
Munich, Germany, 187

Nanchang, 161
Nanchang YMCA, 25
Nankai Middle School, 49, 55
Nanking, 10, 11, 12, 27, 32, 38, 43, 44, 46, 55, 57, 123
Nanking government, 31
Nanking Military Academy, 4
Nanking Normal University, 25
Nanking Physical Culture Institute, 123
Nanking-Soochow, 12
Nanyang University (Shanghai), 6, 16, 55
National Athletic Association, 13, 17-19
   China Amateur Athletic Union, 18, 19
   China National Amateur Athletic Federation, 18, 19
National Athletic Meet Series, 7, 11-17, 19, 26, 28, 45, 51, 203, 204
   Under Nationalist Government, 42, 44
   First, 12, 13, 15
   Second, 13
   Third, 18, 42, 62
   Fourth, 42
   Fifth, 43
   Sixth, 43-44
   Seventh, 44
   Chart, 14
National Athletic Meets under Communists (1959 and 1965), 102, 156, 164
National Committee for Physical Education, 34
National construction, 95
National defense, 93, 135
National defense physical culture (*kuo fang t'i yü*), 133, 143, 147, 148, 164, 204, 206
National Director of Physical Education, 39
National Industrial Exposition (Nanking), 11
National minority groups, 103
National organization of sports activities, chapter 4
National (*min tsu te*) physical culture, 88, 96, 110, 207

Index

National physical director, 9
"National physical education" (*kuo min t'i yü*), 6
National Physical Education Committee (*Kuo Min T'i Yü Wei Yüan Hui*) 47
National Physical Education Law (1929 and 1941), 35-37, 38, 47
"National Physical Education Plan" (*Kuo Min T'i Yü Shih Shih Fang An*), 39
   Kuo Min T'i Yü Shih Shih Fang Chen, 47
National Southeastern University (Nanking), (see Southeastern University)
National Sports Planning Committee (ACAF), 99
Nationalism, 34
Nationalist China (see Taiwan)
Nationalist Flag, 181, 182
Nationalist government, 19, 20, 44, 204
   Early reforms under, 33-42
Navigation activities, 148, 154-155
   Swimming, 153-154
   Swimming with equipment, 154
   Model naval vessels, 155
   Various activities, 155
Navigation Dept. (PCSC), 100, 102
Nepal, 197, 198
New China News Agency (NCNA), 183
New Democratic Youth League (later known as Young Communist League—YCL), 86, 103, 104, 135, 137
"New physical education," 110
New Youth (*Hsin Ch'ing Nien*), 77, 78
New Zealand, 28, 173
Ng Sze-Kwong, 62
Ni Chih-chin, 199
Nieh, C. C., 55
"Nomenclature," 30
Non-military physical education, 7, 31-33
Normal schools of higher education (*kao teng shih fan hsüeh hsiao*), 122-123
Normal technical schools (*shih fan chuan k'e hsüeh hsiao*), 123, 125-126
Normal universities, 27
   In Communist China, 122-123, 206
North China, 6, 12, 15, 17, 18

North China Amateur Athletic Federation, 15
North China Athletic Association, 13, 15
North China Athletic Meet, 15
North China Union College, 15
North Korea, 169, 194, 197, 198
North Vietnam, 169, 191, 194, 197, 198
Northern Expedition, 52
Northwest Border Area team, 84

October 1st, 114
Office of Control (*pao kuan*), 99
Office of Health and Physical Culture (*Wei Sheng T'i Yü Ch'u*) of Central Committee of CCP, 107
Olympia (*Wo-neng-pi-ya*), 45
Olympic Games, 9, 19, 45, 46, 51, 62, 64, 65, 66, 68, 167, 170-189, 195, 200, 201
   1952 Games, 171-174
   Between 1952 and 1956 Games, 174-178
   Soccer qualifying match, 177
   China's preparation for 1956 Games, 178-180
   China's withdrawal in 1956, 180-184
   Events of 1958, 184-187
   Change of status of Taiwan, 187-189
   1960 Games, 189, 192
   Resignation and expulsion of Indonesia from IOC, 190-193
Olympic trials, 179
"On the spot camping," 149
Open International Games, 56-57
Opium War, 3
Organization and Administration of Physical Culture, chapter 5, 205
   Summary chart, 109
Osaka, 61
Osaka City Stadium, 60
"Outer" School, xvii
"Outline for Teaching Physical Education" (*T'i Yü Chiao Hsüeh Ta Kang*), 113
Overseas Chinese, 54, 55

Pai Yu-feng, xvii
Paitou, Hunan, 143
Pakistan, 191, 197, 198
Pan American Games, 68
Parachuting, 104, 152-153
Party fractions, 108
PCSC (see Physical Culture and Sports Commission)

Peasants, 94
Peipiao, Laoning, 143
Peiping, 174
Peiyang (Tientsin), 6
Peking, 15, 27, 57, 124, 128, 129, 130, 135, 144, 154, 155, 160, 161, 169, 170, 179, 192, 197
Peking Athletic Association (*Pei Ching T'i Yü Ching Chin Hui*), 15
"Peking China," 180-181
Peking government, 60
Peking Medical College, 124
Peking National Normal University, 45
Peking Normal University, 25
Peking Physical Culture Institute, 123, 124, 125
Peking Russian Language Institute, 139
Peking Teachers University, 125
Peking Union Medical College, 27
Peking University, 15, 55
Peking YMCA, 8, 13, 20, 25, 27
Pentathlon, 55
People's Committees, 145
People's Daily (*Jen Min Jih Pao*), 107, 162, 179, 180, 193
People's Handbook (*Jen Min Shou Ts'e*), 89, 166
People's Liberation Army (PLA), 87, 94, 117, 149, 160
People's Militia, 147, 149
People's Sports Publishing House, 101
Philippine Amateur Athletic Association, 52-53
Phnom Penh, Cambodia, 198
Philippine Amateur Athletic Federation, 177
Philippines, chapter 3, 178, 193, 195
Physical Culture and Sports Commission (PCSC), 76, 99, 100-109, 112, 113, 119, 120, 128, 131, 136, 137, 139, 140, 141, 147, 156, 157, 160, 163, 164, 205
  General Office, 100, 101
  Cadres Dept., 100, 101
  International Liaison Dept., 100, 101
  Political Dept., 100, 101
  Propaganda Dept., 100, 101
  Aviation Dept., 100, 102
  Ball Games Dept., 100, 102
  Land Sports Dept., 100, 102
  Mountaineering Dept., 100, 102
  Navigation Dept., 100, 102
  Traditional Chinese Boxing Dept., 100, 103
  Mass Physical Culture Dept., 100, 102
  Sports Competition Dept., 100, 102
  Interlocking leadership with ACAF, 104, 105
Physical Culture and Sports Committee (local level), 105, 106, 121, 205
Physical Culture Institute of the PLA, 125
Physical culture theory, 84, 124
"Physical Department Handbook," 30
Physical directors, 10
  Training of, 23, 24
"Physical Education and National Games," 32
Physical Education Committee (*T'i Yü Wei Yüan Hui*), 39-41
  Departments of Planning and Publication, 46
  Department of Research and Publication, 46
  Department of School Physical Education, 46
  Department of Social Physical Education, 46
Physical Education in Communist Chinese Schools, chapter 6
  Primary and middle school program, 110-120
  In schools of higher education, 120-126
  Specialized physical culture schools, 122-130
  In-service training of physical education teachers, 130-131
Physical education period (description), 116-117
Physical Education Quarterly (*T'i Yü Chi K'an*), 33
Physical Education Research Association, 33
Physical labor, 93
Physical program (YMCA), 8
Physical secretaries (YMCA), 9
Physiology, 6
PLA (see People's Liberation Army)
Poland, 167, 169, 173, 194, 197
Political Dept. (PCSC), 100, 101, 107, 108
Political study, 92-93
Politicization of the athlete, 91
Politics, 75

"Politics takes command," 90, 91, 93
Polo, xviii
Popular physical culture (see mass physical culture)
Port Arthur-Dairen, 115
Potsdam Agreement, 186
Prague, 170
Pre-Communist period, part I
Preparatory Conference of GANEFO (1963), 191
President's Council on Physical Fitness, 97
Primary school, 39, 76, 157, 159
 Communist Program, 110-120
Prince Chichibu, 61
Printed material, 42, 101
Productive Labor, 85, 90, 93
Professional physical culture personnel, 104
Progressive physical education, 33
Propaganda and Translation Committee (ACAF), 99
Propaganda Dept. (CCP), 107
Propaganda Department (PCSC), 100, 101
Provincial government physical education appropriations, 49
Pure ideology, 93
P'u T'ung (Common) School, 8

Quemoy-Matsu, 147
Queue, 12, 13
Quisumbing (Mr.), 62

Railroad Construction (T'ieh Tao Chien She), 137
"Ready for Labor and Defend the Fatherland" system, 135-136
"Ready for labor and defense," 140
Records (athletic), 89
Red Flag team (of Central Committee of CCP), 84
Red Guards, 164, 165
Red society (areas), 135
 Sports program in, 82, 83
Reforms of 1898, 3
Regional athletic associations, 11-17, 99
Regional athletic sections, 12, 42
Regional training center system, 24
Religious indoctrination, 11
Republic of China, 7
Republican period, 40, 41, 50, 51, 202
Research Committee (ACAF), 99

Revolutionary Army Committee Team, 84
Revolutionary athlete, 95
Rome, 183, 189, 192
Rule manuals, 30, 42
Rumania, 167, 170, 173, 197
Russian influence, 85, 86, 111, 112, 125

Saavedra, 56
St. John's University (Shanghai), 7, 16, 55
Sanction and justification (for evolving a sports program), 85-88
Saudi Arabia, 194
School Cadres Department (Hsüeh Hsiao Kan Pu K'e), 102
School physical education, 75
"School physical education," 110
School Physical Education Department (T'i Yü Hsüeh Hsiao Szu), 102
School teams, 76, 114
Schurmann, Franz, 93, 107
Schwartz, Benjamin, 4
Scientific (k'e hsüeh te) physical culture, 88, 89, 96, 110, 207
Scientific research, 90
Scotland, 168
Second Conference of Employed Officers of the YMCA, 23
Second Degree Sportsman, 89, 122
Second National Chinese Soviet Congress, 83
Second National Physical Education Conference, 47
Second Revolution, 52
Sectional athletic associations (see regional athletic associations)
"Self-strengthening" movement, 3
"Seminar" (Chiao yen tsu), 131
September 1st Meet (1942), 84
"Service Activities," 19
Shadow boxing, 88, 152
Shanghai, 9, 12, 13, 23, 27, 28, 34, 56, 59, 105, 106, 123, 124, 128, 144, 162, 205
 Municipal Council of, 56
 Municipal CCP Public Health and Physical Culture Department, 107
Shanghai Chinese Girls' Physical Education School, 7
Shanghai-Nanking Railroad, 55
Shanghai Physical Culture Institute, 123, 124
Shanghai YMCA, 9, 10, 16, 20, 21, 23, 25, 27, 54, 57

Shansi-Kansu-Ninghsia Border team, 84
Shantung, 6
Shao lin ch'üan, xv, xvii
Shao Lin Temple, xvi, xvii
Shelter, 80
Sheng Chih-pai, 172
Shensi, 154
Shenyang, 15
Shenyang Physical Culture Institute, 123
Shih Ching (Classic of Songs), xvi
Shihchahai Junior Spare-time Atheltic School, 130
Shoemaker, Dr. Arthur, 15
Shooting (see Marksmanship)
Short course sports training (short term), 94, 122, 136
Shui Hu Chuan, xviii
Sian, 123
Sian Physical Culture Institute, 123
Siler, C. A., 23, 24, 25, 26, 29
"Simplified Regulations" (of PCSC), 120
Singapore, 52, 198
Sino-Japanese War (see Japanese War)
Sino-Soviet Split, 169
Six administrative districts, 99, 103, 136
Sixth "big technique," 162
Small squad *(hsiao tsu)*, 119
Smart, R. D., 16
Snow, Edgar, 82, 154
Soccer, xviii, 10, 15, 19, 45, 46, 54, 59, 61, 63, 106, 124, 129, 156, 173, 177, 183, 191, 192, 198
"Social Sciences," 90, 91
"Socialist Education Campaign" (1957), 117
Socialist production, 85
Softball, 18
Somali, 193, 197
Song of GANEFO, 193
Soochow, 57
Soochow University, 16
Sophia, Italy, 183
South Africa, 173
South African Non-Racial Olympic Committee, 191
South America, 68
South Asia, 167
South China, 6, 12, 17, 18

South China Amateur Atheltic Federation (Kwangtung and Hong Kong), 15
South China Athletic Association of Hong Kong, 17
South Fukien Amateur Athletic Association, 17
Southeast Asia, 45, 183
Southeastern University (Nanking), 25, 33, 42
Southern Fukien Athletic Meet, 17
Southwest China, 20
Soviet Union, 92, 137
Spare-time sports schools, 94, 119, 127-130, 143, 144, 156, 206
  For cadres, 122
"Specialized middle schools" *(chung teng chuan yeh hsüeh hsiao)*, 126-127
Specialized Physical Culture Schools, 122-130
  University level training, 122-126
  Physical culture in middle school level normal schools, 126-127
  Spare-time athletic schools, 127-130
Speed skating, 129
Sports (as an aspect of Communist physical education program), 114
Sports competition, 4, 40, 75, 118
  For elementary and middle schools, 115
Sports Competition Department (PCSC), 100, 102
"Sports departments" *(yün tung hsi)*, 124
"Sports for everybody," 94
"Sports for National Defense," 115, 146-148
Sports medicine, 124
Sports science institutes, 124
Spring and Autumn Annals, xv
Springfield College, 25
Springfield, Mass., 8
Squaw Valley, Calif., 183, 187, 188, 189
Ssu-ma Ch'ien, xvii
"Standard Program for Boys," 22
State Council, 140
State Dept., U.S., 184, 187
Stockholm, 170
"A Study of Physical Culture" (1917) *(T'i Yü chih Yen Chiu)*, 77-82, 96
  Mao's six exercises, 78, 82

Mao's principles of physical training, 81
Su Tung-po, xix
Sudan, 197
Sukarno, 190, 191, 193, 197
Summer seminars, 28
Summer session, 23, 39
Sun Pao-hsin, 12
Sun Yat-sen, 34
Sung Dynasty (960-1279), xix, xviii
Sung, Paul R., 16, 45, 63
Survey of the China Mainland Press (SCMP), 166
Swan, A. H., 16, 20, 23, 24, 25, 26, 28, 54, 55, 69
Swaythling Cup, 170
Sweden, 173
Swedish Curative Gymnastics, 7
Swimming (& diving), 19, 45, 46, 54, 59, 61, 65, 83, 84, 106, 114, 124, 125, 127, 128, 129, 130, 141, 154, 160, 161, 162, 172, 179, 183, 191, 192, 193, 194, 198, 206
  With equipment, 135, 155, 157
Switzerland, 173
Syria, 197, 198
Szechwan, 27, 47

Ta Kung Pao, 193
Table Tennis, 82, 83, 89, 106, 114, 124, 125, 128, 129, 135, 156, 169, 170, 183, 191, 192, 194, 198
T'ai chi ch'üan, xv, xviii
Taiwan, 25, 48, 161, 170, 171, 172, 173, 174, 177, 179, 182, 184, 187, 189, 201
  Olympic Committee, 187, 188
Taiyüan, 15
T'ang Dynasty (618-906), xv, xviii, xix
T'ang T'ai Tsung, xvi, xviii
T'ang Shao-yi (Premier), 55, 57, 68
Tani, 62, 63
Tanzania, 197
Tartars, xviii
Tatu River, 154
Teacher training courses, 41
Teacher training schools, 6, 32
Technical competence, 104
Technical course (*chuan hsiu k'e*), 123-124
Telegraphy, 151-152, 157
Temple of Heaven, Peking, 13
Ten kilometer hike, 115, 138, 139, 142
Tennis, 10, 15, 19, 54, 59, 61, 62, 64, 65, 83, 106, 129, 183, 191, 192

Tent pitching, 57
Textbooks, 42
Thailand, 45
Thatched Hut Among Ten Thousand Trees School (*Wan Mu Ts'ao T'ang*), 3
Third Degree Sportsman, 89
"Thought development," 117
"3-8 work style," 91-92, 157
Three People's Principles, 34
Three People's Principles Physical Education Program, 34, 204
"Three precautions," 157
T'i ts'ao, 5
T'i yü, 5, 75-76, 148
T'i Yü Pao, 100, 101, 157, 190
T'i Yü Pao Publishing House, 101
T'i Yü Wen Tsung (Sports Research Digest), 101
Tibet, 150
Tientsin, 4, 8, 12, 15, 57, 123, 128, 144, 158, 161
Tientsin Naval Academy, 4
Tientsin No. 90 Middle School, 150
Tientsin Physical Culture Institute, 123
Tientsin University, 55
Tientsin YMCA, 8, 9, 20, 25
Tientsin Wool and Feather Factory, 144
Tokyo, Japan, 58, 60, 64, 184, 189
Toribio, 65
Track and field, 7, 9, 15, 19, 45, 46, 54, 59, 65, 83, 84, 106, 114, 124, 125, 127, 128, 129, 144, 179, 191, 192, 194, 198
"Track and Field Technique," 30
Traditional Chinese Boxing Dept. (PCSC), 100, 103
Traditional Chinese sports, xv-xix, 37, 38, 40, 88, 124
"Training center method," 23
Training Commissioner's Department, 36, 37
Translations from Russian, 85, 99
Treaty of Versailles, 52
Ts'ai Shu-fan, 179
Ts'ai Yüan-p'ei, 34
Tseng Kuo-fan, 3, 78
Tsinan YMCA, 25
Tsinghua University, 15, 44, 55, 104, 158, 159
Tsingtao, 15, 45
Ts'un (local village), 142

Tuan lien, 75
Tung Shou-yi, 25, 44, 104, 172, 178, 183
   Correspondence with Avery Brundage, 185, 186
Tungchow University, 55
Tutherly, William, 52
Twenty-one Demands, 52, 56
Tyokansan Sanomat, 173

Uganda, 197
United Front, 52
United Nations, 188
United States, 173
U.S. table tennis team, 169
Unity, 94, 95
University Council (Ta Hsüeh Yüan), 34
University level physical education, 40, 76, 120-126
   In Yenan, 84
Uruguay, 194
U.S.S.R., 167, 169, 173, 183, 191, 194, 195, 197

Vietnam, 158
Virtue, 79
Volleyball, 13, 18, 20, 54, 59, 61, 64, 65, 83, 84, 114, 124, 129, 169, 191, 192, 198

"Walking on two legs," 91, 93, 94
Wang, C. T., 19, 39, 44, 61, 66, 68
Wang Ching-wei, 43-44
War (preparation for), 157, 158
Warlord period, 7, 60
Water polo, 129, 191
Weightlifting, xix, 19, 45, 125, 138, 144, 179, 183, 191, 192, 194, 198
West China, 12, 18, 20
West Germany, 169
"What Is the Labor-Defense System?", 137, 138
"Why China Needs Physical Education," 27
Winter Olympic Games, 183, 184
Women, 4, 18, 32, 34, 38, 61, 65, 203
   Communist Programs for, 85
"World League of Democratic Youth," 173
World Table Tennis Championships, 169, 170
World University Games, 167
Wrestling, xv, xvi, 84, 124, 144, 191
Wu D.M., 62
Wu Shu, xv, 84, 89, 144
Wu Ting-fang (Dr.), 53, 55

Wuchang (Hupei), 16, 27, 57
Wuchang YMCA, 16
Wuchiang River, 154
Wuhan, 12, 154, 161, 162
Wuhan Physical Culture, 123

Yachting, 191
Yang Chang-chih, 78
Yang, Martin, 6
Yangtse River, 154, 160, 161, 162
Yemen, 197, 198
Yen Fu, 4, 78
Yen, James, 150
Yenan, 82, 83, 84, 135
   College level physical culture courses, 84
Yenan College (*Yenan Ta Hsüeh*), 84
Yenan Iron Works, 84
Yenan Municipal School Team, 84
Yenan Municipal team, 84
Yenan New Sports Institute, 84
Yenan Sports Committee (*Yenan T'i Yü Hui*), 83
Yenan Youth Cadre Training School, 84
Yifsaton Island, Canton, 182
YMCA Era, chapter 1, 202, 203
   Involvement in Chinese Sports—1911-1927, 19-30
   Far Eastern Championship Games, chapter 3
YMCA's physical education program, 8-11
YMCA School of Physical Education of the Association College of China, 24
   Failure of, 28
Young Communist League (YCL), 92-93, 106, 107, 108, 119, 121, 128, 137, 141, 147, 149, 156, 158, 159, 160
   Dept. of Military Affairs and Physical Culture, 106, 107
   "Guidelines for Theoretical Shooting Study," 150
Young Pioneers, 119
Young Vanguards, 83
Youth Work Committee of the Central Committee of the Chinese Communist Party, 83, 84
Yu hsi (play, games), 135
Yu Ya-ching, 55
Yüan Dynasty (1279-1368), xvii, xix
Yüan, Dr. T. L., 45
Yüan Shih-k'ai, 52, 55, 56
Yugoslavia, 169, 191, 194

WITHDRAWN
UST
Libraries